Endorsements for *Drawn From Shado*

"Fr. Ray Ryland's *Drawn from Shadows Into Trut.* ... story of how a minister in the Disciples of Christ eventually came to the fullness of Christianity in the Catholic Church together with some excellent apologetics. This splendid book will stimulate those who already have the faith and enlighten those seeking for the truth."

IAN KER
PROFESSOR OF THEOLOGY, UNIVERSITY OF OXFORD

"One of the most amazing men I've ever known, and also one of the holiest, Fr. Ray Ryland shares his life-story in a way that is bound to inform and inspire. Readers will recognize many familiar landmarks in this divinely scripted pilgrimage: from the US Navy to Harvard Divinity School, from the Protestant ministry to the Catholic priesthood; Fr. Ray remains active even still, in his 90s, as a trusted friend and advisor for groups such as Catholics United for the Faith, Catholic Answers, The Catholic Answer and the Coming Home Network. Full of practical wisdom and profound theological insight, *Drawn from Shadows Into Truth* is more than a conversion story; it is a testimony to how God's amazing grace empowered a very faithful disciple to become an extraordinarily fruitful apostle. Highly recommended."

SCOTT HAHN
BEST-SELLING CATHOLIC AUTHOR
FOUNDER AND PRESIDENT OF THE ST. PAUL CENTER FOR BIBLICAL THEOLOGY

"Fr. Ryland has been a dear friend and spiritual guide for many years, but hearing more of the details of his journey has reinforced even more his role as a cherished mentor for all of us on the journey home. *Drawn from Shadows* is a captivating (and agonizing) narrative of a man's quest for God and truth—from a poor Oklahoma farm boy to a naval officer to a Protestant minister to a university professor to a Harvard lawyer to a married Catholic priest with five children and over two dozen grand- and great-grandchildren. The story of a pilgrimage is the story of a lifetime. And what a story this is! Get it. Read it. Enjoy it!"

MARCUS GRODI
FOUNDER AND PRESIDENT OF THE COMING HOME NETWORK INTERNATIONAL

"Fr. Ryland's masterpiece of spiritual autobiography is up there with works of his fellow converts from Anglicism, with Bl. Newman and Robert Hugh Benson—great men who followed the Truth where it led no matter the cost. Fr. Ray's book is a compelling read and will bring many readers to conversion as the new evangelization continues in this still young century."

FR. JOHN MCCLOSKEY
RESEARCH FELLOW OF THE FAITH AND REASON INSTITUTE IN WASHINGTON DC.

"In my career I read many conversion stories—too many, really, since most of them, although written piously, are not written well. A convert will grant a fellow convert considerable literary allowance, having traveled a parallel road and knowing how difficult it is to express what the journey was like. But I am not a convert and am more demanding. I set aside most conversion stories after reading the first few pages, rejoicing to know that the Church has a new member but not rejoicing enough to plow through the rest of the tale.

What a delight it is, then, to pick up—and to be unable to put down—such a well written memoir as Fr. Ray Ryland's! His book is full of well-turned phrases and memorable, even touching, incidents. It also is full of theology and history, but the reader nowhere mistakes it for a catechism or a textbook. I can't remember when I last came across a conversion account that made me wish I had been peering over the author's shoulder the entire time, but that's how I feel about this book.

This is the story of a man who wasn't chased into the Church by the Hound of Heaven but who, from a young age, chased after the Hound, not sure for much of the time where the chase would lead but knowing that he had to follow. That makes this a story of spiritual and intellectual adventure, one that speaks both to converts and non-converts."

KARL KEATING
FOUNDER AND PRESIDENT OF CATHOLIC ANSWERS

"*Drawn from Shadows Into Truth* is the touching story of a life well spent in the enthusiastic search for the true Church established by Christ. In its pages Fr. Ray Ryland provides the reader with keen insights into the misperceptions, prejudices, and doctrinal differences that have separated Protestants and Catholics for half a millennium. In doing so, he brings rich new meaning to timeless theological doctrines. He convincingly proves how the truth of such doctrines is never subjective. He further masterfully demonstrates that fidelity of belief in magisterial teaching leads to authentic religious freedom. This book will serve to inspire and challenge anyone embarked on their own spiritual journey. Those resolute in their search for ultimate truth will find that it provides both intellectual and spiritual enrichment. I wish you joyous reading and a deepened faith as you traverse its chapters with Fr. Ray as your trusted guide."

CHARLES LIMANDRI
LAW OFFICES OF CHARLES S. LIMANDRI, A CIVIL LITIGATION PRACTICE

Drawn From Shadows Into Truth

Drawn From Shadows Into Truth

A Memoir

RAY RYLAND

EMMAUS
ROAD
PUBLISHING

Steubenville, Ohio
A Division of Catholics United for the Faith
www.emmausroad.org

Emmaus Road Publishing
827 North Fourth Street
Steubenville, Ohio 43952

Library of Congress Control Number: 2013932805
ISBN: 978-1-937155-90-2

Cover design & layout by: Theresa Westling
Cover photo: Monica Lahr

For Ruth Margaret—
Next to life and salvation,
God's greatest gift to me

TABLE OF CONTENTS

Part 2
Being Catholic

PREFACE

Every story of conversion is at its root a mystery story. The convert never stops asking himself, "Why was *I* chosen, when so many others close to me, in many ways like me, have not been led into the Church?"

Clare Boothe Luce, a twentieth-century author and playwright, wrote that the convert "never grows weary of reflecting on the variety, the 'passing strangeness,' of the ways in which God, in Francis Thompson's tremendous word, *hounded* him, and brought him to bay." In retrospect, she said, the convert "sees a thousand ways by which *he* might have speeded up the hour of his conversion. . . . Daily he is overcome with contrition for his long recalcitrance, and with gratitude for God's infinite persistence and ingenuity in pursuit."[1]

I recall the misgivings voiced by Blessed John Henry Newman as he undertook to describe the process by which he had been led into the Catholic Church. "For who can know himself, and the multitude of subtle influences which act upon him? . . . It is both to head and heart an extreme trial, thus to analyze what has so long gone by, and to bring out the results of that examination."[2]

Like other converts, I realize that the process of my conversion to the Catholic faith involved my whole life. In my pilgrimage, there were a number of wakeup calls from the Holy Spirit. For many years I ignored them because

---

1   Clare Boothe Luce, "Under the Fig Tree," John A. O'Brien, ed., *The Road to Damascus* (Garden City, NY: Image Books, 1958), 200f.

2   John Henry Cardinal Newman, *Apologia Pro Vita Sua,* ed. David J DeLaura (New York: W.W. Norton and Company, 1968), 81.

of my prejudice against the Catholic Church. Like most prejudice, mine was born of ignorance and misunderstanding.

One of the themes the reader will find in this account of my pilgrimage is an abiding concern for Christian unity. This concern comes to focus on the issue of authority. The imperative of Christian unity arises from our Lord's prayer and command that all members of His Body should be one (Jn. 17:20–23). But what provision did He make for achieving and maintaining that unity? Beyond that, how can we know with certainty what God has revealed in Jesus Christ, not only about unity but also about the entire Gospel? To press this analysis, one would have to confront the ultimate Christological question: What *has* God done in Jesus Christ?

Among the divided followers of Christ, there are four main approaches to determining Christian truth:

1. For Protestants, Scripture alone suffices.
2. For Anglicans,[3] Scripture suffices but must be interpreted in the light of tradition of the first five centuries (the first four ecumenical councils).
3. Eastern Orthodox Christians rely on Scripture and the tradition of the first eight centuries (the first seven ecumenical councils), with a special role for the episcopate.
4. Roman Catholics believe Scripture must be interpreted in light of the *whole* of Tradition under the guidance of the episcopate, with a unique role for the successors of Peter.

And, of course, all Christians seek to rely on the guidance of the Holy Spirit.

* * * *

When folks in my Oklahoma hometown referred to someone of wide experience, they would say, "He's really been around the block." Having shared or seriously examined all these views on authority, I can say that, with regard to this issue, I have "been around the block." For years I embraced the Protestant and then the Anglican traditions. Later I was strongly drawn to Eastern Orthodoxy. My study of the Eastern churches led me beyond them to the Catholic Church in Rome.

Reflecting on and praying about my pilgrimage, I began to see the dim outlines of a testimony to grace. I hoped it would be a testimony that illuminates the issues of unity and authority. I began praying that the Holy Spirit would guide me in writing an account focused on the gradual steps in my pilgrimage without too many tiresome personal details. When Saint Therese of Lisieux was ordered by her superior to write her autobiography, she

---

3 "Anglican" is a generic term for members of the Church of England and its transplanted branches, including the Episcopal Church in the United States.

insisted, "It is not . . . my life . . . that I am going to write; it is my *thoughts* on the graces God deigned to grant me."[4]

I share the Little Flower's intention. I continue to pray that in reading my testimony, Catholics may find their faith strengthened, and others may find answers to their misgivings about, or even their opposition to, Catholicism.

Now I can see that my calling to ministry and my pilgrimage are a single adventure. Had I not entered the Protestant ministry, I probably would have remained a layman in the Disciples of Christ denomination. I might have drifted into a more intellectually oriented denomination. But apart from the study of theology, I might not have faced the issues involved in this pilgrimage. I see now that God's calling me into the ministry was the means He used to call me into His Church.

In this narrative, I will use the first-person singular pronoun a great deal. Yet the truth is, from the time of our marriage, my wife and I traveled the road together. We read many of the same books, discussed and prayed, and sometimes even argued (good-naturedly). At times one, then the other, would pull ahead. All the way we traveled alone. Apart from the priest who instructed us and the priest who assisted at our reception, we had no Catholic friends. When my wife, my five children and I were received into the Church, we had no one except the two priests to invite to our celebration. All our friends were Episcopalians and strongly disapproved of our decision. My parents, who lived in the same city we did, were tearful and in no mood to celebrate. Undaunted, my wife assured us that we would have a grand gathering. "Seven Rylands," she said, "two priests, and hosts of angels and archangels!"

Three days after being received into the Church I went to Mass at our parish church. I was forty-two years old and in excellent health. As I knelt in my pew after Communion, I exclaimed involuntarily (and quite audibly), "Now I'm ready to die!"

What follows is an attempt to explain why I uttered those words—and why now, having shared for a half century in the fullness of grace and truth in the Catholic Church, those words have far richer, deeper meaning for me. I am grateful to Karl Keating and to Chris Michalski for permission to use material of mine that appeared in *This Rock* and in *Crisis* magazines, respectively.

Newman's writings profoundly influenced our pilgrimage and our lives as Catholics. We were greatly blessed by his prayers that we invoked in the latter stages of our journey to Rome. The Cardinal's self-composed epitaph is *Ex umbris et imaginibus in veritatem*. In light of the Cardinal's role in our lives, we have chosen as our title a paraphrase of his epitaph: *Drawn From Shadows Into Truth*.

---

4   *Story of a Soul: The Autobiography of Saint Therese of Lisieux*, trans. John Clarke, O.C.D. (Washington, DC: ICS Publications, 1996), 15.

Part 1
LONG JOURNEY HOME

CHAPTER ONE

PILGRIM ROOTS

For thirty years as a priest, it has been my greatest privilege to offer the Holy Sacrifice of the Mass, to serve my Lord Jesus Christ as His medium through which He re-presents His perfect offering of Himself to the Father. Almost always, at some point in the liturgy—most frequently at the elevation at the Doxology—a thought flashes through my mind: Can this be true? Am *I* really offering this holy Sacrifice?

Countless times outside the Eucharistic celebration I have wondered at the mystery of it all. How after so many theological and ecclesial detours a person raised in a Fundamentalist church in a small Oklahoma town could finally be empowered to stand at the altar of God.

To trace that circuitous path I must choose a starting point. Since Adam and Eve are too remote, I'll start with my grandparents, Ben and Martha ("Mattie") Ryland, and Bill and Nancy Cowling.

I have often imagined my grandfather Ben fingering the reins of his horses as he sat in the high seat at the front of his wagon. It would have been late morning, April 22, 1889. Frequently he would have shifted the reins in his hands to pull out his watch. Beside him would be sitting his wife Mattie, again and again looking over her shoulder at their toddler Franklin, clambering among the household possessions that filled the wagon.

On either side of them hundreds of other wagons and men on horseback lined the southern border of Kansas. All awaited the firing of the cannon that would signal the opening of a large portion of Indian Territory (now Oklahoma) to white settlement. At noon the cannon roared, and the "Run of '89" began. Ben and Mattie traveled about one hundred fifty miles as fast as they could, stopping only to eat and briefly to sleep on blankets on the ground.

Near the center of Indian Territory, Ben staked out claims for three farms. He set aside a forty-acre site for the town of which he and Mattie and Franklin were the first citizens. He named the town Crescent City because of a large fan-shaped stretch of timber at the south end of one of his farms. (In later years, with other, more modest town fathers, he agreed to drop the word *City*.) Ben was the first merchant in the new town, as well as the first farmer. In the years that followed, Ben and Martha had a daughter (who died in infancy) and five sons of whom my father, born in 1899, was the youngest.

Bill Cowling, my maternal grandfather, was a native Texan and a farmer. His wife, Nancy, was born in Illinois. When she was ten years old, her family moved by covered wagon to Texas. She told me that on that long journey she and her older siblings walked behind the wagon a great part of the way. Several years before my mother's birth, her parents had moved their family to the southern part of Indian Territory. There my mother was born in 1901, six years before the territory was admitted to the Union as the state of Oklahoma.

In my early years, my mother shared memories of her childhood among the Native Americans, whom she had always regarded with awe. She recalled their custom of tolling the death of one of their number for two weeks straight with an unbroken heavy drumbeat that could be heard for miles around. She had vivid memories of waking with a vague fear to that drumbeat in the night.

During World War I, her family moved to Crescent, where she met my father and married him in 1920. I am their only child. My parents told me they wanted more children, but my mother could not conceive again. (In my adolescent years I teased them by saying that when I was born, they took one look at me and said, "No more!")

My mother's education ended at high school, my father's at the ninth grade. My paternal grandfather was a prosperous farmer who could have sent his sons to college, but he regarded education—especially higher education—as a waste of time. During his lifetime my father had a number of different occupations, mostly in the grocery business.

As a child, I disliked the name my parents had given me. When I learned to talk, my parents later informed me that I refused to acknowledge that my name was Raymond. I insisted it was Jack. They had no idea why I chose that name, but it stuck. Until the end of their lives my parents called me Jack.

The first vivid memory comes from my fourth year. One winter morning I stood in my pajamas backed up to a red-hot wood stove. My hands were behind me, palms extended to catch the heat. My father opened the front door to let in my dog, Bounce. He ran to me and jumped up, his paws on my chest, pushing my hands flat against the stove. That much I remember; I have forgotten the pain.

Once, when I was five, I was playing with cousins in their backyard. It was bounded on one side by a high fence that enclosed a large apple orchard. A power line in the alley had broken and was lying on the ground. (Later we learned that boys down the alley had taken a long pole and lifted the broken line onto the fence.) I happened to be the first one to touch the charged fence. I remember struggling vainly to free my hands, feeling the electricity surge through my body. My screams brought my aunt to the scene. She tried to free me and was also filled with the charge. With strength born of desperation, she pulled me away from the fence, leaving behind some of the skin from my hands. For several days after that I imagined I could feel electricity pulsating through my body.

My father was fiercely independent. After the market crash in 1929, he lost his job as parts manager for a local auto agency. He despised the thought of taking relief (poverty assistance) from the government. (Today what we called "relief" is called "entitlement"; what a difference in outlook from the 1930s!) On more than one occasion he told my mother and me, "We'll go hungry before we take a dime of relief." His declaration never alarmed me; I knew he would take care of us. For years during the Great Depression he supported our family by working the small farm on which we lived and by finding occasional odd jobs in the town.

Though her education was limited, my mother had a love for learning, which she inculcated in me. I began my schooling at the first grade, there being no preschool or kindergarten classes. We lived five blocks from school, so I always came home for lunch. Evidently my mother had aroused in me great expectations about what I would learn in school. Years later she told me that on the first day of first grade, I came home at noon in tears. When she asked why I was upset, I cried out, "I've been in school all morning, and I can't read, and I can't write!"

Evidently I made progress. The following spring the local paper offered a prize for the best essay from each of the grades in the elementary school. (Do first-graders in public schools write essays today?) Prompted by my mother, I asked my grandmother Mattie to share some memories of her early pioneer days. For my essay I settled on one of her stories about a local man who had driven his team to Guthrie for a load of supplies.

In my time we traveled the fifteen miles between Guthrie (the first capital of Oklahoma) and Crescent on pavement. In my grandmother's day the trip was through wilderness, slow and difficult. Making the trip involved finding a spot where a team and wagon could ford the Cimarron River. When the man in Mattie's story returned one week later, he discovered she had married another man because she thought her husband was not coming back. Even as a child I wondered why the woman gave up her husband for lost so quickly. My essay won first prize: one dollar, to me a great sum of money.

I took delight in school, always looking forward to the end of vacations. Regarding only my fourth-grade teacher do I have mixed feelings. She had a rather unusual punishment for boys who did not confer with her standards of classroom behavior. (None of the girls were ever punished.) She would command, "Put your foot out in the aisle!" With her right heel (she always wore high heels) she would step on our toes and spin around a time or two. Her heel-spinning amused us victims. Evidently she didn't realize that in those depression years our parents bought our shoes in larger sizes so we wouldn't outgrow them quickly. We usually just pulled our toes away from the end of our shoes and grinned at her while dervish-like she whirled on empty shoe space. (She could have been a character in a Dickens novel.)

My most vivid memories of elementary school are of my fifth-grade teacher. Though she had been raised in Crescent, and though I knew her much younger sister, I did not know her before entering her class. We were her first class after she graduated from college. She was not only a good teacher, she was also a sensitive and beautiful young woman. Sometimes when she was on duty at recess, I stood talking to her, telling her she was very pretty and that I loved her very much. She never made me feel awkward for having blurted out my feelings. She would smile her gorgeous smile and thank me, with a slight touch on my shoulder. That for me was being knighted by my queen! The next year I was crestfallen when a man from a neighboring town married her and took her to live in the East. I never saw her again.

Growing up on a small farm gave me many advantages denied my children and grandchildren raised in an urban setting. They have always enjoyed my stories about my pets, especially my horse. During the long summer vacations, Midget, my sorrel pony, was my constant companion. Like the other youngsters I knew, I always rode bareback. Though we had saddles we never used them; saddles were for sissies. I often dispensed with even a bridle, simply tying a rope around Midget's neck and looping it around her nose. Always barefoot in the summer we would hook our toes on the back of our horse's left front leg, grab the mane, pull ourselves up and gallop away. Although the cowboys were always the "good guys" in the cowboy-and-Indian movies we saw on Saturday afternoons, we did admire the Indians' bareback riding.

Two or three of my cousins and I had the daily task in summer of driving our families' cows to pasture on a farm owned by my father and his brothers. In late afternoon we drove them back for milking in the evening. The pasture was a mile and a half from our homes. In the mornings, after closing the pasture gate, we explored the tree-lined creek. Sometimes we waded in the

Family Farm
Oklahoma circa 1905

water, catching crawdads and throwing them back. Except in times of drought, the creek flowed freely. To thirsty youngsters it was inviting. We drank freely, with never a thought of pollution. One day, however, we permanently lost our appetite for creek water. Having slaked our thirst in a remote section of the creek, we waded about twenty-five yards upstream and discovered the badly decomposed body of a cow lying in the water.

Next in my affection for my pets came my goat, Billy, and a small young Shetland pony. Too small for me to ride, the pony followed me around our yard and out in the fields like a dog. Billy usually accompanied us. I often wrestled with Billy, grabbing his horns, pushing him and being pushed, especially as he grew older. When I was with him, Billy would never attack so long as I looked directly at him. If I dared to turn my back, he made his charge. Because the goat and the pony were so dear to me, I found it difficult to understand why my mother would not allow me to play with them in the house, along with an assortment of dogs and cats. Billy developed such a habit of butting everyone in sight that my father eventually gave him to a farmer who had a herd of goats. I never saw Billy again.

Our little town of fifteen hundred people was not lacking in churches. There were more than a dozen churches for white people and several for blacks. The three most prominent white churches were the Methodist, the Baptist, and the Disciples of Christ (commonly called the Christian Church). These were what are called today the "mainline" denominations. I grew up with the conviction that while the Methodist church was almost as good as our church (the Christian church), the Baptists were well down the scale.

People in my hometown seldom visited one another's churches. There was a keen sense of competition among the congregations, especially with regard to the denominational affiliation of the grade school and high school faculties. We kept count of which church had the most teachers among its members. The three "mainline" churches seemed to have a monopoly. For years the president of the school board was a Methodist. We in the Christian Church thought that gave the Methodist church an unfair advantage in recruiting members among the new teachers.

The Methodist church and the Christian church were located on diagonally opposite corners of the same block. The Baptist church stood another block away from the Christian church. A local wag declared he heard a significant concatenation of closing lines of hymns one Sunday morning while out walking. The Methodists ended a hymn that asked the question, "Will there be any stars in my crown?" At that moment he heard the Christian church congregation blare out a last line of another hymn, "No, not one!" Immediately thereafter the Baptists were singing the closing line from still another hymn, "O, that will be glory for me!"

My statement that people did not visit one another's churches should be qualified. During the summer months, a number of people visited one or more of the Pentecostal churches in town. We lumped them all under the rubric of "holy rollers," because in their worship some members would fall to the floor in ecstasy. When I say people visited the holy rollers, I mean they went to watch them. Summer entertainment at night for quite a number of non-holy rollers was to stand outside the large windows of the main holy roller congregation and laugh at the goings-on inside. The holy rollers practiced mutual foot washing, following the example of Jesus. The onlookers regarded this with disdain. Some said the holy rollers who were farmers probably *needed* to have their feet washed. As a child I had no desire to peek in at the holy rollers, and not, I must confess, out of consideration for their feelings. What I heard about them seemed "spooky," to use a boyhood term. I didn't want to see it.

Some of the Christian souls in Crescent were suffused with something other than love for other Christians. One of the most startling events of my church life occurred one Sunday evening, when I was nine or ten. My father invited me to go with him to attend services at one of the local "gospel" churches. As a local businessman he knew many members of the church. He wanted to hear what he thought would be a good, fiery sermon.

The sermon was fiery, all right—much fierier than my father had expected. Shouting at the top of his voice, the preacher bitterly attacked members of other local churches. He declared they did not deserve the name "Christian." My father and I stirred uncomfortably in our pew.

Suddenly, looking straight at my father and me, the preacher shouted, "I'd rather hug a nigger than hug one of those Campbellites!" (In those days

Campbellite was a pejorative term for a person of my denomination, taken from the name of its founder, Alexander Campbell.)

"Let's get out of here, Jack," my father said quietly. As we walked out the center aisle toward the door, the preacher shouted after us, "See there! When you tell the truth, some people can't stand it!"

I had never been so embarrassed in my life. I couldn't look at the faces of the people staring at us as we walked out. My father was quiet on the way home. He said only, "I'm sorry, Jack," and never mentioned the incident again.

I would have received Christian formation in a Southern Baptist church had it not been for a rebellious act by an uncle before I was born. My paternal grandfather, Ben, was the leading layman in the Baptist church in Crescent. When his son Emmett, who was musically gifted, reached his later teens, grandfather insisted that he play the organ for all the Sunday services. My father told me Uncle Emmett resented this duty.

One Sunday morning during a communion service (rare event in a Baptist church), apparently something inside Uncle Emmett. He suddenly pulled out all the stops on the organ, pumped furiously with his feet, and began playing a ragtime tune called "Everybody's Doin' It!" The tune extolled the latest dance craze, the Turkey Trot. Dancing was anathema to those Baptist folk, and so was that music. When Uncle Emmett finished the tune, he walked out of the church.

The minister stopped the worship service and convoked a congregational meeting. Uncle Emmett and my grandparents were "churched"—that is, they were forbidden to take any part in any church activity. In a few weeks, after congregational passions cooled, my grandparents were received back into fellowship. But not Uncle Emmett.

Nor had he any desire to be. For several weeks during the morning service he walked slowly by the church. Through the open windows the congregation could hear him whistling "Everybody's Doin' It!"

My grandfather did not force my father to attend the Baptist church, so he had no religious affiliation until after he and my mother were married. She was a member of the Christian Church, so that became our family church home.

Our town was strictly segregated. The black people comprised about a third of the population. As a child I never ventured into the black sections of town, nor did we see black children in the white sections. A few times, when I was seven or eight, I had a black playmate, the son of a woman who came to our house to do laundry. On one occasion he gave me some startling information. I cannot recall how the subject of human reproduction came up, but in plain terms he told me how I came to be born. I was shocked.

On occasion I would see the principal of the black school on the street or in one of the stores. I held him in awe. He was tall, very dignified, always neatly dressed. All the merchants he dealt with addressed him as "Professor Moon." Their attitude toward all the other black people they served, however, was condescending.

My father was an exception. In his brother's grocery store where he worked, he was unfailingly polite to all customers. I noticed that black customers would often stand and wait for him to serve them rather than deal with other clerks who were available.

My father was fond of one of his regular customers, a black boy about my age, also named Raymond. My father would tease him gently, and the boy seemed to enjoy it. Once or twice a week he would come with a list of groceries his mother needed. Each time, after completing the charge list, my father asked him, "And what else, Raymond?" Raymond would reply, "That's all she wrote." That phrase became a staple in our family vocabulary to denote the decisive end of something.

In all grades of the public school up to high school, we had music classes in which we learned folk and patriotic songs. Many of the songs of Stephen Foster are now in oblivion because they are supposedly racist in tone. My reaction to learning many of his songs was a deep sadness at the quality of life of black people expressed in these songs. The horror of slavery especially impressed me when we sang "Darling Nelly Gray," the plaintive account of the breakup of a black family by the sale of one of the members to a distant slaveholder.

My parents gave me solid moral instruction by word and example, but I can recall no specifically Christian training in my home. My mother read her Bible frequently. As a child I noticed that it was worn from use. I seldom if ever saw my father reading Scripture until much later in his life. Apart from an occasional perfunctory grace before meals, my family never prayed together. My mother did impress on me the necessity of praying silently "Now I lay me down to sleep" before going to bed at night. But apart from the moral training, all my Christian formation came through the activities of my church.

My grandmother Mattie did give me one bit of religious instruction. When I was four or five, she called my attention to how chickens drink. I had already observed how they dip their beaks into water briefly and then raise their heads as if looking upward, before dipping more water and repeating the head raising. Grandmother asked me, "Do you know why the chickens look up like that?"

"So they can swallow, I guess."

"That's not the real reason," she said. "They're thanking God for their drink."

From the age of three or four I attended Sunday school classes every week while my parents were in an adult class. In our church, as in all Protestant churches, formation at all levels focused on the study of Scripture. I still recall many passages I memorized from the King James Version. The formation focused on drilling into the minds of the children and adults a particular interpretation of the Scripture we read. I recall as a kindergartner singing "Jesus loves me, this I know, for the Bible tells me so." I couldn't read; the Bible could tell me nothing. But I had been assured by my Sunday school teachers and my pastor that Jesus loved me, and it was they who imparted the tradition of our denomination.

Though our study of Scripture focused on the New Testament, we learned many stories about individual persons and events in the Old Testament. We learned that the prophets were strong-minded men who declared the truth of God to unreceptive hearers. But the roots of the New Testament in the Old were never brought out. We learned that the prophets had foretold Jesus' coming, but we (certainly I) gained a distinct impression the two Testaments were disconnected. The Old Testament's central emphasis on sacrifice was ignored, as were all sacrificial language and overtones in the New Testament.

We were taught that our "brotherhood" (the term *denomination* was never used) had "restored" the "primitive church." This latter phrase is an abstraction dear to most Protestant hearts. As a child I assumed that the

Mother and infant Ray

earliest Christians probably had the same King James Version of the Bible that we did. My teachers assured me that our worship was just like that of those early Christians.

In retrospect, I can see that the study of Church history was a key factor in my embracing the Catholic faith. Yet Church history played no part in my early formation as a Christian. Apart from a few details gleaned from the book of Acts, I learned nothing about the nineteen centuries that preceded the founding of our "brotherhood." Now I can see the reasoning behind this studied ignorance: If one believes he is sharing in a restored "primitive" church, why should he be concerned about what happened between the first century and the early nineteenth century when his "brotherhood" was formed?

Sundays were busy days. There was a worship service before Sunday school, followed by classes for all ages. Then came the regular worship service with a long sermon for the adults. Children up to the age of twelve worshipped separately in a part of the church built to scale for their worship. The pastor's wife (who was also ordained) conducted what we called "junior church." On Sunday afternoons, especially in the summer, there might be social gatherings at the church. Or caravans of cars might journey to a neighboring town for a get-together with that Disciples of Christ congregation. Back we went to church for the youth meeting called Christian Endeavor. Following that, we went to the regular Sunday evening service, which included a long sermon.

On Monday the adult choir spent an entire evening in practice. For most of my pre-college years, my father was director of the choir. Though not musically trained, he had a melodious baritone voice. He had been taught to read music and direct the choir by the pastor's wife, herself an excellent musician. My mother sang alto in the choir. Until I was thirteen or fourteen I had to go to choir practice with my parents; neither the term baby-sitter nor the practice was much used then.

I always sat in the back of the church for those two or more hours doing homework or reading a book. Wednesday night was "prayer meeting" night. Several dozen of the parishioners, including my parents, regularly attended this meeting. The only prayer was an opening prayer by the pastor, who then spent the evening leading the group in study of Scripture.

But at the age on nine I was still a pagan.

CHAPTER TWO

CHRISTIAN ROOTS

From my earliest days in the Christian Church I had heard "altar calls" after the sermons. This was common practice among Protestants (and still is among the more evangelical traditions). The call was an invitation for anyone who felt moved to come forward and make a profession of faith in Jesus Christ. Those who came might be unbaptized; they might be baptized but not active in the church; they might be active but wanting to rededicate their lives to Christ.

One Sunday evening when I was about six years old, to my great surprise my father went forward and in tears publicly professed his desire to surrender his life to Christ. I did not understand what this meant, but I remember being embarrassed by his show of emotion.

Ordinarily, baptism was administered by immersion in the baptistery located in the front of the church behind the choir pews. My father evidently requested baptism in the river rather than the baptistery. A week after he responded to the altar call, on a Sunday afternoon, several dozen members of our congregation gathered on the bank of the Cimarron River four miles south of town. The minister (a boyhood friend of my father) led my father out into waist-deep water. There he administered trine immersion. I didn't understand the significance of what my father was doing. I was impressed by the solemnity of the occasion but anxious lest my father be lost in the river. (Only later I learned he was a good swimmer.)

Like the Baptists, the Christian Church practiced what it called adult baptism. Ordinarily, children would be baptized around the age of eight or nine, after having made an "adult" confession of faith. I knew I was expected to follow this custom, though my parents never urged me. One Sunday morning when I was nine, without consultation with my parents, I answered the altar call given in the junior church service by the pastor's wife. I "went forward," as it was called, and said I had accepted Christ as my savior. I knew that Baptism would soon follow. My parents seemed pleased when I told them what I had done.

A couple of weeks later I was baptized during the morning service of what we kids called the "big church." I was apprehensive. I had never been underwater except once, when I was about five. At a church picnic beside the river, an older cousin tossed me into water over my head, thinking it would force me to swim. It didn't. My father rescued me after I had gulped a quantity of water.

As a child, I had peered into the empty baptistery. It was a large tank, about ten feet long, six feet wide, five feet deep, with stairs at each end. In a dressing room next to the baptistery a deacon helped me don a long white robe after I had stripped to my underwear. He led me out into the open where the congregation could see me.

The pastor in his shirtsleeves was standing in the water. As I started down the steps he took my hand. I could not swim. Going into water that deep frightened me. The pastor gave me quick whispered instructions. "I'll hold the napkin over your nose. Fold your hands on your chest. Stand stiff. Take a deep breath each time before I immerse you." Standing in the middle of the baptistery, facing the congregation, he placed his left hand at the back of my head. Raising his right hand, he said in a loud voice, "I baptize you in the name of the Father—"

Backward I went. Underwater again!

("Oh, Mr. Harman! *Please* don't let me fall to the bottom!")

Up he lifted me. I took another breath.

"—and of the Son—"

Back into the water. Not so frightening this time. I had survived the first plunge.

Up out of the water. Another breath.

"—and of the Holy Spirit. Amen."

Down, under, and up for the last time.

I climbed the stairs out of the baptistery much faster than I had stepped in. The deacon draped a large towel around my shoulders and led me back to the dressing room to change into dry clothes. I joined my parents in the congregation, jubilant at having the rite behind me. At our noonday meal afterward my parents were rather quiet. They did not discuss my baptism. I knew that I had made a serious resolve, which I understood in purely moral terms. Though I had been an obedient child, I knew I must be especially vigilant in minding my parents. After my baptism I was a model child—that day and part of the next. The memory of my baptismal resolve faded rather quickly.

At that time in my life, since both my parents were in the choir, I sat with my friends at Sunday morning and evening services. We were mostly attentive during the morning service, but our mood on Sunday evening was different. Perhaps after having spent several hours in church we had had our fill. We amused ourselves by turning to the index of the hymnal, which listed the hymns alphabetically according to their first lines, and adding certain phrases to the titles.

The first phrase I remember using was "under the bed." We stifled our giggles to avoid adult stares of disapproval but found great amusement in "Brighten the corner where you are—under the bed" or "We're marching to Zion—under the bed" or "Yield not to temptation—under the bed." As we approached puberty, a couple of the boys from farm families widened our horizons. They introduced "without pants," which we eagerly put to use: "Just as I am—without pants" or "Abide with me—without pants" or "Onward Christian soldiers—without pants."

In those days, and still in some Protestant traditions, the social activities of families centered in the church. There were seasonal parties for whole families: Independence Day, Memorial Day, Thanksgiving, Christmas, New Year, Easter. My favorites were the summertime ice cream socials. They were fundraisers. Women of the parish would gather at the church in the morning and make several large freezers of ice cream, using thick cream brought in by the farmwomen. These events were held on the church lawn illuminated by strings of lights overhead. The rich ice cream was served in large cereal bowls, heaped to the brim, at a price of ten or fifteen cents.

For the children these were delightful times. After filling up on ice cream we ran around the church lawn and played hide-and-seek in the shadows while our parents chatted over their empty bowls.

Most Protestant congregations love to sing, and most sing well. To some extent, their hymn singing is to their corporate life what the sacraments are to the corporate life of Catholics. In non-liturgical worship such as that in which I was nurtured, singing is the only active part the congregation can take, except for an occasional responsive psalm. Growing up in the Disciples of Christ tradition, I learned more of basic Christianity from the hymns we sang than from any Bible reading. I did read the Bible in Sunday school, but seldom at home.

But the hymnal—that was a different matter! I loved singing hymns in and out of church. We had few books in our home. For some reason my parents never made use of the public library in a larger town fifteen miles away, where most of our family shopping was done. I often read the words in the hymnal, but more often sang them. Many times I went through the entire hymnal. Even today many verses of those hymns come to my mind.

Our hymnody was individualistic, focusing on the person's relationship with Jesus. It seems strange to me that I knew and loved those Christ-centered hymns but had little awareness of a personal relationship with Jesus. Our Sunday school lessons, the sermons both in junior church and in the adult church, the worship service itself—all urged us to trust and love Jesus. I accepted what I had been taught, that Jesus is the Son of God, the third Person of the Blessed Trinity (though the word *Trinity* did not appear in our hymnal).

I think that as a child I was Unitarian without ever having heard the word. Not in rebellion, but in ignorance. I did not receive—or at least did not understand—any specific instruction on committing one's life to Jesus and growing in that commitment. I only remember warm, friendly feelings associated with my thoughts of Jesus. Only years later in seminary did I begin to grow in personal devotion to the Lord Jesus Christ.

As a high school student I attended meetings of Christian Endeavor, the Sunday evening youth group. It was a fairly serious study group with a bit of social activity afterward. We were required to answer roll call each week by reciting a Scripture verse we had learned for that meeting. I suspected some of the boys had not done their homework. Their favorite verse, often used, was John 11:35: "Jesus wept." After Christian Endeavor ended, we went straight to the evening worship service, in which our pastor preached his second long sermon of the day. That service ended just in time for many of us to catch the second showing of the latest movie at the local theater two blocks away.

As I reflect on growing up in a small town, several characteristics of that life come to mind. We children had astonishing freedom. Everyone knew which children belonged to which family. People in general watched out for the children of the town. Many of us even knew which wandering dog belonged to which family. We were free to ride our bicycles anywhere in town. I still recall the thrill in early adolescence of riding my bicycle at night along the sidewalks and streets of the town, proud of my dual headlamps and my taillight.

In a small town there is much less privacy than in a city. People knew a great deal about each other, and gossip flowed freely. As a child, I noticed much of my parents' conversation with their friends tended to focus on other friends.

But along with the gossip came compassion for persons we knew were troubled or suffering. I recall my parents sharing from our meager resources with others in greater need. When there was 25 percent unemployment in our nation, I think no one in that town went to bed hungry. This small-town familiarity created a deep sense of safety. No one locked house doors. No one took keys out of car ignitions. There was no crime.

And along with compassion came remarkable acceptance of eccentric behavior. And as I look back on that life, Crescent seems to have had an unusually wide assortment of eccentric persons. I have amused my children and now my grandchildren with stories about the characters I knew there. In the telling, much of that conduct seems strange and comical. Yet other townsfolk accepted those eccentricities as natural for the persons themselves. One scarcely heard a critical comment about behavior that my children and grandchildren consider humorously odd.

My childhood was happy, except for the parts of the "dustbowl" years (1933–1935). Ordinarily, springtime was my favorite season. But the beauty of spring in those years was blotted out by the clouds of dust that made life miserable.

Ten years later in a wartime journal I reflected on those years: "I can think of nothing in all my experience which can compare with a dust storm in its ability to sap the joy from living. For days and days the dirt would blow unceasingly and unmercifully, filling every cranny and crevice, oftentimes reducing the visibility in broad daylight to fifty feet or even less. And then one night the wind would suddenly stop blowing. After that, for days and days the air would be filled with dust. Dust everywhere, enveloping everything in a gloomy shroud. One would think it would certainly settle after a day or so with no wind, but the dust seemed suspended in midair. As in a heavy fog, we lived and moved and had our being. Yet 'fog' is an inept description. Fogs are sometimes refreshing; the dust was not."

Both my parents worked. For several hours after school I was alone. Those were the loneliest days of my life. In those years of devastating drought, the well from which we pumped household water dried up. We had to carry drinking water from the home of our elderly neighbors a block away. As I carried water I often became so saturated with the melancholy atmosphere I thought I hadn't the strength to carry those two buckets back to our house. An occasional light shower—no rain for months—was a minor disaster for housewives who had hung their washing to dry. (No electric dryers in those days.) The rain shower did not bring water. It brought light mud. They had to take their clothes in and wash them again.[1]

---

1   Though we suffered from dust and drought, our part of Oklahoma was only on the edge of the "dust bowl" area. My family had no accurate knowledge of the devastation and suffering of millions of persons in the "dust bowl." For a gripping account of this disaster, see Timothy Egan, *The Worst Hard Time* (Boston: Houghton Mifflin, 2006).

In Sunday school I had read Jesus' warning, "No one who puts his hand to the plow and looks back is fit for the kingdom of God" (Lk. 9:62). The truth of His words was impressed on me when I was ten or eleven. I spent much of that summer on my grandfather's farm. He knew my eagerness to drive one of his teams of horses. One morning he told me I could help him by driving one of his cultivators in the cornfield. The cultivator had two large wheels and a seat where the driver sat while guiding two sets of three small plows with both hands and feet. The cultivator straddled each row of new, short stalks of corn to loosen the soil and keep the rows clear of grass and weeds. Since both his hands were engaged, the driver looped a single line of reins from both horses over his left shoulder and under his right arm. He guided the team by leaning backward with one shoulder or the other.

From watching my grandfather I knew what to do. My first hour of plowing went well. Then I began to wonder how my freshly plowed rows looked. I turned in the seat to look back over my right shoulder. My turning signaled the horses to pull to the right. As I was looking back to admire what I had done, I suddenly realized I was plowing not along the row but *across* several rows of new stalks.

In panic, I stopped the team. Grandfather had been keeping an eye on me from where he was working in the field. He came quickly to my rescue. Without a word, he smiled at me and drove the team back on course. Then he entrusted the line to me again and went back to his cultivator. I saw then even more meaning in Jesus' words. Not only is one who sets his hand to the plow and looks back not fit for the kingdom of God. He's also not fit to run the plow.

My first awareness that there were Catholics in the world came in early childhood. Frequently I saw nuns on the streets of Guthrie, the county seat, where I went occasionally with my mother on her shopping trips. I do not know how I learned they were nuns. I cannot recall having asked my mother about those ladies so strangely dressed. Once when we drove past a convent on the outskirt of Guthrie I asked my mother what it was, and she said it was a Catholic convent. I think I had never heard the word *convent* before. She offered no explanation. I asked for none. My impression then was that anything Catholic was not subject for discussion.

As years passed, on trips to Oklahoma City I saw more nuns, always in pairs. (Now I know they were mostly Carmelites. And now for years I have been nourished by Carmelite spirituality. Harbingers, those chance encounters on the street?) Their long, heavy habits and huge coifs always caught my eye. Even in the hottest days of summer with the temperature well above one hundred degrees, the faces of the nuns on the street always seemed cool and calm.

This fascinated me. Out of politeness I restricted my curiosity to quick glances. The thought often came to me, "These people seem to mean *business*." This remained my primary impression of Catholicism. I cannot recall when I first recognized a man as a Catholic priest. Somehow I learned that nuns and priests did not marry. Celibacy (the word was unknown to me at that time) did not seem strange to me, since I knew some women and even a few men who never married.

Wearing the Church's uniform is an essential part of the apostolate of religious and clergy. Suppose these nuns had been wearing ordinary clothing. I would not have known they were Catholic religious. Today, so far as I know, not a single order that has discarded religious garb is being blessed with vocations. (If religious refuse fully to embrace the life in their outward appearance, God evidently does not intend to preserve their orders.) Some religious who insist on civilian dress have argued with me that they are now "more approachable" than when they wore religious habits. My response is, "How can you as a religious be more approachable when the person in need can't tell that you *are* a religious?"

The only conversations about Catholics I heard in my home concerned the only two known Catholics in Crescent. Friends of my parents, this middle-aged couple owned a department store where they worked long hours. On Saturday their store was open from early morning until 11 o'clock at night. My parents knew that early every Sunday morning the couple drove 15 miles to Guthrie to attend Mass.

Several times mother expressed pity for them. "They work so late and hard and have to get up so early on Sunday morning. That old Catholic Church has a terrible hold on them," she would say. I agreed. But I wondered at their loyalty to their Church. I knew my parents in similar circumstances would not make such a strenuous effort to attend an early church service. But I assumed from my parents' attitude that Catholic loyalty was grievously misplaced.

I referred to my parents' friends as the only "known" Catholics in town. There was another Catholic whose faith we did not know. She was a Native American who seemed to live apart from the community. I never saw her visiting with other people. Years later, when my family and I were living in Oklahoma City, I met her (then widowed) at the cathedral. All those years she lived in Crescent, married to a local truck driver, we never knew she was practicing the Catholic faith and unobtrusively driving fifteen miles to Mass.

When I was fifteen I underwent a tonsillectomy performed by a doctor who used an electric needle. The surgery caused little pain and I recovered quickly. But a couple of years later I began having trouble with a portion of a tonsil the doctor had failed to remove. A specialist determined that the muscles of my heart were being adversely affected by poison from the diseased tonsil, making me weak and lethargic. It was necessary to undergo a second tonsillectomy, this time at Saint Anthony's Hospital in Oklahoma City.

I had never been a patient in a hospital before. The fact that the hospital was Catholic added to my apprehension. Everything Catholic was so foreign to my little world. Why couldn't our doctor have worked on me in a nice public (that is, non-Catholic) hospital? The doctors decided it was inadvisable to give me general anesthesia because of the poison in my heart. I could hardly believe what I was hearing. They were going to take that piece of tonsil out while I was awake?

Now I was really frightened. They put me in a surgical gown and hauled me into the operating room. Then I climbed into the chair that would be my resting place while they operated. I almost held my breath as I watched a nurse lay out surgical instruments on a tray beside me. She put them in place, side by side, very deliberately. Was she trying to scare me? I counted them. Thirteen! I have never been so frightened, either before or since.

Both the injection of the anesthetic and the operation were quite painful. A couple of times during the procedure I fainted. I cannot remember being taken to a room. Shortly after I realized I was in bed in a room, a nurse came into my room. A nun! I looked at her and immediately vomited a great quantity of blood at her feet. Not intentionally, of course.

She said nothing. Smiling gently at me, she began cleaning me and my bed and the floor. I have never forgotten the look on her face: kind, sympathetic, reassuring. I wanted to apologize, but the words didn't come. I closed my eyes in a wave of nausea and mentally thanked her for her kindness. May God richly reward her!

I recovered my strength slowly. By the time I started college in the fall I thought I was back to normal. The doctor gave me an excuse from compulsory gym class in college. I used this excuse all four years and engaged in no athletic activities in college. When I went to enlist in the navy in the spring of 1942, I assumed I would be rejected because of a weak heart. I was greatly surprised— and, I must say, elated—when I passed the physical exam. I suspected the navy doctor somehow missed a weakness that must be in my heart.

Throughout my two and a half years aboard ship I occasionally had chest pains, always in the middle of night, that awakened me from sound sleep. They frightened me because I assumed they were heart attacks. Each time I prayed for God to preserve my life. I promised Him that if He would save me from the heart attack, I would never smoke again. (I was then a confirmed cigarette smoker, having begun my addiction with pipe smoking in college.)

Each time my prayer was answered; I drifted off to sleep again and awakened the next morning. And each time I went right back to smoking as usual. (I am thankful to report that ten years later I finally kept that promise to stop smoking.)

When I was discharged from active duty I had to take another physical. After the doctor pronounced me fit, I confessed to him that I had had a good many heart attacks while onboard ship. I described them to him and he snorted, "Heart attacks! Nothing but pleurisy." I had never heard the word before. He explained what it was, and I was enormously relieved.

Despite early favorable impressions of Catholicism, I was infected with anti-Catholic prejudice from the conservative Protestant air I breathed. The prejudice first manifested itself in this way. At the height of singer and actor Bing Crosby's popularity in the 1930s and early '40s, my parents and I regarded him as a family friend. Only in rare circumstances did we miss listening to his weekly radio program. Once in those years I turned on the radio and recognized Bing's speaking voice. I could hardly believe what I was hearing: Bing—our old friend *Bing*!—was repeating certain prayers over and over with a group of Catholics. (I knew nothing about the Rosary.) I literally groaned and said to myself, "*Not* old Bing?" It was as if I had suddenly learned of some serious moral defect of his.

I wanted to hear no more. I turned off the radio, the only time I ever tuned Bing out. I remembered having read that he was Catholic but had put it out of my mind. Though I continued to be a fan, the realization Bing was a Catholic remained a regretful memory.

After graduating from high school in 1938, with half a dozen friends from my church I attended a weeklong summer conference outside Siloam Springs, Arkansas. The conference was sponsored by the Christian Church. Several hundred young people came to the conference. There I came under the influence of a young, gifted, attractive minister named Bill Alexander. Before entering the ministry he had been a nightclub entertainer. The son of a minister, he was beloved by all the conferees. Like everyone else I was deeply moved by his preaching and the impact of his personality. During the conference I began to think I would like to be a minister—as much like Bill as possible. An immature thought, yes. But it was the beginning of my call to ordained ministry.

From early years I had always assumed I would go to college. Yet I gave little thought, even in high school, to which college I should attend. Now it seems strange to me that my parents and I did not discuss this important decision. In my senior year of high school I decided I would enroll in the University of Oklahoma to study journalism. I knew my parents couldn't give me much financial support in college. That spring a woman friend of our family offered me a scholarship to attend her alma mater, Phillips University in Enid, Oklahoma. It was a small denominational school affiliated with the Disciples of Christ. I knew nothing about Phillips but a lot about the limitations of my parents' finances. I accepted the offer and enrolled in the fall of 1938.

One Sunday afternoon in early September my parents drove me to Enid and saw me settled in a room in a private home near the university. (There was no men's dormitory.) After my parents left, I had never been so lonely. I briefly met three or four house fellows and then spent the evening alone in my room. I asked myself, "What am I doing here?" I did not yearn to be at home again; I simply yearned *not* to be in a strange room in a strange house in a strange town.

But from the moment I walked on the campus Monday morning and began the enrollment process, I sensed I had begun an exciting new life. My college years were by far the happiest years I had known. The student body, numbering about five hundred, was a warm, friendly community. I came to know almost everyone by name and formed some deep, lifelong friendships. I served in a number of positions of leadership—president of the freshman class, editor of the yearbook, president of the student body, president of a literary society—that greatly increased my self-confidence.

There were no teaching assistants in Arts and Sciences. All my classes were taught by seasoned professors. My freshman instructor in rhetoric was a gifted teacher who coaxed us into greater facility in writing. She urged us to develop what she called the "dictionary habit": make a mental note of any new word, and look it up as soon as you can. That habit has remained with me. She encouraged my admiration for Walter Lippman, a journalist whose columns I collected and studied. "Perhaps that's your calling," she said. "Think about it."

I set aside thoughts of becoming a minister. I would become a writer. The summer after my freshman year in college I charted my course in a journal

High School Graduating Class, 1938

Freshman year in college

entry. I would absorb all the knowledge I could from a general education and then set out to travel the world. I would "learn more of men, their ways, and their social ills," as I noted in my journal. (This plan was carried out in an unexpected way: three years in the U.S. Navy.) After living abroad for several years, I would return to my native land and settle down to writing.

I conceded in my journal—with Olympian disdain—that I might have to do "hack work" at first, like working for a newspaper. Eventually I would become independent so that, like Lippman, I could offer sensible solutions to the problems of our democracy. I declared all this was not "the ephemeral pipedream of an older adolescent" (I had just turned 18) but "the map by which I shall steer my life." I even decided on a name I would adopt. Not liking my given name, Raymond, I combined its second syllable with my middle name, Olin. Some day I would be known (far and wide, I hoped) as Ray Mondolin. (Years later, in reading that entry, I realized that proposed name is almost identical with the name of my least favored musical instrument.)

I chose history as a major, with a minor in political science. From my mother I had inherited a deep interest in history. All but one of my history courses were taught by the head of the department, who immediately became my favorite. He was a gruff, demanding teacher. Students who did not know him well were intimidated and tried to avoid him. He was not only an inspiring teacher but also a very colorful man with whom I developed a deep friendship.

"Prof," as his students called him, had a keen sense of humor, which overflowed with students who were privileged to become better acquainted with him. He was a keen observer of student life. One day in conversation he referred to a couple I knew who had been dating for some time. "Not much there," he said. "Do you know what that is? It's a 'platonic' relationship: a 'play' for her and a 'tonic' for him." I thought he was joking. A few weeks later I noticed the couple had stopped dating.

Meanwhile, in my history courses I was introduced to Catholic doctrine and history since the Middle Ages. (I had no course dealing with earlier times.) The textbooks Prof used in a sophomore course in modern European history were written by Carleton J. H. Hayes. (Years later I learned he was a Catholic convert who eventually became the U.S. ambassador to Spain.) The textbooks gave much more detail about Catholic doctrine than does the average history text. I learned about monks and bishops and popes and sacraments and interdicts and penitent kings standing barefoot in the snow, begging papal absolution. Though fascinated, I felt no attraction to Catholicism itself. It was a world totally different from mine.

My ambition to become another Walter Lippman did not entirely replace my attraction to the ministry. My motivation was a vague desire to help people solve problems and lead better, happier lives. I did not think of it as a calling. It was simply something I thought I probably should do. Yet I kept putting the thought aside and tried to concentrate on my ambition to be a journalist.

In my younger years I almost never missed going to church on Sunday, except when in summer I visited my maternal grandparents. They were kindly, good people who never went to church. During college, however, I attended church only occasionally, usually when whichever girl I was dating at the time chose to go. I admired the pastor of the university church, an intellectually disciplined man who preached carefully crafted sermons. Many of my friends did not appreciate his skill in preaching; they preferred a more emotional, dramatic type of preaching.

In those years I lived by a general Protestant ethic. I believed that Jesus is the Son of God and that there are three Persons in the Trinity. I had a vague sense that there is something called heaven for those who live good lives. But these were only opinions, not based on a personal relationship with Jesus. I reacted negatively to anything that sounded "pious." A friend told me that when another student we knew was greeted with the usual "How are you?" she always replied, "Oh, I just love Jesus more and more each day!" Without any reason to, I doubted her sincerity. I was even annoyed by her response. I know now that I reacted that way because her piety was foreign to my experience. She may well have known Jesus personally. But I didn't.

Because of a mistake in enrollment, at the beginning of my senior year I still lacked two freshman courses. One was introductory psychology. With another upperclassman I sat in the back row, rather superciliously surveying the freshmen and sophomores in the class. Almost from the first day I noticed a young woman who walked into class with a confident stride. She had long dark hair and an olive complexion—in the slang of that time, a "real beaut." I soon learned she was Ruth Silvee from Galveston, Texas.

She sat in the front row next to a loud-mouthed freshman also from Texas. One day he came with a small garden snake in his hand. Before class he pretended to ask the girls near him to admire his snake. They all shrieked and recoiled appropriately. Then he turned to Ruth. She was seated at her desk, looking at a book. He thrust the snake near her face. She looked coolly at the snake, then at the snake's captor, and then resumed her reading. I was impressed.

Through all my joy-filled college years I could not stop thinking about the ministry. Early in my senior year I told myself that for almost four years I had wrestled with the thought of becoming a minister. "It's time to shape up," I told myself. Given my interest in government, I decided that after graduation I would enroll in the school of public administration at Harvard. (In those years, with my academic record, it was not an unrealistic goal.) Making the decision brought immediate relief to my unsettled spirit.

Then came Pearl Harbor.

Less than a week after the Japanese attack on the U.S., I took part in a debate tournament in Texas. In a journal entry later, I noted the reactions of the one hundred fifty college students at the final banquet of the tournament. Beneath the usual gaiety there was an undercurrent of anxiety about the war. It surfaced when one of my colleagues gave a reading of a poem, "Whisperin' Bill," about a disabled Civil War veteran that was a stinging indictment of war. Many eyes (including mine) were wet as people realized that the very thing about which Tom was reading was upon us—war—WAR—in all its awfulness. "Tears in eyes," I wrote, "yes, but this is only the beginning. Many an eye will be wet before this thing is over."

A couple of months later I gave in to God's call. With the help of the seminary dean at my college, I arranged to enroll in the fall to prepare for ministry. Not yet twenty-one, I had not been classified in the military draft. Without telling me, the dean arranged with my draft board to give me seminary status (4-D) when I registered a month or two later.

As soon as my future was settled I began having second thoughts. Patriotic fervor was widespread, and many of my friends were enlisting in the armed services. I shared the common conviction that the war against Nazi and Japanese imperialism had to be prosecuted to victory. I began to realize I could never be content to sit in a seminary classroom while my friends fought a battle that was as much my responsibility as theirs. I decided to enlist in the navy and go on active duty after graduation that spring.

By the time I had decided to enter seminary, I had begun to believe I had a true calling to the ministry. Now, as I prepared to enlist, I thought serving in the Armed Forces would be a good test of that calling. If I survive the war, I told myself, and if that calling persists, it must be genuine.

In the spring of 1942, shortly before graduation, I enlisted in the navy. My orders to active duty did not come until October. In the interim I lived with my parents and worked for a friend in Crescent. I drove a tractor pulling a wheat combine, did much plowing and planting, hauled construction sand from my friend's sand pit. I worked long, hard hours and greatly enjoyed the exertion.

During those many weeks of driving a tractor and planting ("drilling") summer wheat, an obvious but important lesson impressed itself on me. A journal entry from that time noted the necessity of a fixed goal for success in one's venture. In planting wheat, so long as I watched the preceding row near me, I could keep all my rows parallel. But they were far from straight. It's impossible to detect slight veering from side to side when one looks only at the rows near at hand. But if I kept my eye on some post, tree, or bush at the far end of the field and steered the tractor by that, my rows were straight. Let the planter keep his eyes fixed on the goal at the far end of the field. So I repeatedly told myself that if I want to succeed in this world, I must always look far ahead to a worthwhile goal.

Countless times during my years in the navy this thought returned. My goal was to serve Jesus as one of His ministers. Imperfect though that goal was, keeping my eye on it helped me avoid many moral and spiritual blind alleys and detours. How much straighter would have been my course had my focus been Jesus Christ Himself and my love for Him, my Savior!

In God's good time, that was to come.

When the fall term after my graduation began at Phillips I visited friends there on two different weekends. Those visits were sources of untold blessings for me. For the first time I dated that notable girl from psychology class, Ruth Silvee. Thus began the romance that led to our marriage three years later. And not just because she had shown no fear of snakes.

God had led me to my lifelong companion in pilgrimage. Next to my Redeemer and to life itself, she is God's greatest gift to me.

CHAPTER THREE

OFF TO WAR

In the fall of 1942 my orders to active duty came. At the train station in Guthrie my parents and I said our good-byes. Father cried; mother held back her tears. It was hard not to cry, but I kept smiling at them. I wondered, would I ever see them again? I was apprehensive yet excited as I climbed aboard the train that would take me to New York to begin my naval training. As the train began to move, I knew I was on my way to the war.

This was my first long trip on a train. I was so interested in my pullman car that I gave little thought to what lay ahead in New York. When the train stopped for half an hour in Kansas, I called the mother of Bette, a young woman I had dated during most of my junior year in college. She told me her daughter was married. I knew—a "Dear John" letter had brought me the news the previous year. Then the mother told me something I did not know: Her daughter's husband was an instructor in the midshipmen's school at Columbia. My destination.

"Small world," I thought. "Weird, too." She proudly told me they were living in a penthouse in New York City.

The trip from Oklahoma City to New York was pleasant. En route I met a number of young men also headed for the midshipmen's school. We soon discovered none of us could give the rest any hint about our new life soon to begin. So we talked of other things.

Arriving in New York, we scarcely had a moment to stretch our necks in awe as we saw Grand Central Station for the first time. A cab deposited us at John Jay Hall in Columbia. There we joined hundreds of other confused young men and were processed with startling speed. We were signed in, assigned rooms, given uniforms. We chased up and down fourteen flights of steps several times in getting settled. The officer in charge of our floor (the "mate of the deck") lectured us on how to succeed as a naval officer. Exhausted, I fell asleep that night with a copy of *Bluejacket's Manual* in my hand.

The following three months flashed by. We marched in formation an hour or two each day. For what purpose, except exercise, we never learned. Our coursework was demanding, our study hours long. My friends and I agreed our ordnance course was the most difficult. We spent days studying and diagramming the intricate breech mechanism of a 5-inch 25-caliber gun. (Once aboard ship we learned the navy had discontinued use of that gun years before.)

We were drilled in naval nomenclature. Certain words were banished from our vocabulary. Aboard ship, one must never say "floor" but "deck." Never "wall" but "bulkhead." Never "stair" but "ladder." The list seemed endless. Once at sea I was somewhat surprised but grateful to hear graduates of the Naval Academy, including our captain, speak of "floor" and "wall" and "stair." Early in our course one of the instructors solemnly catechized us in what he called standard naval operating procedure: "When in trouble, when in doubt, run in circles, scream and shout."

Our instructors were newly commissioned officers who had finished their course a day or two before my class arrived at Columbia. Their knowledge of matters naval exceeded ours only slightly. Several weeks into our course, in the middle of winter, a group of us were taken across the Hudson to New Jersey for "whaleboat drill." A new ensign sat in the bow of a whaleboat, facing us six who vainly tried to row in unison. I had never had an oar in my hands. None of the others seemed to be any more experienced. We rowed out from the shore for some distance, expecting to be ordered to maneuver the boat in a different direction. It was necessary to avoid the heavy river traffic. But the ensign sat facing us with a grim look on his face. He glanced over his shoulder frequently.

No words were spoken. Yet all of us knew we were getting too near the path of large boats and ships going up and down the river. "Why don't we turn around?" I thought. "Doesn't this guy know the proper terminology for turning us around?" Finally, in a resigned voice, the ensign said, "Alright, guys, turn the damned thing around and take us back to the shore." Awkwardly but eagerly we obeyed.

The discipline was strict at midshipmen's school. The officers gave us demerits for the slightest offenses, even for putting one's hands in one's pockets while walking down the hall. Twenty-five demerits and you were out and on your way to boot camp as an apprentice seaman. None of us wanted to make that trip.

And yet that fate almost befell me. I led my company in demerits: twenty-four. For various small offenses I had received a total of four demerits. Nothing to worry about. Then one evening my demerit total skyrocketed.

During evening study hours several classmates had come to our room to ask my roommate about a troublesome assignment. Each one left the door ajar as he went out. An ajar door was against the rules. Since my desk was nearer the door, each time I had to interrupt my study to close the door. The last time I didn't get up. Instead I took my *Bowditch*, a large navigation manual, and tossed it at the door to close it. As the book left my hand it slipped from my fingers. Instead of hitting the bottom half of the door, it hit the top half and went right through the translucent glass window. The sound shattered the quiet of the hall.

Alarmed men popped out of their rooms. A man next door had been depressed; some feared he had tried to commit suicide. The officer on duty rushed down the hall. He demanded an explanation. He listened with scornful disbelief to my story. On the spot he gave me twenty demerits and ordered me to clean up the mess. The men returned to their rooms. As I swept, I could see the gates of boot camp opening before me. Not till graduation day many weeks later could I be certain those gates were closed.

In my days at Columbia midshipmen's school, chapel attendance on Sunday evening was compulsory. (The following year some midshipmen objected on grounds of religious freedom. After that, chapel attendance was optional.) Our liberty extended from early Saturday afternoon following inspection until six o'clock Sunday evening. A few minutes after six on Sunday, we were mustered according to companies and marched off to worship. Jewish midshipmen were taken to a nearby synagogue. Catholics went to a nearby Catholic Church. The rest of us marched to Riverside Church. It is an enormous Gothic structure, surely one of the most imposing Protestant churches. (We were told that one of the Rockefellers underwrote the cost of construction and endowed the institution. After the war, when I was a seminarian at Union Theological Seminary a block away from the church, I learned to refer to it as "Rockefeller's fire escape.")

It was mid-winter. Our only protection was a light raincoat. Winds blowing from the partially frozen Hudson River cut through us. We generic Protestants marched vigorously through the streets from John Jay Hall to Riverside Church. At the time there was a popular song about a chaplain who in the thick of battle forgot his non-combatant status. Supposedly he shouted, "Praise the Lord and pass the ammunition!" As we marched we shouted our version, "Praise the Lord and give me my commission!"

It was warm inside the church. More than a thousand of us packed tightly into the pews. To understand the congregation's behavior, remember that liberty had just ended. Many—most—of the men had been drinking since Saturday night, some of them heavily. As soon as we finished a hymn and heard a bit of Scripture, we settled back. The sermon always sounded dull at the start, but we welcomed it. Fifteen or more minutes was time enough for a delicious nap. (Years later the chaplain and I were fellow clergymen in the Episcopal Diocese of Washington, DC. I never brought up his tour of duty at the midshipmen's school.)

Almost all of us went to sleep. Fatigue and ingested alcohol made our collective slumber sound. I use the word *sound* as both an adjective and verb. Our sleep was sound. Our sleep sounded. With hundreds of men gently snoring, Riverside Church sounded like a giant beehive. I include myself in the chorus, though I had not been drinking. (Parental training and Woman's Christian Temperance Union conditioning as a child led me to abstain from alcohol in my navy years.) After the benediction, the organist would sound a thunderous chord on the giant organ. We all snapped awake, stood up, and began the navy hymn. More than a thousand young manly voices lustily sang "Eternal Father, strong to save." The memory is still emotionally stirring.

Several weeks into the program an officer came to my room and asked for me by name. I guessed his identity before he introduced himself: he was my replacement whom Bette's "Dear John" letter had announced to me. He invited me to dinner with him and his wife at their nearby apartment the next liberty night, Saturday. Of course, I accepted.

Their penthouse turned out to be a very small apartment on the top floor of a modest apartment building a few blocks from John Jay Hall. I had not seen Bette for over a year. She looked radiant (how *could* she, I thought, with another man), but the meal was a disaster. Meat badly overcooked, vegetables the consistency of lumpy mashed potatoes, a dessert I could not identify. Soon after dinner I pleaded a need to study. My departure was probably as much a relief to them as it was to me.

One day I received a letter from the sister of a college friend. She asked me to pray for him because he was critically ill with a kidney infection. Though he had been an outstanding athlete in college, to his deep regret the military rejected him. As soon as I could get permission to leave my dorm, I went to the nearby Episcopal Cathedral of Saint John the Divine to pray. I had never been inside an Episcopal church. There were other churches in the neighborhood, though none so grand. Why did I go there? Was I led to that Episcopal cathedral, as I would be led into the Episcopal Church six years later?

Kneeling in the cathedral (I had never knelt to pray in a church before), I prayed earnestly that the life of my friend "Snoop" would be spared. Though my decision to become a minister had been largely forgotten during the rigorous naval training, now I bargained with God: "Let Snoop get well and I promise that I will go into the ministry after the war." Bargaining with God is bad enough. Trying to offer in the bargain something I had already given to God made the effort even more deplorable. Snoop did not recover—God rest his merry soul!—but I did keep my promise.

During my Saturday evening "shore leaves"—naval parlance for liberty—I often walked alone for hours among the crowds in midtown Manhattan. Often I thought of a radio program from my college years, "Broadway Is My Beat." The police protagonist in the series introduced each segment by speaking of his part of Broadway as "the loneliest mile in the world." In the midst of those crowds I not only experienced intense loneliness, I actually savored it.

I was fascinated by the fact that with thousands of people around me I could feel utterly alone. I asked myself, is it because none of these people has the slightest interest in me? Is this sense of isolation caused by seeing so many people who probably wouldn't help me if I were in trouble? Often I asked myself how I would feel if I had no money, no home, or even had a family to support with no way to care for them. A few times I even began to feel somewhat homeless and hungry and friendless. God have mercy on those who live what I tried only to imagine.

Just before graduation we received inoculations for various diseases we might encounter in the tropics or the Orient. Wearing t-shirts, we lined up, bared our upper arms, and placed our hands on our hips. Then we ran a gauntlet of four pharmacist's mates, each armed with the world's dullest needle. None of us looked forward to this inoculation and the feverish reaction produced by some of the shots.

Ahead of me was a man who kept jeering his apprehensive classmates. "What are you guys scared about? Four lousy needles. Nothing to it!" His turn came. He stepped forward briskly, grinned left and right at the first two pharmacist's mates as they jabbed both his arms. Another step forward. More grins, two more jabs. He grinned again, triumphantly, took two more steps, and fainted. We cheered. When the corpsmen revived him, he went quietly.

More than three months after beginning our training, we received our commissions as ensigns in the United States Naval Reserve. (Those of us, that is, who had not received twenty-five demerits.) Our diplomas declared to the world that, by an act of Congress, each of us was "an officer and a gentleman." I received orders to report about two weeks later to an officer pool at the navy yard in Bremerton, Washington. I had time to visit my parents in Oklahoma City. I also returned to my alma mater to visit old friends and especially to see Ruth. We had corresponded while I was in New York. Now, through this time with her, the plot of our romance thickened.

During the three weeks in Bremerton, the two or three dozen of us new officers awaiting orders were subjected to a number of courses. Orders came for me to report to San Francisco for duty aboard an escort aircraft carrier, the USS Nassau (CVE 16). In San Francisco I came in contact with half a dozen other newly commissioned ensigns with the same orders. In wartime San Francisco, the demand for hotel accommodations far exceeded the supply. Five of us were given one medium-sized double room in the Fairmont Hotel.

The next day was Sunday. I had my second contact with the Episcopal Church. All but one of us (who was a Catholic) went to morning services at Grace Episcopal Cathedral near our hotel. I had never shared in liturgical worship before. The beauty of the liturgy impressed me. Even more impressive was the conviction that flooded my mind during the service: more than anything else in the world, I wanted to be a minister.

Yet after leaving the church service I realized my determination had faltered. On many other occasions I had resolved to enter the ministry during a worship service and then wavered afterward. Why this pattern, I wondered. That night in a journal entry I decided what really faltered was my sense of worthiness to be a minister. "It is such a glorious calling that I could never give myself up to it, even though I was burning with a zeal to serve (as I am now), if there were the slightest doubt in my mind (as there is now) as to my capabilities."

As a Unitarian (though I did not think of myself with that term) I was "living under the law." From being a Marcionite as a child (divorcing the New Testament from the Old) I had become a Pelagian. I had an exalted, unrealistic ideal of the kind of person a minister should be. I believed I must make myself into that kind of person if I dared to enter the ministry. Now I can see that with those presuppositions I was bound to falter in my determination. My indecision reflected my sense of personal unworthiness for what I regarded as the highest of callings.

After a few days in the hotel, the accumulation of our soiled laundry became a problem. The hotel charges for laundry service were prohibitive, and there were no laundromats on Nob Hill. We decided we must wash our own underwear and socks. We bought heavy cord and strung four lines the length of our room, over our beds. For longer than an hour we took turns washing clothes in the basin and the bathtub. When we finished, more than two dozen pairs of black socks and an equal number of T-shirts and shorts hung sodden on the lines above our beds. None of our laundry was marked. We had to remember where each had hung his socks and underwear.

Late that night, Hank, one of our crowd, came in quite intoxicated. He went to the phone, dialed a room number at random, and began talking incoherently—nothing obscene or profane, just babbling. His monologue ended, he put the phone down, undressed and went to bed.

We soon learned he had dialed a room occupied by an elderly lady on our floor. Though he said nothing threatening, his call disturbed her. She reported the incident to the manager, who traced the call. Early the next morning he called our room while we were still in bed. He said he was coming up to talk to the man who had made the call.

Panic set in. We grabbed damp socks and damp underwear and piled them in the bathroom then yanked down our improvised clotheslines.

When the manager came, Hank confessed. The manager upbraided Hank while he and the rest of us sat on our beds, still in our pajamas. Hank was contrite and apologized. All of us apologized, eying Hank. The manager left after being assured nothing like that would happen again. Then he went to the room of the lady who had received the call. When he told her we were a group of new ensigns awaiting the arrival of our ship, her motherly and patriotic instincts prevailed over her resentment. Through the manager she accepted our apology and even ordered a rich assortment of delicacies sent to our room.

As soon as the manager closed the door, we looked at each other. Our laundry! All five of us tried to rush into the bathroom at the same time. There was no way we could sort the identical socks and underwear. We replaced the clotheslines and hung the clothes to finish drying. We were all approximately the same height, so we agreed to divide the laundry equally. But my feet were larger than anyone else's, so for months I wore tight socks.

The news came through the desk clerk that we were to report to our ship, which had just docked in San Francisco. A taxi took us to the pier where the Nassau was docked. We were all excited. Near the middle of the ship the taxi discharged us with our gear (the navy term for luggage and anything else one travels with). We huddled at the foot of the gangplank, looking nervously at the officer of the deck. He was watching us.

Why were we nervous? We had been taught the procedure: One goes up the gangplank, salutes aft (toward the stern of the ship where the American flag normally flies), then requests permission of the officer of the deck to come aboard. That much we knew. But what we couldn't decide was, which end is aft? We kept urging one another to go on up the gangplank and make a guess. No volunteer. The officer of the deck came to the railing and stared at us.

Someone thought of walking the length of the ship as if casually inspecting it from the dock. No, that would be too obvious. We were supposed to go aboard, not stroll like tourists. Besides, this was wartime; no tourists were allowed. One thought was uppermost in our minds. Here we are, newly commissioned naval officers who couldn't tell one end of the ship from the other. Could the officer of the deck from high above us see how red our faces were?

Our salvation came in the person of an enlisted man who came on the dock. He scrambled up the gangplank and saluted in a certain direction. We grabbed our gear and stumbled over one another in our eagerness to go up the gangplank and salute what we now knew was aft. Faultlessly we requested permission to come aboard. Though I have forgotten the name of the officer of the deck, I remember his face and clearly remember his expression as we filed past. Not contempt—only amusement.

Our skipper was Irish, a colorful aviator who was well liked by his crew. After the ship departed San Francisco, we learned our assignment. While the captain had been on leave in Washington, he had snooped around the Navy Department. Friends there had told him about plans to recapture the island of Attu, westernmost island in the Aleutian chain off Alaska. A carrier had never operated in the Bering Sea. He persuaded those in charge to include the Nassau in the task force being assembled. The officers I spoke with lamented his voluntarism.

My first Easter in the navy came while we were going to Alaska. It seemed ironic to me to be on a mission of destruction on that day. I could not even attend divine services (the term used for non-denominational worship services) because of being on duty. The only reminder of that day's significance was a Scripture passage and a paragraph by the chaplain in our daily newssheet.

Ray's navy portrait

But, I noted in a journal, "Easter Sunday, like Christ and the message of truth which he brought to earth, cannot be ignored." I assumed as fact, as always, that Christ rose from the dead. But I was still Unitarian: the risen Christ was my teacher, my guide, my example, not my Lord and Savior.

I had to admit to myself that I had given little serious thought to God and His loving care for me. My piety was confined to perfunctory prayer before going to sleep. So I prayed about the coming hour of battle. I did not pray for deliverance, but for God to help me to do His will, to give me the grace to commit my safekeeping into His hands. That was the beginning of a much deeper prayer life than I had ever known. I felt no fear in the face of the coming action. Whatever I would be called on to do as a crew member of the Nassau was simply a job to be done. In fact, I realized I had somewhat the same attitude toward the imminent action as I used to have toward examinations in college.

For the first time I was among men facing dangerous situations, casually discussing the possibility of being killed or wounded. Our primary concern was enemy submarines. In a matter-of-fact manner we were reminded that our aircraft carrier had none of the heavy armor plating below the water line that regular navy ships have. The skin of our ship was a half-inch thick. The water temperature in the Bering Sea at that time was thirty-two degrees Fahrenheit. Our doctors speculated on how long a man could survive in the water: maybe half an hour, maybe less.

The quarters assigned to junior officers were at the water line, which would be the point of entry for an enemy torpedo. Everyone referred to our quarters as "Torpedo Junction." Since the ship's skin was so thin, we who called the Junction our home cheerfully told one another we had no reason to worry. We said that if a Japanese torpedo hit our ship on either side, the torpedo would probably go clear through the ship without exploding.

Though I never discussed the issue with my shipmates, I believe that men in battle generally hold an implicit fatalism. "If it's my time to go, . . . If it's not, . . ." This fatalism is not consistent. Those who live by it in battle make every effort to avoid death. In those war years it was often said there are no atheists in foxholes. I have never polled occupants of foxholes. Still, I doubt that generalization.[1] In the times when we were in action in the Bering Sea, I was too intent on getting to my battle station and doing my duty to think of praying.

---

1   Tony Hillerman, noted novelist, was a much-decorated infantryman in Europe during World War II. In his autobiography, *Seldom Disappointed* (New York: Harper Collins Publishers, 2001), 146, he writes, "I always wondered who invented the absurd lie that proclaimed there were 'no atheists in foxholes.' Where else could atheism better thrive than in the killing fields where homicide was honored?"

For me, and I think for my shipmates, living dangerously was exciting, even exhilarating. One tends to forget petty details in the zest for living and the determination to do one's duty well. In later years I read and agreed with William James's essay on the moral equivalent of war. He argued that there can be no lasting peace until mankind finds some constructive activity that brings out the good qualities (forget the bad ones) involvement in war brings out in people.

One of the many wardroom rumors was that our captain had secured the involvement of the Nassau in the Attu campaign because he wanted to prove what an escort carrier could do in that part of the world. He did. He also proved what an escort carrier operating in the Bering Sea in early spring could *not* do. The Nassau catapulted her planes into flight, but she required twenty-five or thirty knots across the flight deck in order to land them. Her top speed was eighteen knots. Do the arithmetic: We had to have ten to fifteen knots of wind or our planes could not land.

Unfortunately, the Bering Sea was remarkably calm. For days one could hardly see a whitecap. As I looked at the sea hour after hour I thought it was like steaming through an ocean of oil. On some days, no wind at all.

Result? After doing their strafing and bombing missions on Attu, several of our planes had to circle the ship to use their fuel, and then crash-land into the water ("going into the drink," we called it). One of our destroyer escorts rescued the flyers from the water and kept them until a convenient time to return them to the Nassau. All but one.

The flyer in question was a handsome, happy-go-lucky Polish man from Chicago. As we learned later, after he was rescued and given dry clothes, he went to the bridge to chat with the officer of the deck. The destroyer was steaming on our port bow (to the left and well ahead of us) to screen us from enemy submarines. The officer of the deck asked the flyer to take the con of the ship (take command) so he could go below for a few minutes. The flyer readily agreed. As soon as the o.o.d. left the bridge, the flyer leaned over to the speaking tube and called to the helmsman, "Left full rudder, full speed ahead." Immediately the destroyer pulled out of formation, leaving the Nassau unprotected on her port side, and sped away from the task force.

Alerted by the abrupt change of course, the o.o.d., the captain, and the executive officer rushed to the bridge. The captain checked the course, turned to the flyer and demanded to know why he had given that order. His cheerful explanation was, "I saw a movie once about a destroyer. At a critical point they gave that command. I just wanted to see what would happen if I gave it."

The captain brought the destroyer back into formation. Breaking radio silence, he called our skipper and said he was coming alongside immediately to transfer personnel. The destroyer came parallel with our port side, twenty-five or thirty yards away. A breeches buoy was rigged—a line between the ships, with a seat for the person being transferred. As the errant flyer was being pulled across the water, the destroyer veered toward us slightly, causing a slack in the line and momentarily submerging the flyer in the freezing water. He came out grinning.

The destroyer's captain had had his revenge.

CHAPTER FOUR

VOCATION UNFOLDING

After the Attu campaign and a return to the States, the Nassau headed for Australia and other South Pacific ports. It was on this cruise that my prayer life truly began. Until then, prayer had always been a bedtime duty not always fulfilled. One night, about to drop off to sleep, mentally praying, I suddenly began thinking about what I was praying. Almost as if I were eavesdropping on someone else's prayer, I realized I was praying, "Dear God, help me to be a good boy." Suddenly wide awake, I thought, "I'm still praying the same prayer I prayed as a child. And I'm twenty-two years old. Grow up, Ray!"

Never before had I known deep joy in prayer. I had never yearned to pray as I did beginning in those months after the Attu campaign. Early in the morning or late at night, I would go topside to the flight deck or to the catwalk alongside it and give thanks to God for the gift of life. I began praying prayers of repentance, prayers of adoration. Some of the wide reading I was doing was helpful. I recall reading Thomas àKempis's *Imitation of Christ* without thinking of it as being Catholic. (I steered clear of all things "Catholic.")

Earlier I spoke of the time when I prayed in New York's Cathedral of Saint John the Divine for my friend Snoop's life to be spared. Other than that, my prayers had always been perfunctory, purely a matter of obligation. In retrospect, I see that God used the majesty and wonder of the sea to open my heart to him and grant me the grace of earnest prayer. Almost sixty years later I read of my favorite saint, Saint Therese of Lisieux, that "it was in the great book of nature that she discovered the ways of prayer." She was especially impressed by gazing at the sea.[1]

---

1   Angel de los Gavarres, *Therese, The Little Child of God's Mercy* (Washington, DC: Institute of Carmelite Studies, 1999), 45.

From my journal I recall late nights when, greatly fatigued, I looked back on a day that had not gone well. Disgusted and sad, I forced myself to go up in the night to the flight deck. The ship always traveled totally darkened. At times it was so dark I could scarcely see an arm's length ahead of me. And at length I would pray, pouring out all my disappointments and frustrations and regrets. I prayed to God. I had been taught that He is our Father, but I did not know Him as Father. This was because I did not have a personal relationship with His Son. But even my Unitarian prayers were sources of healing. I always went back below refreshed and renewed.

In those days a poem from my childhood came to mind. A copy hung in a frame in my grandparents' home. I read it so many times it remained in my memory.

> If radio's slim fingers
> can pluck a melody
> from night and toss it over
> a continent or sea;
> If petalled white notes
> of a violin
> are blown across a mountain
> or a city's din;
> If songs like crimson roses
> are culled from thin blue air,
> why should mortals wonder
> if God hears prayer?

My early morning and night prayers were primarily prayers of thanksgiving for the privilege of being alive. I looked forward to each new day with keen anticipation. I felt compassion for a fellow officer in my department who told me he greeted every morning with, "Oh, hell. Another day."

On my first Thanksgiving Day aboard ship I noted in my journal many reasons for being thankful. "As in the past I am thankful for parents, friends, food, shelter, clothing, the freedom I enjoy in my native land, but today my gratitude goes much deeper. Over and above all other things I am humbly and deeply grateful for the privilege of being alive. I have no fear of death, but I have an immeasurable zest for living. I have so much to live for, that the very fact of being alive fills me with an inexpressible sense of gratitude."

My prayer was not confined to early morning or late night. In my leisure time I often went to the sponson on the port side of the ship. The sponson was a small platform jutting out from the side of the ship, equipped with anti-aircraft guns. Our sponsons were on the same level as the hangar deck of the ship. Ordinarily I was alone there. I spent many hours in reading, in thinking about my life and about the future, and in prayer. My daytime prayers were mostly petitions. I continually asked for guidance in discerning the direction my life should take if I persevered in my calling to the ministry.

Sometimes I would go on the sponson at night, when it was totally dark. There came moments of adoration, looking at the stars that shone brilliantly when we were thousands of miles from any city whose lights would dim the stars' brightness. Often I was filled with awe at the mystery and grandeur of God's creation. As I stood looking at the panoply of stars, I thought about the immensity of the heavens. Pondering the dimensions of the universe impressed me with the fact that, in the total scheme of things, my own efforts count for so very little.

One evening I stood on the bridge as the stars were becoming visible. I noticed one of our destroyer escorts silhouetted against a particularly heavy cloudbank to the northeast of us. The sun was just below the horizon, and its reflected rays added to the darkness of the background of that noble ship. (We loved our escorts; they were our only protection against enemy submarines.) Immediately I was impressed by the thought of eternity. It seemed to me that beyond that cloudbank lay great ages and histories and horizons of thought that I would never have the privilege to encompass, or attempt to encompass. A deep sense of humility came over me as I realized what an infinitesimal, ephemeral speck I was in the scheme of things. I felt shame for being anxious about the petty details of my own life. There and then I perceived my humble place in the universe. There and then I realized dimly the urgency while in this world of preparation for the next.

Yet as I recall those days and nights, and as I read about them in my journal, I wince at the thought of how superficial was my understanding of prayer. If someone had asked me if Jesus were the Son of God, I would have replied affirmatively. But this was only an opinion, a vestige of my childhood training. I had no awareness of a personal relationship with Jesus, nor did I direct any prayer to Him.

As I noted in my journal, I thought of prayer "not as a device, a communication channel through which requisitions for miracles are sent, but rather as an opportunity for opening my heart and soul to God and in that process finding an almost unbelievable peace of mind which allows me to think clearly and logically as I can never do at any other time. God has given me a mind and the power of reasoning. Through prayer He allows me to take a mental and spiritual bath, as it were, to cast out all irrelevant thoughts and concentrate on the great problems of my life. If He gives me the tools and the atmosphere for solving my own problems, what more can I expect?"

I spent hours on the sponson, sometimes not reading or praying but simply looking at the sea. I could sit or stand there for long periods of time looking across the sea, staring at the waves. The sea is always the same, and never the same. Each wave is different. On occasion I would pick out a particular wave and follow its movement as far as I could keep track of it. It seemed to me that the sea had a personality. At times it seemed cheerful, even playful. At other times it seemed lazy and complacent, and at other times angry. I thrilled to watch rough seas, of which we had a great deal in the "williwaws" along the south side of the Aleutian chain.

On our long voyages we often traveled unescorted. I found much pleasure in gazing at the horizon that surrounded us. When on duty on the bridge I could scan three hundred sixty degrees of the compass and see nothing but horizon. I even imagined at times that I could catch a gleam of the eternal. It seemed to me that we were surrounded by a great circle that was itself moving while we remained stationary at the center. To this day I long to look across those wide spaces uncluttered by distracting objects.

When one is at sea in the tropics, twilight lasts only a few minutes. One evening at twilight my roommate and I had gone to the well deck at the bow of the ship to enjoy the cool breezes. We looked out over the rail on the port side and saw the last rays of the setting sun mirrored in the clouds as a delicate shade of pink. Then we looked over the rail on the starboard side and saw the light from the rising moon clearly reflected across the water. It was a sight of singular beauty. We stood in silence for several minutes. Then my roommate said, in a hushed voice, "If that wouldn't make you think of your favorite girlfriend, then you need to get another girlfriend."

Another time at sea my roommate and I had gone to the flight deck to take a look at the escort with which we had just rendezvoused. A light rain was falling even though the sun was shining. This mixture produced the most unusual rainbow I have seen. The rainbow was of brilliant hue, perfectly shaped. But what amazed us was that the end of the rainbow was plainly visible in the water at the bow of our ship. It looked as though one could jump off the bow of the ship and land right at the end of the rainbow. I looked in vain for the pot of gold which proverbially rests at the foot of a rainbow. In my journal that night, reflecting on not having found one, I wrote, "Now I am a sadder but wiser man."

From early in my days aboard the Nassau, in my spare moments I wondered with deep concern what I was to do after the war. The thought of the ministry never left me, nor did my sense of unworthiness. I decided that I should steer my life toward the goal of the ministry and pray and read my Bible more when I felt my resolve weakening. I had a mortal dread of being what I called a "half-hearted preacher," apparent examples of which I had known.

Not long after, I began to sense that I was about to decide to enter the ministry of my denomination. I prayed often and intensely for strength to make the decision. One Sunday morning during divine services on the hangar deck I suddenly felt the decision had been made for me. Despite much thought and prayer in this matter, the thought of my decision having been made hit me with the same shock one might receive from a sudden dash of cold water. Instantly my whole being was concentrated on this thought. I was immensely happy. I felt such a great eagerness to get started on my life's work that I squirmed in my chair. It was difficult to restrain myself from leaping from my chair in the middle of the chaplain's sermon and shout what I intended to do.

After I went to my room, I felt calm and serene. It seemed to me then that nothing would be too great for me to attempt. I repeated to myself the words from Scripture, "I can do all things in him who strengthens me" (Phil. 4:13). I viewed my feelings with some trepidation, however. They seemed too good to last. In my journal I summed up this event: "Oh, would that I could retain forever the inspired eagerness which fills my whole soul now!"

About that time I came across Matthew Arnold's poem "Self-Dependence." The poet's yearning, and even the context in which he uttered it, were remarkably like my own. These stanzas struck a responsive chord in my mind and heart:

> Weary of myself, and sick of asking
> what I am and what I ought to be,
> at this vessel's prow I stand, which bears me
> forward, forward, o'er the starlit sea.
>
> And a look of passionate desire
> o'er the sea and to the stars I send:
> "Ye who from my childhood up have claimed me,
> calm me, ah, compose me to the end!
>
> "Ah, once more," I cried, "ye stars, ye waters,
> on my heart your mighty charm renew.
> Still, still let me, as I gaze upon you,
> feel my soul becoming vast like you!"
>
> From the intense, clear, star-sown vault of heaven,
> on the lit sea's unquiet way,
> in the rustling night-air came the answer:
> "Wouldst thou *be* as these are? *Live* as they.

"Unaffrighted by the silence round them,
undistracted by the sights they see,
these demand not that the things without them
yield them love, amusement, sympathy.

"And with joy the stars perform their shining,
and the sea its long, moon-silvered roll;
for self-poised they live, nor pine with noting
all the fever of some differing soul.

"Bounded by themselves and unregardful
in what state God's other works may be
in their own tasks all their powers pouring,
these attain the mighty life you see."

At that time Ruth and I were not engaged, but there was no doubt in my mind we soon would be. Therefore in a letter to her I discussed my concern about my vocation. I told her that in thinking about the ministry I always tried to look on the dark side, "at the heartaches, worries, disappointments and innumerable cares which must inevitably pile up on the shoulders of a minister who is really doing his work." And yet, I said, as I think of life after the war is over, I can think only of the ministry.

"This subconscious tendency of mine carries over in my reading and studying. I find myself at all times on the alert for apt quotations, illustrations and other bits of relevant matter which might someday make good sermon material. [This reflects the Protestant focus on preaching as the chief task of the minister.] Even my associates here on the Nassau do not escape my attention. I have carefully analyzed many of them as best I could, and asked myself, 'How would I approach that person if he were a member of my congregation?' Or 'What would I tell that man if he some day came to me, seeking help with a great problem confronting him?'"

I confessed to Ruth that many times I had shut out thoughts of ministry from my mind, saying that it must be work for others. But that effort only made me feel miserable. Then I would turn again to consideration of the ministry and be caught in a deep feeling of exuberance and happiness.

So much for my soul-baring to Ruth at that time. Recall that I was wavering like this only weeks after the time when I suddenly became convinced during worship service that the decision for the ministry had finally been made. Even though it was gradually unfolding, my call to vocation was dampered by my vacillation for months to come. In my indecisive state I think I may have been what my roommate facetiously called me: "a would-be dilettante."

Meanwhile, the Nassau was engaged primarily in ferrying aircraft and air squadrons around the Pacific theater. After we left Australia we were scheduled to load damaged aircraft in New Caledonia for return to the States. New Caledonia was an overseas territory of France. In preparation for going ashore, for several days at odd moments my roommate and I practiced what we could remember from our college courses in French.

When I went ashore I learned from navy personnel that the army had taken over the island well before naval or marine forces arrived. Soldiers had warned the French families—and especially the young women—not to trust any sailor or marine when the navy and marines came to the island. Sailors and marines, they assured the French people, are all ex-convicts—immoral, lawless characters of the worst sort. This campaign of slander achieved its desired result. Sailors and marines were still pariahs when we put into New Caledonia. Neither a French girl nor French family would speak to us.

When sailors land in a foreign port, they always look for souvenirs. We found that the soldiers and sailors stationed there had cleaned out the curio shops. At one point I stopped at the door of a butcher shop. Glancing inside I saw a large roomful of beef carcasses (or what I took to be beef) hanging with no evidence of refrigeration. I saw an older Frenchman behind a counter on which laid a goodly quantity of what I took to be French currency. "There's my souvenir," I thought.

I spoke to him in my best French, telling him I wanted some money. My vocabulary was confused. Instead of asking for *l'argent* or *monnaie*, either of which would have communicated my intent, I asked for *montre*, which means a watch.

The old fellow looked puzzled. His watch was there on the table before him. I repeated my mistaken request. He looked at me. He looked at the gun at my side. (Officers were required to be armed when going ashore.) He looked at his watch. I became impatient. "Can't these birds understand their own language?" I thought.

Finally a local man who spoke English intervened. "Do you know what you're saying?" he asked. "You're telling him to give you his watch!" With his help I apologized to the shopkeeper, who was greatly relieved. He gave me some French money for my American money. He even gave me without charge some French coins that were then rarely circulated in Nouméa.

That fall we had to send our Christmas cards at least two months in advance because of being in the South Pacific. It would be my second Christmas away from home. As I addressed cards and added notes to some, I reflected on Christmas celebrations of years past. I recalled, according to my journal, that in those celebrations there had been "something joyful and sweetly solemn and even a bit sad that always clutched the strings of my heart."

(Now, nearly seventy years later, I understand that sadness. It was caused by my lack of a personal relationship with the Lord Jesus. It was like standing outside a window and looking in on elaborate festivities in which one yearned to share. Yes, and not even knowing that the door was open to me to come in and be part of the celebration. Since I came to know and seek continually to surrender my life to Him, I have never known that sadness. Only as one knows Jesus as Savior and Lord can one enter into the true joy of Christmas. Only then can he really know and live what Christmas means. There *is* still some sadness for me in Christmas. But it comes from realizing that the Holy Family had to suffer even at the time of the holy birth.)

The least coveted assignment in my department (communications) was custodian of publications. All confidential documents for the ship were checked out to the custodian. He was responsible for their safekeeping, regardless of who else might be to blame if any were lost or compromised. Each one of the six or eight major departments of the ship had dozens of confidential documents checked out to it by the custodian. He was also responsible for keeping them up to date in accord with corrections that came through regularly and in great abundance.

During my first year aboard the Nassau I was appointed custodian. Because my predecessor had fallen far behind in making corrections, I faced a mammoth task. For weeks I was taken off the watch list and worked ten or twelve hours a day catching up. Friends in the department teased me about my being court-martialed if someone lost a document. I needed no reminder. Providentially, I was able to pass the custodian's mantle onto a successor the following year and remained free of prosecution.

I fondly remember a stowaway we had on board for several months. She was a medium-sized dog that one of the crew smuggled aboard in an overseas port. He kept her hidden until we were out to sea. She was dubbed "Queenie" and had the run of the ship. We could never understand how she quickly learned the bugle calls that sounded over the loudspeaker. She loved frolicking on the flight deck with sailors who were not on duty. But when the call for "flight quarters" (to launch or to receive aircraft) was sounded, immediately she ran down a ladder to a lower deck. The hangar deck was also one of her haunts. On Sunday morning when we were not mobilized for action, chairs were set up on the hangar deck for the chaplain's worship service. When the bugle call for divine service was sounded, Queenie would disappear. And I'm certain she must have learned first of all the meaning of the bugle's chow call.

One day we realized Queenie had disappeared. She had jumped ship in our last port.

The most unpleasant aspect of my life in the navy was being often surrounded by drunkenness when we were in port. By virtue of parental training I was a teetotaler. I can honestly say my attitude toward the widespread abuse of alcohol was not self-righteousness but sadness. I saw so many of my shipmates whom I liked and otherwise respected make utter, drunken fools of themselves. And worse. In their drunken states some (according to their own stories) engaged in immoral behavior from which they abstained when sober.

Some of the younger officers said they found it necessary to drink, often heavily, with their superior officers in order to get along with them. I was convinced they were wrong and were only rationalizing their behavior. I think my last fitness report proved that it was not necessary to abuse alcohol in order to get along with one's superior officers.

But first a bit of background. I liked our executive officer and worked well with him when we were at sea. In port he was one of the heaviest drinkers of all our officers. His drunken antics were appalling, even to some of the other officers who were his drinking buddies. He knew my attitude toward drinking.

Now back to the fitness report. Navy regulations provided that an officer could not see his fitness report unless it was unsatisfactory, in which case he would be given an opportunity to defend himself. Shortly before my last fitness report was turned in, this policy was changed. Now officers could see satisfactory as well as unsatisfactory fitness reports. The head of my department had rated me highly, probably more highly than I deserved. One thing about the report impressed me. In addition to my department head's general comments on my ability and my conduct, the hard-drinking exec wrote in blue pencil: "His military and moral conduct is beyond reproach."

During my two and a half years aboard the Nassau, I spent most of my spare hours reading. When we were in port I would head for a bookstore if one were available. Many more books that I ordered by mail followed us around the Pacific, sometimes for months, before they caught up with the ship. I borrowed books from some of my fellow officers. I read countless short stories and a wide assortment of poetry. I read the Bible, but almost entirely the Old Testament. I pored over many of the classics of English literature. I discovered and agonized over Dostoyevsky's *Crime and Punishment* and *The Brothers Karamazov*. After reading *Crime and Punishment*, I vowed in my journal that I would never read it again. The moral and emotional suffering so powerfully described by Dostoyevsky literally nauseated me.

I read philosophy; Plato was my favorite. I read and re-read his dialogues. I read *The Republic* three times, the third time in Basic English (a 1,200-word English vocabulary developed by two semanticists). I puzzled long and hard over *The Republic*. Socrates gave his blueprint for the just society, but it would have been intolerable to live under the system he propounded. Occasionally one of his auditors would voice this concern. Yet Socrates would answer them by saying, in effect, "But it *is* perfectly just."

Years later one of my professors in the philosophy department at Columbia offered an interpretation of *The Republic* that made sense. He claimed it is a study in irony. Through the person of Socrates, Plato was making it clear that *any* ideal that becomes an absolute thereby becomes tyrannical and even demonic. Reinhold Niebuhr at Union Theological Seminary made the same point, drawing on both the French Revolution and the Communist Revolution for illustration. The French Revolution started out as highly idealistic. But it made absolutes of "liberty, equality, fraternity," and soon the streets of Paris flowed with the blood of its victims. The Communist Revolution was even more idealistic than the French Revolution. Yet in the name of egalitarianism its leaders slaughtered countless millions of Russians and others, and it became the worst tyranny the world has known.

But while my intellectual horizons were expanding, my theological horizons were still cramped. I wrote a letter to Bill Alexander, the well-known Disciples of Christ minister who had inspired my first thoughts about the ministry. It was a newsy letter about my reading and thinking. At one point I told him rather proudly that my understanding of God had "developed" a good bit. I said I no longer thought of God in grandfatherly terms but understood Him as "the Great Dynamo of the Universe." I cringe in recalling that assertion. I had exchanged an anthropomorphism that had some validity for a concept of an impersonal God.

Bill answered my letter. He was Trinitarian, so far as I knew. He should have blasted me out of the water for such gross error. Because of my admiration for him, I would have taken seriously any correction he offered. His only comment was to commend me for giving thoughts to God.

One evening I sat at my desk in my stateroom, about to start writing in my journal. My mind suddenly turned to the Japanese soldiers on the island that our task force was attacking. I wrote, "Cut off from reinforcements, decimated in ranks, hopelessly outnumbered, these few remaining have only a matter of hours to live. I cannot help feeling sorry for them." I knew they were just as eager to live as I, just as full of love for those they had left behind.

Suddenly I heard a loud noise that caused the Nassau to shudder. General quarters sounded. I rushed to my battle station in the communications office. There I learned that one of our destroyer escorts had depth-charged what it was certain was an enemy sub quite close to the carrier. Several of our men topside saw an oil slick rise at the spot where the depth charges were dropped. It could have meant the sub was damaged, perhaps fatally. It could have meant that the sub released a quantity of oil to give that impression and get away before more depth charges were dropped. We never learned the truth.

After general quarters was secured (declared no longer in effect), I went back to my room and to my writing. I must confess that the sympathy I had felt earlier for the enemy was weakened by the submarine scare. It brought to my mind a favorite poem evoked by the First World War. Its author is James Stephens, its title, "Hate":

> My enemy came nigh and I
> stared fiercely in his face.
> My lips went writhing back in a grimace,
> and stern I watched him with a narrow eye.
> Then, as I turned away, my enemy,
> that bitter heart and savage, said to me:
> "Some day, when this is past,
> when all the arrows that we have are cast,
> we may ask one another why we hate,
> and fail to find a story to relate.
> It may seem to us then a mystery
> that we could hate each other."
> Thus said he, and did not turn away,
> waiting to hear what I might have to say.
> But I fled quickly, fearing if I stayed,
> I might have kissed him as I would a maid.

Like most Americans, I was convinced this war had to be fought and won. It was a deadly grim business on a vast scale. Decoding dispatches from all areas of the Pacific to pass on to our captain and executive office confronted me with this fact daily. Yet at the same time I believed that war is idiotic.

"To think," I wrote in my journal, "that millions of human beings, endowed by their Creator with power to reason and plan, with ability to iron out differences by rational means, will attempt to exterminate each other is a revolting thought."

And it still is.

Even if a war becomes unavoidable.

CHAPTER FIVE

VOCATION ON FIRE

When I went aboard the USS Nassau, the chaplain was a young, newly married Methodist minister. He was very shy. Some of the older officers, veterans who had come up through the ranks, teased him continually and (I thought) rather cruelly. We rarely saw him except at general quarters or at meals or at brief Sunday religious services on the hangar deck when we were not in action. Otherwise he was always in his room and, according to his neighbors, always in his bunk. Our exec became exasperated with the chaplain's hibernation. Ignoring the chaplain's non-combatant status under navy regulations, the exec assigned him to work with us six days a week in the communications office.

"At least he'll have to stay awake while he's on watch," the exec said grimly.

Our next chaplain was a young Episcopal clergyman. By his behavior and demeanor he commanded more respect than his predecessor. He and I quickly developed an acquaintance. He told me that when he was transferred from his previous station, his bag containing all his sermons had gone astray. (It reached the Nassau months later.) Until his missing gear arrived, each Saturday he sought me out and bemoaned the fact that he didn't have his sermons. Each time he said he would have to throw something together for divine service the next day. He seemed to have a block against writing new sermons. Or perhaps he believed he had said everything he had to say in the old sermons.

The next chaplain became a good friend and benefactor. Herb was in his late thirties, a Congregationalist, a thoroughgoing, no-nonsense Yankee.

Prior to enlisting in the navy he had been pastor of a large congregation in Massachusetts. He was a brilliant man, well trained, and devoted to his ministry to our crew. When he came aboard he asked for a room next to enlisted country (quarters). He wanted the enlisted men to be able to come to his room without having to pass through officers' country. My room was nearby. Day after day when I was in my room I heard the door from enlisted country open and close as a constant flow of men came to talk to him. Every night at 2100 (9 p.m.) when we were at sea, Herb read a well-crafted evening prayer over the ship's loudspeaker.

Herb clarified my thinking about my calling to the ministry. I became convinced that God was calling me into His service, and began to yearn to answer that call. Because of Herb, humanly speaking, my vocation was no longer under fire—it was on fire.

In a long talk not long after Herb came aboard, I told him about my problem of trying to decide about the ministry. To my astonishment he said with a smile, "Your problem sounds much like the decision I had to make. You might well be telling me the story of my entrance into the ministry." From his junior year in college he had wanted to be a minister, but because of uncertainty about his calling he went to law school. In his second year there he decided he must try something else. He went into the newspaper business for a few years and was rather successful. At the same time he founded, financed and directed a missionary chapel with a membership of eight people. Finally, at the age of twenty-eight he knew he could no longer remain out of the ministry, so he went to seminary at Harvard Divinity School.

Even more encouraging was his assertion that the indecision, the questioning I had been undergoing, was typical of the experience of many ministers whom he knew. Toward the end of our conversation, with a broad smile, Herb spoke words that closed the door on all my previous indecision: "Speaking for the clergy, I would say come into our ranks. We need you! We must have more sincere young men willing to devote themselves to this work and raise the level of the ministry far above what it is."

Not long afterward, I made a list of reasons for wanting to be a minister. The first reason reflected the Unitarianism I had held all my life: "I am convinced that the only way to live is the way Jesus Christ showed the world when he was among men." The second reason: "I want my life to count for something. The thought of going through life being merely a wage-earner, of not being a part of something bigger than myself to which I can give my wholehearted support and allegiance, which can be both vocation and avocation, leaves me cold." Other reasons were that in the ministry I would have a fine corps of coworkers and that my love of study would stand me in good stead.

I was looking for fulfillment through the ministry. Here is one of my reasons (from my journal): "I am at the peak of my efficiency when I pray and meditate and concentrate as much as possible on my duties as a Christian. In the ministry it would be naturally impossible to work at top speed all the time, but I do believe that in this sort of endeavor I would have the fullest possible possession of my faculties." (That assumed, of course, that I had faculties worth possessing.) My final reason for wanting to be a minister was purely subjective: "I feel so much at home in the church, so completely as-if-I-belonged-there."

I reasoned that, after all, I had made a decision for the ministry in the spring of 1942, when I was a senior at Phillips. The decision had never been reversed, though there were times when I wondered whether I should persevere in it. I wrote, at the end of my list of reasons, "I do feel that I have what would have been denoted in former times as a 'calling.' How else to describe this unshakeable something which has made me constantly aware that only in the ministry can I ever find happiness?"

Herb showed me a recent letter from his friend Willard Sperry, dean of Harvard Divinity School. Sperry, himself a Congregationalist (with a Unitarian flavor) had given a talk to a group of Congregational officials. He had told them "the serious theological disciplines in a seminary are the backlog which kept the fires of genuine piety." He added, "One can get up quite a blaze with excelsior and kindling in the front of a fireplace, and that is what a great many ministers do, but it is only the steady fires coming from hard wood at the back that keep alive genuine religious interest." Because my orientation to religion was then so largely intellectual, I agreed with Sperry. Now I note with wonder the lack even of mention of disciplined prayer, both private and corporate.

One of Herb's sermons on the purpose of faith made me realize I had many questions in my mind about faith. If I am to be a good minister, I admonished myself in a journal entry, I must find answers to these questions. When I mentioned this to him at dinner, he said. "That's what makes it so much fun—there are always unanswered questions."

So in those days I envisioned the academic side of the ministry as a continuing search for truth. The question of a criterion for truth did not enter my mind. I never asked myself, how will you separate truth from falsehood? I was determined to follow truth wherever it led. I would have been appalled had I been told that my quest for truth would lead me into the Catholic Church.

Many of my waking hours when off duty—and sometimes when on duty—were filled with thoughts about the ministry. I had a horror of crowd-pleasers. I copied in my journal Ezekiel 33:32 (King James Version), in which God speaks to the prophet about the effect of his preaching on his contemporaries: "And, lo, thou art unto them as a very lovely song of one that hath a pleasant voice, and can play well on an instrument: for they hear thy words, but they do them not." This to avoid at all costs! After Herb was transferred from the Nassau, I wrote him a letter in which I expressed my concern about ministers I had known, "especially young ones, who had sacrificed their intellectual integrity on the altar of denominational taboos." This observation reflected my anxiety that in the pressures of the ministry I might do the same thing.

Still, my decision for the ministry was not free of wavering. Encouragement came one morning from an unexpected quarter. A black steward's mate came to my room to carry out his usual duties of tidying up the room and shining shoes. I had known Greene for some time and enjoyed talking with him. (It was customary for officers to call enlisted men by their last names.) He had lost both parents when he was young. He had been unable to go beyond high school because he had to support himself and a younger brother. Before the war he had worked for the postal department in Florida.

In a previous conversation I had said I intended to go to graduate school after the war. This morning, as he set about to make up our bunks, his first question was what I intended to study. I smiled and said, "Oh, I don't know. I might be a lawyer or a preacher or a teacher or something like that." (Little did I know that I would eventually become a lawyer and a preacher and a teacher and perhaps even a "something like that.")

Greene assured me it would be a fine thing if I were to become a preacher. (Later I noted his remarks in my journal because of his quiet eloquence.) He said that good preachers are "respected," that there is a "great need" for them. "If you're trying to do the right thing," he said, as he gave the sheet on my bunk an extra tug, "you'll be taken care of. People whose hearts are right can always get help. And if a man wants to be a preacher, he will never be happy doing anything else. It will never leave you."

This remark left me silent for several minutes. Was it coincidental that our conversation should have taken this turn at a time when I was wrestling with misgivings about my decision? Or was it providential? The sincerity of his interest in my future led me to tell him about the decision I had made in the spring of 1942 and the further decision to postpone seminary until after the war.

By this time Greene was shining shoes for my roommate and me. He told me how hard he tried to interest the other steward's mates in prayer and Bible reading; how he pleaded with them not to get drunk and use foul language. All with little success, he said sadly. While passing through the galley of our wardroom I had overheard him gently remonstrating with his shipmates—both black and white—about their behavior.

After he left our room, I wrote, "Greene's theology is simple, his faith undisturbed by academic perturbations. As he continued talking and shining shoes, accenting his points with especially vigorous swipes of his brush, I saw someone else sitting in that chair. The person I saw was not just another colored boy [this term was a reflection of my early conditioning] shining shoes, but a shining spirit. Suddenly I felt an almost irresistible urge to take those shoes from his hands, finish them and then shine his own shoes for him. I realized I could learn so much from him about matters of faith and singleness of purpose. In my opinion, Greene is a true Christian gentleman— untutored in many ways, yes, yet firm in his belief in the essential rightness of the universe and God's saving spirit. He wasn't aware of it, but he made me ashamed of myself and my vacillations about the ministry. Right then and there I thanked him silently from the bottom of my heart for having set me once again on the right track."

My intention was to return to Phillips University and enroll in seminary there. I told myself it would be Phillips rather than Harvard or Union Theological Seminary in New York or some other place back East. (These are words taken from my journal. Six years later I had gone not to Phillips, but to Harvard and Union Theological Seminary and to "some other place back East," Virginia Theological Seminary in Alexandria.) I thought that if I went to an Eastern seminary for three years, I would lose contact with my denomination and with my fellow clergy. This prediction came true—not because of geographical isolation but because my pilgrimage led me beyond the Disciples of Christ denomination.

One day as we lay anchored in the harbor of a large South Sea island, through powerful binoculars I could see natives on shore. There were two women and one man, all seemingly middle-aged, sitting in front of their hut. They were watching the dozens of warships anchored in the bay. Occasionally one of them would come down on the beach, near the water's edge, and walk back and forth, gazing out toward where we were anchored. After sauntering up and down the beach for a few minutes, he or she would return to a chair, never taking eyes off the assembly of ships. I yearned to know what they were thinking. I imagined it might be something like, "So this is how the 'civilized' people spend their time. If this is 'civilization,' then deliver us from it!"

False propaganda is a feature of modern warfare. Some time after we had taken part in the recapture of the Marshall and Gilbert Islands in the central Pacific, the Nassau briefly revisited the area. One of the naval officers stationed there told us of having taken part in the interrogation of one of the Japanese prisoners who could speak English. At one point he exclaimed defiantly, "You may take these islands, but you'll *never* recapture San Francisco!" That part of California, he believed, was safely under the control of Japanese forces.

One of the books I relished in my days at sea was Thoreau's *Walden*. I copied from chapter 11 this statement: "I found in myself, and still find, an instinct toward a higher, or as it is named, spiritual life as do most men, and another toward a primitive rank and savage one, and I reverence them both. I love the wild not less than the good."

Pondering this, I wrote in my journal, "I share Thoreau's feeling in this respect. Many times have I stood on the flight deck or the bridge, especially at night, with the wind tearing at me with a million tentacles as if to divest me of the thin veneer of civilization which is mine, and exulted in its wildness. At such times I could imagine myself some fifteenth-century explorer, sailing into the awful darkness to reach I-knew-not-what land, relying on the most primitive methods of navigation and seamanship. I wanted to laugh and shout and hurl defiant curses at the elements, challenging them to do me any harm. At such times it would have taken little more inspiration to provoke me into a wild chant or savage dance, so great was my animal spirit. I cherish those times, and shall never forget them. Nor am I ashamed of the me that was revealed there."

Starry nights at sea in the tropics: magnificence I have never known since those years on the Nassau. Often late at night, off duty, I would go to the flight deck and let my soul bathe in the clear, brilliant light of the stars. I gazed at the immensity of the heavens. As noted in the previous chapter, I always marveled at my own infinitesimal stature in the universe. I pondered how little my life's efforts would count in the total scheme of things. That was the closest I came to humility in those days.

One Saturday afternoon I heard someone in the chaplain's room playing a small organ, practicing hymns for divine service the next day. The sound of that familiar music, even though it was inexpertly played, awakened again in me a deep desire to be in the church and a part of the church's work. Hearing "Faith of Our Fathers" reminded me of bold missionaries carrying the Gospel to all parts of the world. I prayed, "Keep me to the faith of our fathers, and in that faith help me to persevere ever for the right." At that time, for me "fathers" simply meant forebears. I had no knowledge of the Church Fathers. Not until years later did I learn that the composer of the words to that hymn was a Catholic priest.

In my years as a naval officer, navy men were intensely loyal to their ship and their shipmates. This loyalty is perhaps largely due to the fact that a sailor's ship is his home. I wondered then whether an aviator would have as deep personal regard for his plane, since he does not live in it, does not entrust all his belongings to it. Sailors would speak disparagingly of their ship; they would call it all manner of derogatory names. But woe to the outsider who cast aspersions on it.

I had a deep regard for the Nassau, which was my home for two and a half years. She was proud, often haughty, in the presence of other CVEs (escort aircraft carries). She had accumulated a list of firsts: first CVE to operate as a combatant ship, first carrier to operate in Aleutian waters, first carrier to enter the harbor of Brisbane in Australia. Yet there was a strong tint of sham in her personality, for she knew as well as I that she had weaknesses she could never overcome. When at the end of a long voyage I went ashore and viewed her from the dock, it seemed to me she looked tired. Conversely, she always seemed eager to be on her way when she had been loaded and refueled. She was my home. I can understand the deep sense of personal loss that sailors feel when their ship goes down.

Our pilots did not make their landings on carriers by computer, as pilots do today. The landing signal officer waved them in (and sometimes waved them off). He stood at the port side of the aft end of the flight deck with paddles that looked like huge ping-pong paddles. As a plane approached for a landing, with arms extended he would signal by his paddles whether a plane should lift or lower one of its wings. When it touched down he would signal the pilot to cut power and let the arresting gear catch the tail hook to bring the plane to a halt. Sometimes he would have to wave off a plane when its approach was wrong. Below him was a safety net into which he jumped when a wave-away plane roared just over his head to circle for another try at landing.

The Nassau's landing signal officer, Jim Brickett (himself an aviator), composed a song entitled "In Praise of the USS Nassau." It was to be sung to the Gilbert and Sullivan tune from "HMS Pinafore," in which the Lord of the Admiralty sings of being "the ruler of the Queen's navy." In his tribute, Brickett referred to our ship as the "Nasty Maru." "Nasty" was his corruption of "Nassau." The "Maru" was added because it was part of the names of all Japanese ships. The "Tojo" referred to the prime minister of Japan. When he complained about the landing patterns of the combat squadron then aboard, as landing signal officer he had personal reason for ribbing the pilots. The planes' speed about which he complained was far in excess of a safe speed for landing. "Betty" was the term used for a particular Japanese fighter plane. In Gilbert and Sullivan fashion, the last two lines of each stanza were to be repeated:

Of combat ships we have quite a few,
but the best one of any is the Nasty Maru;
she knocks down planes—wouldn't Tojo groan
if they'd only been Japanese and not our own.
The crew fights heroically but just for sport—
the only time they do it is when they're in port!

We've spirit such as none before,
though we'd all abandon ship if someone slammed a door.
If the ship's on fire hardly anyone knows;
they'd complain about the smoke but never man a hose.
Oh, a tougher carrier you never saw
than the God-forsaken, widow-makin' old Nassau!

As crowning glory of this awful fix,
we've got Composite Squadron Sixty-Six.
With nonchalance and a hundred-forty knots
they make their landings in the damnedest spots.
Oh, we love them dearly and we don't mean to crab.
But they don't know a betty from a taxicab!

Now the fleet may reach the stateside shore,
but the Nassau stays to fight the blankety-blank war.
We go to conquer islands and if we get through,
then the Admiral says that we can do it next time, too.
But what's the use of having medals big as plates,
if the liquor's all consumed before we reach the States?

My classification as a naval officer was C-D (Communications, Deck). Since coming aboard in San Francisco, I worked in the communications office. In the last year of my duty, I was assigned to be assistant navigator. In midshipmen's school I had received intensive training in celestial navigation. I learned a great deal more and very quickly doing navigation with the navigator and a competent chief petty officer. The navigator was an easy-going man who tried to work as little as possible. At one point he broke his glasses—his only pair, he said. For weeks I took over the navigation. It was the most interesting work I did in the navy.

Precise calculations of our location in that vast ocean were made just before sunrise and just after sunset. The time in which one could take star sights was limited to a very few minutes: that short interval when the stars first peeped out and the horizon was still visible. Whether we were north or south of the equator, we had favorite stars for navigation. Using sextants, we measured the angle of elevation of five or six stars in various parts of the sky. Each time, a quartermaster with a chronometer noted the exact second at which we had taken the sight. With five or six good star sights and the navigation tables, we could plot within a few hundred yards the exact location of the ship at a given time.

This fact never failed to cause me wonder. Here we were using points of light from stars hundreds of light years away—stars that even might no longer exist—to determine our location. The orderliness of the universe was astounding and mysterious. I knew it was all God's doing. Sometimes I even thanked him. Only in clear weather, of course, could we make these calculations. If the weather in the morning or evening was cloudy, there could be no star sights, no calculation. It would be years before navigation by satellite would make the navigator relatively independent of the weather.

Many times we made the run from Pearl Harbor in Oahu to San Diego, a voyage of about five days. On one of those voyages we took star sights the first evening and had cloudy weather the rest of the way. We had to rely on dead reckoning navigation. ("Dead" comes from *ded*, meaning *deduced*.) One takes into account whatever information one has from navigation charts about the set (direction) and drift (speed) of the currents through which one is steaming. Knowing one's speed, one then makes an educated guess as the courses to be followed to arrive at one's destination.

The captain did not disguise his anxiety about our not having precise calculations to guide us. As we stood on the bridge he often teased me. He said he figured I was taking the ship to San Francisco (my favorite port) but he said he didn't mind, since his family was living in nearby Berkeley. Providentially, at the time we had calculated, our radar picked up the first buoy in the San Diego channel.

Both the captain and I were greatly relieved.

Ray with sextant

CHAPTER SIX

HEADING FOR SEMINARY

Eager to prepare for seminary, I asked Chaplain Smith where I should begin. At his suggestion I ordered a copy of Robert H. Pfeiffer's *Introduction to the Old Testament.* Pfeiffer had been Herb's professor at Harvard Divinity School. Herb wrote to him about my using his book, and Pfeiffer wrote back asking me to send him any questions. I wrote several times, sending postage for the replies. Each time he quickly responded, returning my postage and asking for more questions. Over a period of months I checked every one of the many hundreds of biblical references in the book.

I found quite a number of mistakes and listed them in a letter to him. He replied and gave three reasons for the errors. The first was the differences between the Hebrew and the English version in the numbering of verses. Then, too, he had written the book over a period of twenty-five years, when time lapses allowed mistakes to enter. Finally, he said, the author (himself) was "not smart enough to keep them out." This confession from a world-famous scholar endeared him to me even more.

Pfeiffer's large book was a detailed exposition of the documentary hypothesis. According to that hypothesis, the first five or six books of the Old Testament are a blend of four basic documents. The scholars who held this hypothesis labeled the documents *J, E, P,* and *D.* Pfeiffer had added one more, *S.* I laboriously color-coded the first six books of my Old Testament according to Pfeiffer's specifications. For five or six months this task took much of my spare time. I had invested so much work in the project that one time I thought of putting my Bible next to my life jacket so I could easily take it with me if I had to abandon ship.

Though it never spent time in the ocean, that particular Bible did become relatively worthless—except for once, when it brought brief recognition. William F. Albright, a leading biblical archaeologist, came to Union to give a lecture. My favorite Old Testament professor, James Muilenburg, introduced me to Dr. Albright as one of the very few persons who had checked all the references in Pfeiffer's book. (All my professors in Scripture were committed to the documentary hypothesis.) But over the years equally learned scholars more and more questioned the documentary hypothesis. Now that polychrome Bible is nothing more than a souvenir of countless hours of study while aboard the Nassau.

Back to life on the Nassau. A fellow officer, Bill Rader, once encountered an interesting juxtaposition of cultures. It occurred when the ship had anchored briefly at a South Sea island. Walking alone, he explored a native village. He saw several army and navy officers going into the largest native hut in the village. He decided to follow them, thinking that there must be something of interest there. When he entered, he discovered he had barged into the hut of the village chief. The other officers were invited guests. Bill was embarrassed, but the chief insisted that Bill remain. He stayed for a serving of tea and native cakes of some nondescript variety.

In the hut, behind the chief, sat six large native women, the wives of the chief. They said nothing during the proceedings. In broken English the chief described with great gusto a fishing trip from which he had just returned. He dwelt at length on the size of the largest fish he caught. As his enthusiasm for his story grew, so did the size of the fish. Before long he was describing a fish as along as his arms could stretch. At the climax of his story, one of his wives broke her silence by calmly but firmly, in a loud voice, uttering a single word: "B---s---."

Dead silence. The chief had evidently heard the word before and did not know what to make of his wife's remark. After the silence became strained, one of the officers smoothed over the situation. With solemn face he explained to the chief that back in America the "b---s----ers" are a select group of individuals. They tell great tales, he said, but they are highly honorable, and do not lie. This mollified the chief and saved the day. The wife probably had added the highly descriptive noun to her vocabulary after overhearing the conversation of sailors at a nearby naval base. She may not have known what she was saying, but she spoke truly.

In journal entries I continued to exult about the daily joy of being alive: "If my voice were not so ill-adapted to singing, I should probably be bursting forth at all hours with Manna-Zuca's triumphant song, 'I Love Life and I

Want to Live!'" Much of my *joie de vivre* was due to my having dedicated my life to the service of God and the church.

At the same time I sensed an importunate voice within that could not be stilled. "You're grateful for the privilege of being alive. So what? How are you going to show your gratitude? What are your intentions?" I thought of a great trial in process. The courtroom was the world, the prosecuting attorney was spokesman for the "new morality" we were beginning to recognize. The defendant was the ideal of truth, integrity, and morality that I had long cherished but had done little to support. What was I doing in the battle?

This brief analogy reflected my continuing distress over the moral degradation I had witnessed both at home and overseas, since coming into the navy. I can recall standing on the quarterdeck when the ship was in port, watching the men go on liberty. Such handsome, enthusiastic lads, resplendent in their uniforms, shoes brightly polished, every hair in place. So eager to get ashore!

Always there was sadness in my heart as I watched them leave. I knew that many would return throughout the night, until 8:00 the next morning, in dreadful condition—staggering drunk, uniforms awry and soiled, hair messed up. Yes, and a certain number would be bringing new cases of venereal disease aboard. Ashore I had seen hundreds of men lined up for blocks before brothels in Honolulu and New Caledonia, each waiting hours to spend a few minutes with one of the women inside.

Despite all this, by God's grace I was preserved from cynicism and disillusionment and (I honestly believe) from self-righteousness. I never lost faith in the enormous possibilities for good in all those men—indeed, in all men. Seeing them at their worst strengthened my desire to minister to these veterans and others like them after the war. It also further convinced me it was wise to have postponed seminary training until after the war. I went into the navy wanting to know the war first-hand. I believed that I could profit from my seminary training far more from having been in the military.

At that same time, I knew that much of the war remained foreign to me. I could never know what went on in the mind of a young man who prowled through thick jungles, expecting at any second to be struck down by a bullet from an enemy gun; what exhausted infantrymen thought and felt as they slogged through mire in the battlefields of Europe; what the emotions of our flyers were as they braved ground fire and attacks from enemy planes to accomplish their mission. But I did learn something of the moral temptations these men faced when they were back from the front lines, still far from home.

With regard to the ministry, and indeed, life in general, when he was our chaplain Herb Smith wielded by far the greatest influence on my life. He and I usually sat together at lunch and dinner in the wardroom. Except when we were in combat or at general quarters, our meals were leisurely affairs with much time for conversation. We had many long talks, in his room or mine, that revolved around the ministry. Herb was unusually articulate, with occasional dry wit shining through.

Looking back on our friendship, I can see that Herb was rigorously honest within the framework of his liberal Protestant presuppositions. Though I did not recognize it at the time, either in him or in myself, there was strong Unitarian flavor in both of us. Neither in conversation nor in his sermons did I ever hear Herb speak of a personal relationship with Jesus Christ. Always he emphasized the teachings of Christ.

Herb always tried to be rigorously intellectual in his approach to "religion" (a term he used more than he did "Christianity"). The preacher, he said, must search for the truth, and, having found it, try to share it with his congregation. At the time it did not occur to me to ask how a preacher will know whether what he has found is the truth. Later I began to see that is the key issue in all Christian disunity: the question of authority. How does one find the truth? How does one test the truth? Now I can see that Herb's job description of the preacher contrasts sharply with the role of a Catholic priest. The preacher tries to find the truth to share with his people. The priest receives the truth to share with his people.

Though he never spoke critically of the Catholic Church, I can see now that his assumptions were anti-Catholic. He deplored what he saw as a Protestant tendency to adopt some of the architectural and liturgical "practices" of Catholicism. He saw this as part of a universal trend toward "authoritarianism" in government and other phases of life. To combat this tendency, he said, he always tried to adhere strictly to what he called "the tradition of Protestantism in its true historical sense." I didn't know what that meant, but I assumed it meant something good or Herb would not have appealed to it.

Herb told a story related to him by Dean Sperry of Harvard Divinity School. A new church at the University of Chicago was built in the late 1920s or early '30s. Its architecture reflected traditional Gothic lines. Dean Sperry was given a tour of the new building and thought it a beautiful structure. He asked the pastor what he intended to preach in that church. The pastor mentioned several themes he had in mind. Dean Sperry asked him, "Do you think those things will fit in this church?"

The pastor was surprised at the question. After a moment's thought, he admitted they wouldn't; he said he had never thought of that. Herb's point in telling me the story was that the uniquely Protestant message, its emphasis on the worth of the individual and the sacredness of personality, would be entirely out of place in such architectural surroundings. (Herb thought these emphases were uniquely Protestant because he knew so little about Catholicism.)

The blame for the "catholicizing" tendencies in Protestantism, Herb said, lies with Protestant ministers who are ignorant of "church history and church tradition" (his terms). He said I should choose a seminary which offers "hard, cold facts" and not "dogma or doctrine." He urged me to make church history my major field of study. It's ironic that what he urged on me is precisely what led me into the Catholic Church. Frequently I recall Blessed John Henry Newman's dictum, "To be deep in history is to cease to be Protestant." Each one of the many hundreds of Protestant clergy converts to the Church in recent decades has become what I call a "victim of the dictum."

So strong was Herb's influence on my thinking that I decided I must try to secure seminary training like his. That meant going to Harvard Divinity School. My decision pleased Herb. Before I told him, he said, he had picked me out as the type who would go to Union Theological Seminary in New York. (I later did go to Union.) Though I had never been to New England, since childhood I had felt an attraction to the region. As I thought with keen anticipation about living there, I thought with a smile I must have had some New England ancestors. (I do. Recently a friend traced my family tree and disclosed a number of Yankee forebears.)

Incongruous would best describe some of my most memorable spiritual experiences on the Nassau. I have stood on the catwalk on the port side of the ship, offering my morning prayers as the wings of catapulted aircraft soared a few feet over my head. I have stood on the bridge during early morning general quarters, as junior officer of the watch, expressing my gratitude to my Creator for the privilege of being alive. As I kept a sharp lookout on the horizon under the watchful eye of the captain and the officer of the deck, I sometimes wondered if they knew I was praying. They might have interpreted my silence as sleepiness. Many times I have leaned against a gun on the platform just off the flight deck, praying for peace, for an end to what I thought of as a holocaust.

Alexander Campbell, the founder of the denomination in which I was raised, had a passion for Christian unity (which did not include Roman Catholicism.) To his dying day he claimed he had founded not a denomination but rather a brotherhood for Christian unity. Despite his noble intentions, his movement was a *de facto* denomination from the beginning. I will always be grateful to that tradition for nourishing in me an ecumenical concern. Yet as I thought of going to Harvard Divinity School, my loyalty to the Disciples of Christ began to waver. I was not certain that I wanted to stay in the denomination or even to preach in the Middle West. My denomination was not one of choice but of inheritance. I assumed that during my seminary training I would find my rightful place.

In my adolescent years, I had devoured a series of books by Richard Halliburton detailing his travels in other continents. The titles are still fresh in my mind: *New Worlds to Conquer, The Flying Carpet, Glorious Adventure.* Once while on leave in Los Angeles, I picked up and re-read some chapters of *The Flying Carpet.* I smiled to myself as I realized that the old thrill was gone. I had known adventure in the war years. I was not tired of adventure. I realized, however, that my youthful ideas about adventure were quite romantic. Now I was convinced that the greatest adventure in the world is living. As I mused over Halliburton's book I asked myself, what could be more rigorous or demanding than growth in righteousness? What higher peaks could one scale than those of spiritual experience? What greater worlds to discover than the vast, unexplored areas of deeper and deeper communion with God?

Or take the matter of courage. I had seen many examples of courage in my years aboard the Nassau. In the heat of battle men do death-defying stunts. The exploits of aviators, submariners, paratroopers, and infantrymen thrilled me. They filled me with a sense of pride in my comrades-in-arms. But toward the end of the war I realized I was even more impressed by the everyday courage of people I had known in my small hometown. I even wrote part of a sermon I wanted to preach some day:

"I would not disparage the exploits of our fighting men, the deeds they have done in the heat of battle. Their acts were for the most part unpremeditated. It was the extra adrenaline, the excitement, the devotion to duty that led them to do these things suddenly. Far more impressive to me now—I never realized it before I got into this war—is the quiet, unassuming courage of those people back home. People who have always led Christian lives. People who have sacrificed much for their children, who have never let down through all the busy years of their lives." I went on to speak of my grandparents and my parents as examples of quiet courage that expressed itself in countless sacrifices for their families and friends. "Heroism?" I asked. "Yes, *that's* my idea of heroism." And then I quoted lines from Edna Lyall's *To Right the Wrong*:

> Glory of warrior, glory of orator, glory of song,
> Paid with a voice flying by to be lost on an endless sea—
> Glory of virtue, to fight, to struggle, to right the wrong—
> Nay, but she aimed not at glory, no lover of glory she,
> Give her the glory of going on, and still to be.[1]

---

1   Edna Lyall, *To Right the Wrong* (London: Hurst and Blackett, Limited, 1894), v.

In what turned out to be the closing months of the war I sometimes envied the seminarians who were preparing for the ministry while I was in the navy. I knew ministerial training must go on in wartime. I did not doubt the sincerity of those who had been exempted from military service to continue their studies. I, too, could have avoided military service. I chose to postpone seminary training until after the war, and I believed it was a wise choice. I think the temptation to envy was due largely to my impatience. I was so eager to begin seminary. I believed my experience in the service would be beneficial to me in my ministry, but I did want to get to work: to study, to ask questions, to seek answers. Truth Incarnate was beckoning me, but I knew Him only as teacher, not as Savior. Unbeknownst to me, He was calling me into His Church, which I then regarded as a (I might even have said "the") bastion of error.

Shortly after the war ended, the Nassau tied up briefly in the harbor of Okinawa. A typhoon had devastated the area a week before. We saw numerous patrol vessels and landing craft piled up on the coral reef guarding the south side of the harbor entrance. One night before turning in I climbed to the flight deck for fresh air. It was a peaceful scene, presided over by a tranquil moon nearing its full stage. I thought of the extreme contrast between the serenity I saw and the living hell that was Okinawa a few months ago when it was still being wrested from the Japanese. I imagined the moon admonishing me in a gentle voice, "*This* is how things should be—just as you see them now, not as they were in the days about which you are thinking. Remember that. Ponder it well."

With regard to my vocation, one troubling thought returned many times. "Am I going into the ministry simply because I can't think of anything else to do?" God gave me reassurance. Within a few months, two job offers came to me. One was from my navigator, who in peacetime was official of a large firm in Honolulu. The other offer came from a friend in San Francisco. His company made documentary and training films. I found his offer especially attractive because of my interest in history. I was thankful for the offers, taking them as a sign from God confirming my vocation to the ministry.

How did Catholicism impinge on my life in those days? Very slightly. Just before going into the navy I read a book by Henry Link, *Return to Religion*. Condemning certain modern educational dogmas, Link said they were "no less naïve than the dogma of the immaculate conception or the second coming of Christ." I had never heard of the Immaculate Conception but guessed (wrongly) that it had something to do with the Virgin Birth. In my journal I saved a copy of Sigrid Undset's re-telling of a touching Norwegian legend about church bells lost in a lake. Her name was unknown to me. (Now that I have read and re-read her two masterful novels, *Kristin Lavransdatter* and *Master of Hestveiken*, I regard her as the greatest Catholic novelist of modern times.)

Without knowing both writers were Catholic, I read a couple of poems by Hillaire Belloc and a short story and nine poems by G.K. Chesterton. One of Chesterton's poems was his stirring "Lepanto," though I had no conception of the event he was celebrating. I wonder now what the poem meant to me then. I read *Imitation of Christ* by Thomas àKempis, not meditatively but simply straight through. His insistence that we must strive for knowledge of God, of self, of one's fellow men, and not other kinds of knowledge, impressed me. I read Willa Cather's *Death Comes for the Archbishop*, thinking it was a murder mystery when I started it.

The first priest I ever admired was fictional Father Chisolm, protagonist in A.J. Cronin's *Keys to the Kingdom.* I read almost the entire book at a sitting but suddenly quit reading. I felt incapable of sharing in any more of Father Chisolm's woes. Each time in the story something else happened to that poor priest, I wanted to exclaim, "Come now. This is enough. No more, please! Let him have a bit of sunshine in his life for a change!" I was deeply impressed by the priest's humility. I wrote in my journal, "There is so much we all could learn from a man of his spiritual caliber. Truly, he was Christlike." I considered Cronin's portrait of the priest "magnificent."

In July 1945, the Nassau steamed from the Philippines to the States. This was the voyage that took me to my wedding in San Francisco. Because of navy censorship, I could not tell Ruth that our ship was scheduled to return to San Francisco in late July. I did send her several letters telling that in late July she should visit my friends the Walkers. (She knew they lived in San Francisco.) We left for the States the day after I wrote her, and for a couple of months the ship's mail did not reach us. I did not know whether she had received my letters. I did not know whether she could come to San Francisco. In the war years air travel for civilians was uncertain.

On the way back to the States I contracted a near-terminal case of pre-marital jitters. I was convinced that God was calling us into marriage. My anxiety centered on the thought of being responsible for the life of another person. Though slender in build, I lost fifteen pounds in a three-week voyage, none by intention.

A few days before our ship reached San Francisco, our captain honored me with a bachelor dinner. Four of my close associates and I were his guests in his quarters. As we settled back in our chairs after dinner, one of the guests asked me to tell them about my future wife. I said that Plato once observed that men in love like to hear praises of their beloveds because that praise redounds to their own credit. I smiled at my questioner and said, "Therefore, gentlemen, my own modesty forbids my speaking of my own beloved—for more than half an hour—at a time!" When we left the skipper's stateroom, he facetiously warned me about the breeze that usually plays around the bridegroom's pants legs and makes them flutter. It was a warning I should have heeded.

The next night I went to the flight deck before going on watch at midnight. A full moon enhanced by light, fleecy clouds and a black horizon made visual poetry that I yearned to capture. The breeze across the deck was cool. Our weather in recent days had amazed us. Instead of the usual conditions of rough seas, cold winds and an overcast sky, we had smooth sailing and sunshine almost every day. The temperature within the ship, when compared with that observed on previous similar cruises, was comfortably warm. Several times I wondered, "Can all this be a divine augury of a peaceful voyage on the seas of matrimony?" I could not believe the weather was a good omen, but I did try.

The day before the Nassau arrived, my bride-to-be did reach San Francisco after many hectic flights and delays because she had no military priority. It took her eighteen hours to get from Houston to San Francisco. The next morning the Nassau came in under the Golden Gate Bridge. The home of the Walkers, Ruth's hosts, overlooked the bridge and the bay. Ruth's hostess and her husband had been my guests aboard the Nassau in times past. She recognized the ship from afar.

She awakened Ruth and led her to the bedroom window from which she could see the ship arriving. When the ship docked I phoned Ruth and arranged to meet her at the marriage license bureau. She was waiting for me there, but I saw her first.

Ray & Ruth in LA

To understand her greeting, one should remember that I was gaunt from weight loss and deeply tanned by hours of exposure on the flight deck every day for three weeks. As I rushed to embrace her, Ruth turned to me, her eyes widened, and she said, "You look just like a cadaver!" When she recovered her composure, she did say some more endearing words. But I have never let her forget that greeting.

Our friends had arranged a wedding for us in a Swedenborgian chapel. (Ruth had never heard of the Swedenborgian tradition. I knew it only from an essay on Emmanuel Swedenborg by Ralph Waldo Emerson.) It was a popular place for weddings, on Pacific Heights in San Francisco. My roommate on the Nassau, Fred Wellmerling, was my best man. We were both quite nervous, I far more than he.

When the ceremony began, I thought I had lost my voice. What could I do when time came to repeat my vows? In desperation I even wondered if our marriage would be legal if I *wrote* my vows. Then the minister looked me in the eye and said, "Repeat after me," followed by "I, Raymond, take thee Ruth . . ."

Almost in panic, I forced air through my throat and sound came out. Relieved that I could speak, I stared straight ahead and said, now in a strong voice, "I, Ruth, take thee, Raymond . . ." Silence. Long silence. I glanced at the minister. His Adam's apple was bobbing rapidly. "What's wrong?" I thought. "Didn't he hear me? Okay, I'll say it again." Then the right words came out: "I, Raymond, take thee, Ruth—"

The day after our wedding we went to church. The church nearest our hotel was the Episcopal cathedral of San Francisco, where two years before I first shared in formal liturgical worship. Again I was moved both by the beauty of the music and the sonorous Elizabethan grandeur of the Book of Common Prayer. Attending that cathedral was another unrecognized step in my pilgrimage. That morning I could not have imagined that three years later when I worshiped a third time in an Episcopal Church it would be to receive confirmation.

After our two-week honeymoon, I returned to duty. It was difficult to find housing in San Francisco in those days. Our friends who had arranged our wedding introduced Ruth to one of their woman friends, a charming retired colonel of the Salvation Army. She graciously invited Ruth to share her small apartment. While the Nassau was steaming toward Pearl Harbor, the war with Japan suddenly ended.

Our ship was tied up in Pearl Harbor for a week while naval authorities tried to cope with the abrupt end of the war. Then we went back to San Diego for several days. Ruth meanwhile had gone to work in a branch of the Bank of America. A week after she started work, she went to her supervisor and asked for a week off to meet me in San Diego. He knew she would quit if he refused, so he grudgingly gave permission.

From San Diego the Nassau was ordered to the Far East, putting in at the southern Philippines, Guam, Okinawa, and China before returning to the States. While ashore in Tsingtao, China, with several other officers, I visited the Catholic cathedral. It was the first time I had entered a Catholic church. It pains me now to think that when I first came into our Lord's sacramental presence, I knew nothing about His being there. I briefly inspected the interior of the church and then went next door to a gift shop. There for the first time in my life I chatted briefly with some nuns who were in charge of the shop. One of them, I learned, was from Dubuque, Iowa.

When we returned to the States I bade good-bye to the Nassau and went on terminal leave. Ruth and I went back to Oklahoma and Texas to visit our families. Then we drove to Cambridge, Massachusetts, in January of 1946 to begin our new life.

Recently my eldest son, Chris, called my attention to a website that provides descriptions and pictures of naval ships active in World War II. Visiting the site, I saw an aerial photograph of the Nassau. There she was, bravely ploughing through the ocean. Now she is no more. Sold for scrap. Gazing at this picture of an old beloved friend, I couldn't help shedding some tears for my Nasty Maru.

U.S.S. Nassau

CHAPTER SEVEN

SHEDDING MY UNITARIANISM

We arrived in Boston in mid-January along with thousands of other veterans rushing to enroll in the dozens of colleges in the area. The housing office at Harvard could offer us nothing for months to come. We rented a room in a house not far from Harvard Yard and began our frantic search for an apartment. For a week I went out at 5:30 a.m. to get the morning papers and study the classified sections. We did locate a number of apartments, but all were too far from Harvard for our purposes. Then we put an ad in the *Boston Globe*. We received half a dozen calls from people with furnished apartments, all in outlying districts. One call came from a naval officer who was leaving Cambridge. His apartment, very near where we were staying, was on the third floor of a six-unit apartment building. We took it, gratefully.

We learned quickly from our neighbors that our building superintendent had some peculiar habits. When sober, he tended to neglect keeping the boiler in the basement to the temperature necessary for heating all six units. When he drank heavily, his neglect of the boiler must have hurt his conscience. He over-compensated, giving us more heat than we needed. Some days we were cold in the apartment. Some days we had to open windows (in January and February in Boston!) to make the apartment comfortable. Still, we were thankful we had a place to live. It was only a few blocks from the Divinity School and within walking distance of the personnel office where Ruth had found employment.

As I prepared to enroll in the Divinity School, I realized a profound debt of gratitude to God who had brought us there. So many things *could* have happened to me and to Ruth in the previous three years to prevent our being in Cambridge. Indeed, as I looked back over my life from earliest days, I thought God had been guiding me to this point. This gave me a deep sense of responsibility for making my best effort to prepare to serve God's people in churches of my denomination.

Two years before I had finally accepted my calling to the ministry I was convinced it was a calling to search for the truth, a calling to find answers for myself and for those whom I served. Answers to the deepest questions in life: who I was, what the purpose of my life was, how to achieve that purpose. Apart from some theological generalities, I had no sense of a body of truth bequeathed to me by my denomination, no tradition that I must pass on. (The Greek word for tradition, *paradosis*, means literally a handing on.) It was up to me to find the truth about God and about life and to pass that truth on to others.

From the outset of my seminary study, then, I had almost a compulsion about study and learning. Driving this compulsion was my concern about the shortness of time. A sonnet by Wilfrid Scawen Blunt, "On the Shortness of Time," had long been a favorite:

If I could live without the thought of death,
forgetful of time's waste, the soul's decay,
I would not ask for other joy than breath
with light and sound of birds and the sun's ray.
I could sit on untroubled day by day
watching the grass grow, and the wild flowers range
from blue to yellow and from red to gray
in natural sequence as the seasons change.
I could afford to wait, but for the hurt
of this dull tick of time which chides my ear.
But now I dare not sit with loins ungirt
and staff unlifted, for death stands too near.
I must be up and going—aye, each minute.
The grave gives time for rest when we are in it.

Gradually I realized that I must be most concerned about the spiritual aspects of my life and my training. I knew that I could learn the practical aspects of ministerial work—church management, religious education and so on—by experience. The intellectual side of my preparation would have to come by my own efforts. But what about the spiritual side? In my journal I often returned to the subject of the struggle for spiritual growth. (The word *sanctity* was not in my vocabulary.)

My basic reason for concern about my spiritual life was utilitarian. I kept telling myself I must grow spiritually so that I could be a more effective minister. I gave little thought to the universal call to holiness of which the Second Vatican Council would speak eighteen years later. Ruth and I prayed together at meals and in the evening. But my life in the Divinity School community contributed little or nothing to my spiritual growth. Chapel services were a sometimes thing. I cannot recall a single class that was opened with prayer.

When I went to church on Sunday I went as a spectator. Part of the reason for that detached attitude was the requirement of a scholarship I received from the Divinity School. When I applied for admission, a grant had been given to me for fieldwork in a local church. I elected not to do the fieldwork but to concentrate on my study. As an alternative to fieldwork, the dean assigned me the task of visiting a different church each Sunday and writing a reaction to what I saw and heard. We visited a Greek Orthodox church, a Unitarian church, a Jehovah's Witnesses church and many others. It never occurred to me to visit a Roman Catholic church.

I was somewhat amused by the perplexity of the preacher in the Jehovah's Witnesses congregation. He dwelt at length on portions of the Book of Revelation but bogged down on the reference to the 144,000 who would be gathered around the heavenly throne. He assumed they would all be Jehovah's Witnesses, of course. He took the number literally. Then, it seemed, in the middle of his sermon he suddenly realized that there are far more than 144,000 Jehovah's Witnesses in the world. Who of them would have to be excluded? He made some unenlightening remarks in response to his own question and then went on to another subject.

Though the divine liturgy of the Greek Orthodox church we visited was foreign to my experience, two things impressed me. One was length. I had never before been in a church service that lasted for three hours. It seemed even longer because of my total lack of understanding what was going on. The other impression was the casual attitude of the worshipers. While the liturgy was being celebrated (my word then was "performed"), many persons—more men than women—drifted in and out of the church, standing outside in a corridor to chat and smoke. Some smokers took more than one leave of the liturgy in that three-hour period.

We had never heard a sermon preached by Dean Sperry of the Divinity School. One Sunday, when he was preaching in Harvard Memorial Church, I received permission to depart from our church visitation schedule in order to hear him. A few days before, the dean had told me he was working on a sermon whose theme was the tragedy of wasting experience. He had also written me a warm note of praise for a statement I had written as part of the requirement of my scholarship. The statement gave my reasons for entering the ministry and for coming to Harvard.

His sermon was strong. At one point he referred to "one of your number here at Harvard." I held my breath. I knew he was about to refer to what I had written. He introduced his illustration by saying it was a statement by a Harvard student who had been in the navy and had written about his reaction to life in the service. He paraphrased it slightly to conceal the fact that the author was a Divinity School student. This is what he read:

"During . . . my three years' duty aboard an aircraft carrier as a communications officer . . . I saw so many men floundering in disordered lives which lacked a central integration. I saw them seek that integration in almost every conceivable form. It was plain to see that only those men with spiritual backbone were the ones who withstood not only the rigors of combat duty but also—and this is infinitely more difficult—the rigors of moral combat duty which one constantly undergoes in the service. These years in the navy were a profound experience—spiritually, mentally, morally—and it is my sincere desire to use wisely the lessons learned during them."

I was so surprised this eminent man would use one of my statements to illustrate his sermon that I could hardly breathe. I felt my neck and ears and face turning a fiery color. I knew everyone in the congregation must have been looking at me. How could they look elsewhere, when I was on fire? But I kept my eyes glued on Dean Sperry. After reading the quotation, he underlined it as pointing toward the lesson he was drawing. I knew never again would Dean Sperry quote me. But at least it had happened once. In the words of an old friend, "That was glory enough for one lifetime!" At least for a seminary neophyte.

A theological eye-opener jarred me when I began my classes at the Divinity School. Some of the professors and a number of the students were Unitarian. I had scarcely heard the word before. The professor of theology was Unitarian. Indeed, I later learned he was so liberal that even some of the Unitarians apologized for his apparent lack of belief. The professor of New Testament, a Quaker, was also Unitarian. Early in the semester I noted in the journal that the lectures in theology would be "stimulating instead of reassuring."

The largest contingent of seminarians was Church of Christ fundamentalists. All of them were graduates of Abilene Christian College in Abilene, Texas. (As a college senior I had once participated in a debate tournament there.) I never knew why these men came to Harvard. (It may have been the Divinity School's very generous scholarship program.) Most of them became Unitarians in the course of their three years at the Divinity School. A few retained their fundamentalist faith by closing their minds to the watered-down theology being taught at the school. At the time I was disdainful of those who remained fundamentalist. Now I realize they were wiser and more faithful to Christ than I was. (My disdain for fundamentalists was somewhat diluted by hearing the dean say that if ever there were Christian martyrs in this country, they probably would be either fundamentalists or Roman Catholics.)

In those days my capacity for disdain was great. I also looked down on the fundamentalists who did become Unitarians. Only years later did I realize that when I was at Harvard I was one of them: a fundamentalist (of sorts, in my youth) who years before had become Unitarian.

Two months after the semester began I made this journal entry: "Unitarianism has much to commend it, I find. Upon closer examination of its beliefs, I find that *much of its thought has been latent in my own mind*. Fundamental, of course, is its opposition to the Trinity. In all sincerity, I must admit that the Unitary view of the Godhead makes much better sense to me. [I did not realize that *Godhead* is itself a Trinitarian term.] Its consequent view of Jesus not as the actual Son of God but as the most divine of men [whatever that could mean] is *one to which I have long tended*" (emphasis added).

And then I added I would have to ignore what Disciples believe and hold to my beliefs. "In my work with the Disciples Church, my only recourse, it seems to me, will be to ignore that part of the church's teaching [as if the Disciples had 'teachings'] and cling to my beliefs. I have no zeal to impress my own views on others, for it might lessen their complete set of religious convictions." (To have urged Unitarianism on a congregation might well have lessened—or dissolved—many people's convictions.) I ended on an optimistic note: "But it is a grand experience to begin this examination of what one might believe in the light of what one has tacitly believed from childhood. A most exhilarating experience!"

Yes, heresy *is* exhilarating when first embraced. And note the matter of examining "what one *might* believe." Or to be more specific, "what one might *choose* to believe." This is Protestantism at its logical purest.

One of the former Church of Christ seminarians who had become Unitarian stopped me in the hall one day. "Have you heard the Unitarian creed?"

"Go on," I said. "You guys don't have a creed. You just believe anything you want to believe."

"No," he said earnestly, "we *do* have a creed."

"All right. What is it?"

"We believe in the fatherhood of God and the brotherhood of man in the neighborhood of Boston."

The course in the history of Protestantism as taught by the Unitarian professor raised many questions in my mind. So did my beginning course in New Testament. I asked myself, how much of the Gospel accounts of Jesus' life can we accept as true? I asked myself the absurd question, how much of His divinity can we accept? I had long ago given up trying to make sense of the miracle stories. That professor gave me reasons why I should abandon the attempt; for him they were merely pious legends. But, I assured myself, my religious faith was not shaken. I told myself it was being daily strengthened. I told myself it was doing me no small amount of good. I even wished that some of my ministerial friends could share this experience with me of reveling in Unitarianism!

One of my courses was an undergraduate course, "Types of Philosophy," in the college of Arts and Sciences. On the first day of class the professor told us he would not spread out a whole series of philosophies before us. Instead, he would take us as deeply as possible into the one philosophy that he considered the most adequate: Aristotelianism. As a graduate student in an undergraduate course, I was required to write an extra paper. He assigned me the five arguments for the existence of God. Initially I had little interest in the assignment but developed a deep interest as I prepared the paper. This was my first delving into the philosophy of Saint Thomas Aquinas.

The philosophy class included one hundred fifty or more students. Apart from the general lecture sessions, we were divided into a half-dozen sections with a graduate student as discussion leader for each. The young man in charge of my section later became a well-known Greek Orthodox theologian. After one of our section meetings I asked him what the professor's religion was. He said the professor was an Anglo-Catholic.

"What's that?" I had never heard the word before.

The section leader spoke briefly about "high church" Episcopalians and their claim to be "Catholic." The explanation made no sense to me. (Near the end of my pilgrimage, when as an Anglo-Catholic I saw clearly what Anglo-Catholicism *is*, it made even less sense to me.)

The professor of New Testament was a small, winsome man. He occupied the oldest endowed chair at Harvard University. He was known internationally as a scholar and translator, having been a key member of the group that produced the Revised Standard Version of the New Testament. (That version was published just as I was beginning seminary at Harvard.) When we came to the Book of Hebrews he made a remark that greatly surprised me. I can remember his exact words: "I must confess I don't know what this author is talking about!" And so, he said, we would skip the book in our class. And we did. My initial reaction was that if he couldn't make sense of the book, neither could I. (After I became Trinitarian I understood why a Unitarian would be puzzled by a book which focuses on the sacrificial life and death of God's Incarnate Son.)

As we studied the book of Romans, he said Paul always shared his religious experiences with his church people, regardless of how primitive those experiences were. (I wondered what made the experiences "primitive.") All ministers, our professor told us, might well learn to do the same thing. My reaction, as noted in my journal that day, was "undoubtedly it would be highly beneficent for ministers to share their religious experiences—*if* they have had any." Projecting my own spiritual immaturity on others, I wondered if the average minister has had notable spiritual experiences or even consciously cultivates spiritual experience.

One day in his class I passed a milestone in my pilgrimage. He digressed from study of the New Testament books to explain inspiration of Scripture. He assured us that Scripture is inspired in the same sense that Shakespeare and Milton and Dante are inspired. Inspiration, he said, means noble thoughts expressed in beautiful language. Period.

This came as a shock to me. Despite my Unitarianism, I had always thought that biblical inspiration meant a great deal more than that. Now I saw that on the basis of Scripture itself I could neither refute his definition nor defend my previous understanding. That was when the walls of *sola scriptura* began crumbling.

The professor of church history was a former Catholic. I was told he had left the Church over some issue of "modernism." (I didn't know what the term meant, even though I was immersed in it at the Divinity School!) I also heard he was a former priest (a Jesuit, some said), but this may have been only rumor. (My informer and I did not know that a priest is a priest forever.) He sometimes spoke critically of the Catholic Church, but at the time I did not sense bitterness. I even thought I detected a bit of wistfulness in his attitude and tone.

Had I been Catholic in those days, that impression could have been wishful thinking. Because I was strongly prejudiced against the Church, I think my impression of his wistfulness was accurate. Many years later in Boston one of his acquaintances told me the professor had lived into his nineties. A Divinity School colleague of his had faithfully visited him during his dying days. After much effort, that colleague prevailed upon him to be reconciled to the Church shortly before he died. The colleague, George Huntston Williams, himself a distinguished historian, was Unitarian. May God bless him for this great act of mercy.

During my eight months at the Divinity School I lamented in my journal that my prayer life was not nearly so intense as it was when I was at sea. I missed the inspiration of gazing at the ever-changing ocean. I missed the star-clustered nights when I stood alone on the flight deck looking up at the heavens, "lost in wonder, love and praise," as one of the hymns puts it. I missed going topside and being bathed in the total darkness of an overcast night while saying my night prayers. Yet I had no desire to return to navy life.

On Easter morning I was cleaning the kitchen after breakfast while Ruth dressed for church. I turned on the radio. The "National Radio Pulpit" on NBC came on. As Dr. Ralph W. Sockman, a distinguished Methodist minister in New York, the weekly host, proclaimed the Resurrection of Christ, I was filled suddenly with perhaps the deepest longing of my life up to that time. I yearned to *believe* that what Dr. Sockman was saying was *true*—that Jesus Christ was truly raised from the dead as the Son of God. That He was raised for *me.* I left the kitchen sink and tried to share my longing with Ruth, whose faith was much deeper than mine. She shared her own faith and tried to reassure me in my longing.

That was the beginning of my conversion from Unitarianism.

* * *

My initial enthusiasm for my classes at the Divinity School waned. The Unitarianism of the theology professor became less and less attractive. One day in a pensive aside he spoke about his own lack of faith. "It's not easy," he said, "to come to the end of your life and not know whether there is anything beyond this life." His plaintive observation served as a wakeup call for me. "Not easy, indeed," I thought. "Also terrible."

In my journal I wrote at length about my growing discontent with my work at the Divinity School. I thought the theology professor's lectures were far too discursive. He spent much time defending or attacking certain philosophers and theologians. I thought many of my voluminous notes from his class were of little value. The New Testament classes seemed haphazard. Too much time was given to longwinded students expounding their opinions. I wanted the professor's ideas, not those of my verbose and relatively ignorant classmates.

The philosophy professor's lectures were very low-grade. I found that my attendance at his lectures had little effect on my comprehension of the material under discussion. My complaint about the church history course was that the professor talked too much about Catholicism. The course was supposed to have focused on the relation of the church to society from the time of the Reformation. I expected the course would be devoted to Protestant church history. Instead, the Catholic Church was clearly his major concern.

I told myself I needed to know Protestant history much more than I needed to know Catholic history.

I decided to go to the dean and tell him what was bothering me. I even rehearsed part of a little speech I would give him. I would tell him that if the courses of my first semester are fair indication of what to expect, I should find it necessary to go to Union or Yale next fall. I would use strong language: Schooling at Harvard was costing Ruth and me too much in living expenses to accept mediocre instruction.

Just before calling the dean's office to make an appointment, I came across a quote I had copied from one of his sermons. He had cautioned against trying to find a church or a college that fits us when we join it. He said we might well outgrow it. That seemed true. Perhaps I was being too hasty in going to him with my dissatisfaction. I decided to give the Divinity School a little more time.

But not much more.

A few weeks later I did go to the dean and say I had to make a decision about future schooling. I spoke as tactfully as possible, but my point was that I must move on. If what I'm getting here is what Christianity is all about, I said, then I shall forget about the ministry. My alternative is to go to another seminary and see what's being taught there. My choice, I said, would be Yale Divinity School.

The dean, who was a graduate of the Yale seminary, advised me to go to Union Theological Seminary in New York. He said it was a "more cosmopolitan environment," both in academic courses and in the range of student representation. Soon thereafter I went down to New York on the train and met with several U.T.S. staff members. Union Seminary was part of the neighborhood familiar from my days as a midshipman at Columbia. Because I had been favorably impressed by what I heard at Union, when I returned to Cambridge we decided I would enroll in Union and we would move to New York in the fall.

Because the Divinity School offered no summer courses, I spent the entire summer in my own reading program. Dean Sperry had told me about studying church history at Oxford, where he spent three years under the direction of noted New Testament and patristics scholar Canon B. H. Streeter. The dean chuckled as he recalled that in three years' study and instruction he and Canon Streeter had never got beyond the first Council of Nicaea (AD 325).

Following the dean's lead, I concentrated on early church history and the history of doctrine, especially the early Christological struggles. All my sources but one were Protestant, but they necessarily dealt with patristic teaching. The one Catholic source was a three-volume history of the early Church by Father

Louis Duchesne. (Herb Smith had recommended these to me when we were aboard the Nassau.) Only recently I read that these books had been placed on the Church's now-defunct List of Prohibited Books in 1912. Still, even from a Modernist I could learn much of value. I ignored as Catholic special pleading everything Duchesne said about the role of the papacy in early centuries.

During that summer of study I began to see more clearly the gigantic leap Protestantism tries to make from the end of the apostolic age to the time of the Reformation. More and more I realized that the attempt to ignore all those intervening centuries is disingenuous.

An analogy occurred to me. It was as if I decided I did not like what happened in my life between the ages of one and sixteen, and I simply chose to ignore those years. I could no longer accept this basic Protestant discontinuity. (More about discontinuity later.) Those early struggles that had convulsed the life of the early Church were too basic to Christianity to be ignored, as Protestants seek to do.

My denomination, the Disciples of Christ, claimed it had "restored" the "primitive church." Alexander Campbell, the Disciples' founding father, decried denominationalism. He was determined to unite all [Protestant] Christians by a return to "the primitive church." His battle cry was, "no creed but Christ, no book but the Bible." All human traditions must be cast aside.

"I will read my Bible as though it had just fallen into my hands from heaven," he declared. And what did he find in that Bible from outer space? Precisely what one would expect from an early nineteenth-century, frontier, ex-Presbyterian. Campbell's attempted "restoration" was in fact a reconstruction of the early Church on the basis of his presuppositions.

Closely related to the matter of restorationism is the issue which figures prominently in many accounts of conversion to the Catholic Church. It is the issue of *sola scriptura*, Scripture alone. Along with *sola gratia*, it is the key slogan of Protestantism. It is the declaration that every Christian belief must be clearly proved from Scripture.

Ironically, the belief itself—that all must be proved from Scripture—cannot be proved from Scripture. Scripture nowhere asserts what Protestants have always assumed. By this time in my pilgrimage I was beginning to realize that the very notion of going back to what Protestants like to call "the pure Word of God" untouched by human interpretations is essentially restorationist. And therefore it is a reconstruction of the message of Scripture on the basis of Protestant presuppositions. (For an expansion of this theme, see chapters 14 and 15.)

During that summer of study I lost all interest in claims and efforts to "restore" the early Church. I began to yearn for historical *continuity* with the early Church. But it was yearning for *institutional* continuity. (It was not a yearning for a personal continuity with Christ Himself through His appointed spokesmen. That yearning developed late in my pilgrimage.) I knew nothing about the Episcopal Church except the stereotype that it catered to the rich. But without realizing it, I had become open to its appeal. Two years later I became an Episcopalian.

At the end of the summer I noted another result of my study. It had softened my Protestant disdain for monasticism. My yearning for deeper communion with God gave me sympathy with those who betake themselves to the monastic life for that very purpose. Monasticism makes sense, I realized, only to the person who has made serious effort to come into closer communion with God.

Still, at the end of this reflection in my journal I wrote, "But Heaven forbid that *I* take the holy vows!"

CHAPTER EIGHT

My First Ordination

A t summer's end 1946 Ruth and I moved to New York. At Union Theological Seminary we lived in the men's dormitory, three floors of which had been assigned to married students. We took our meals in the refectory. Those were stimulating years. Theological discussion, sometimes heated, was our consuming interest. We were immersed in the theological bedlam that is Protestantism. Representatives of half a hundred denominations and many competing theological approaches created a lively, fascinating environment. Ardent Brunnerians argued with equally ardent Barthians. Niebuhrians battled with Tillichians. But so far as I knew, everyone was Trinitarian. At Union I heard Jesus Christ powerfully proclaimed by outstanding preachers and theologians. By God's grace I became a believing Christian, and Ruth's faith in Christ was strengthened.

Prevailing thought at Union was in full swing against Protestant theological liberalism, especially in its view of human nature. The reaction was known as neo-orthodoxy. Its most famous exponent was a Swiss theologian, Karl Barth. The neo-orthodox movement claimed that liberalism in theology had downplayed the sinful nature of man and his possibilities for evil. Despite its inherent anti-Catholic animus, neo-orthodoxy was closer to Catholicism than was its opponent, liberalism. The faculty of Union Seminary was known throughout the Protestant world. Because several of its members were such prominent figures, I noted in my journal, there was "much slavish aping of their attitudes and thoughts by impressionable students."

In two important respects, our life at Union was quite different from life at Harvard Divinity School. The academic pace was faster, the requirements more stringent. Unlike Harvard, Union had daily chapel worship. It also had a noted school of sacred music, training organists and choirmasters in conjunction with the Julliard School, which then was located across the street. The music of the chapel was high caliber, as was the preaching done by professors and visiting dignitaries. I think this atmosphere of worship was responsible for my feeling that I had finally embarked on my real training for the ministry.

Over the courtyard entrance to Union's refectory these words were engraved in stone: *Cognoverunt eum in fractione panis* ("They knew him in the breaking of bread," from Luke 24:35). I seldom climbed the steps leading to that entrance without reading those words. Like dripping water on stone, those words gradually wore down my understanding of Holy Communion as a purely symbolic act. They never failed to remind me that the Lord's Supper must be more than a mere reminder of an event long ago. This reminder later began to take shape as I became interested in the Episcopal Church.

During my three years at Union I did field work on weekends. At the beginning of my first year I obtained a position at Christ Church Methodist at Park Avenue and 60th Street. Though not a Methodist, I wanted to hear the preaching of the pastor, Ralph Sockman, whose Easter sermon on NBC that year had aroused in me a yearning to know Christ. After a year working with a high school group there, I decided I should work in a church of my own denomination.

For the next two years I worked with a young adult group at Park Avenue Christian Church at Park Avenue and 85th Street. Those young people were budding careerists: mostly musicians, some actors, some artists. All were working at odd jobs to support themselves while they sought the lucky break that would launch their careers. Only one whom I remember achieved some artistic success. The others drifted back to their hometowns or the hometowns of spouses they had wed while living in New York. I felt sorry for them. They were so eager to excel. Some were exceedingly talented. But the breaks didn't come. How many thousands like them there must have been in New York at the time! And doubtless still are today.

When I began working in Park Avenue Methodist Church, a women's group was planning to start a nursery school in the Italian section of East Harlem. They asked Ruth to take charge. She had no experience with nursery schools but bravely tackled the project. This was her introduction to life in the slums. She was devoted to the families whom the nursery school served and appalled by the conditions in which they lived.

That year of administering and teaching on the nursery level motivated Ruth to enroll in Teachers College at Columbia University. During the next two years she completed a master's degree in early childhood development while teaching in the nursery school at Riverside Church, across the street from Union Seminary. At my graduation from Union in 1948, along with the other working wives of students she was solemnly granted a Ph.T. degree ("Putting Hubby Through") with appropriate diploma.

One of my unfulfilled resolutions while in the navy was to read widely in philosophy before going to seminary. At Union I discovered that the anti-intellectualism of the Reformation was still in full swing. Despite the presence of many brilliant scholars on the faculty, there was a distinct and often articulated prejudice against the study of philosophy. We were told in class that the worst possible preparation for studying theology was to have studied philosophy. I knew students with degrees in philosophy from Ivy League colleges who, under the impact of this ideology, had become ashamed of their academic background.

Why was philosophy so denigrated? The answer was simple: Rome trains her seminarians first in philosophy, then in theology. If Rome does it that way, it *must* be wrong. This is not an exaggeration of the faculty's logic.

Anti-Catholic prejudice carried over into the classroom in various forms. One of the Old Testament professors told us of the "shameful" way in which the Catholic Church had tinkered with the Ten Commandments. Protestants claim that the first commandment is "You shall have no other gods before me." The second is "You shall not make for yourself a graven image . . ." Now look at what Rome does, our professor said. To cover up the fact that Rome *does* worship graven images, they combine the first two commandments. (Rome was always referred to as *they*, never as *she*). This is an attempt to bury the restriction against worshipping graven images inside the first commandment, or at least to soften it. But there have to be ten; Rome is one short. What does Rome do? "They" split the rightful tenth commandment against covetousness in two, giving them the requisite number.

I was shocked by Rome's deceit. How dare "they"?

(Only after entering the Church did I understand. To begin with, what Protestants call the second commandment is only a specification of the first. We are commanded to have no other gods. That commandment also excludes the worship of graven images. Then there is the charge that Rome splits the last commandment in order to have the full number. Rome splits the last commandment of the Protestant version because it incorporates two very different kinds of covetousness. The ninth commandment is directed at "lust or carnal concupiscence," while the tenth "forbids avarice arising from a passion for riches and their attendant power.")[1]

---

1   *Catechism of the Catholic Church* (Washington, D.C.: United States Catholic Conference, 1997), second edition, sections 2529 and 2552.

Or take the exegesis of John 2, the story of the marriage feast in Cana. One of our New Testament professors assured us that when Jesus addressed his mother as "woman," he was reprimanding her. He was "putting her in her place" for interfering in the festivities and asking him to do something about the lack of wine. For us students, the implication was plain. This was also a criticism of the Catholic Church's veneration (we believed, worship) of the Virgin Mary. No one mentioned the clear distinction between veneration and worship. We were not told that "woman" was a formal, respectful title. Nor were we reminded that Jesus used it affectionately of his mother in his dying moments (cf. John 19:26).

The one good word for Catholic veneration of the Virgin I did hear at Union came from the English Anglo-Catholic professor of church history. (He was primarily responsible for my becoming an Episcopalian.) In his course on the history of liturgy he surprised me by saying that Protestant theology had been "excessively masculine" and that Roman Catholic devotion to the Virgin Mary had been "a good corrective." He did not dwell on the point, perhaps because he realized that any commendation of Rome, and especially of the Virgin, took him onto thin theological ice in that academic atmosphere.

A passing comment by another of my professors, Paul Tillich, has stuck in my mind. Dr. Tillich team-taught a course in religion and psychiatry at Columbia. One day in class he referred to the irony of Protestants who look askance at Catholic confession but unhesitatingly flock to the couches of psychiatrists to tell all.

A number of times in Reinhold Niebuhr's classes I heard him declaim against the "arrogance" of Rome. The Catholic Church, he declared, dares to put herself *above* the Word of God by claiming that she is the authentic interpreter of Scripture. (The next chapter gives a Catholic theologian's response to Niebuhr's charge of Roman arrogance.) Each time I heard this allegation, like my classmates, I was duly appalled at Rome's presumption.

In five years of Protestant seminary training, my most inspiring teacher was James Muilenburg, professor of Old Testament at Union. He was voted Union's most popular professor once or twice while I was there. His love for the Hebrew people and their religion was deep. In an unusual way he was quite dramatic in his lectures. He spoke much of "covenant" but gave no attention to the subject of sacrifice. Like the other six professors of Scripture under whom I studied as a Protestant, he ignored the allegorical interpretation of Scripture. The general impression we students were given was that the allegorical interpretation is purely fanciful and to be avoided.

(In later years when I studied Blessed John Henry Newman's *An Essay on the Development of Doctrine*, I doubted that my Protestant professors of Scripture had read it. In early centuries, Newman wrote, the School of Antioch, bastion of literal interpretation, was also "the very metropolis of heresy." However, in all ages of the Church her teachers have refused to confine themselves to the literal interpretation. The Church's "most subtle and powerful method of proof . . . is the mystical sense" of Scripture. "It may be almost laid down as an historical fact," Newman wrote, "that the mystical interpretation and orthodoxy will stand or fall together."[2])

At Union I heard a lecture by one Catholic theologian, John Courtney Murray, S.J. He was a friend of Reinhold Niebuhr. I knew little, and cared less, about contemporary Catholic theologians, but I had heard that Father Murray was well known. The lecture hall was filled. I cannot recall anything Father Murray said. Early in his lecture I stopped attending to his words and thought about the man himself. He was handsome, I thought, tall with gracious bearing in well-fitting clerical attire. He spoke deliberately; he was articulate and polished—obviously an intelligent man. Throughout his lecture I looked at him in amazement and kept asking myself, "How can such an intelligent, highly educated man be a *Roman Catholic*? How can he stand to let his church do his thinking for him? How can he *tolerate* the oppression of his church? What terrible sacrifices he has had to make!" In my ignorance, these were thoughts of genuine compassion for this Jesuit.

Nor was I alone in my thinking about Catholic priests. John Foster Dulles was then a distinguished international lawyer, active Presbyterian layman, and prominent member of the World Council of Churches. He was also a director of Union Seminary. We saw him fairly often in the refectory when he came to visit. When we learned that his son Avery had become a Roman Catholic, we were greatly saddened. We told one another that Avery had disgraced his father; that Avery was clearly the black sheep of his family. But our sympathy for Mr. Dulles intensified when we learned that not only had Avery become a Catholic; he had become a *Jesuit*! In our minds, this was adding insult to injury of his family. (After becoming Catholic I had the privilege of relating this to the late and revered Father [later Cardinal] Dulles. It gave him a good laugh.)

In retrospect I can see that my professors in the four Protestant seminaries I attended labored under many misapprehensions about the Catholic Church. Many times I heard assertions about the Church that I know now are untrue. Strange that those professors could be so well read, so well informed about many subjects yet so ill-informed about the Catholic Church. In my opinion, none has so well explained this phenomenon as Newman (long

---

2   *An Essay on the Development of Christian Doctrine* (Notre Dame, IN: University of Notre Dame Press, 1989), 342-44.

before he was made a cardinal). Start with the fact that "tradition" is anathema to the Protestant mind. Catholics believe in tradition; Protestants believe in the infallible Word of God; this apparent antinomy is axiomatic in Protestant thinking.

In 1851 Newman gave a series of talks that were published under the title *Lectures on the Present Position of Catholics in England*. His second lecture was titled "Tradition—the Sustaining Power of the Protestant View." These are startling words, in light of the Protestant abhorrence of tradition. Newman pointed to the vast amount of misinformation about Catholicism that Protestants accept as true. With regard to what Catholicism is, he declared, "Englishmen go by that very mode of information in its worst shape, which they are so fond of imputing against Catholics; they go by *tradition*, immemorial, unauthenticated *tradition*." In other words, "Englishmen entertain their present monstrous notions of us mainly because those notions are received on information not authenticated, but immemorial."[3] Another word for that source of information about Catholicism is *prejudice*.

The only member of the staff at Union Seminary I knew to be Catholic was the assistant dietitian. She was an attractive young woman, rather shy, well liked by students and faculty. Her acquaintances knew she had planned to go on a cruise during one of her holidays. Then we learned that at considerable expense she had canceled her reservation shortly before embarkation. Why? She had learned there would be no priest aboard and therefore no daily Mass. We chatted among ourselves about this. We felt sorry for her but thought she was being rigid. None of us would have canceled a cruise merely because there would be no Protestant service on board. And yet in my heart I admired her for the courage of her convictions—even though I thought they were wrong.

Living in New York in the late 1940s, despite my prejudice I could not ignore the Catholic Church. In those days the Church was consistently portrayed with sympathy in Hollywood movies. Producers didn't dare do otherwise, so powerful was the Catholic League of Decency in turning Catholics away from objectionable movies. In those years the *New York Times* gave full coverage to Cardinal Francis Spellman's activities. He was a powerful figure in the city because he forcefully advocated the Church's position on many different issues. The aggressive, self-confident stance of the American hierarchy in those days evoked admiration even from the Church's bitterest critics. I know. I was one of them.

Over a period of weeks, Cardinal Spellman and Bishop Garfield Oxnam, the local Methodist bishop, feuded in the columns of the *New York Times*.

---

3   John Henry Newman, *Lectures on the Present Position of Catholics in England* (London: Longmans, Green and Co., 1913), 45.

Finally the well-known pastor of a Catholic parish in Manhattan was quoted in the *Times* as saying, "Why don't *both* of you be quiet?" In a day or two the rumor went through Union that the priest had gone on an extended leave of absence. The dean of the Episcopal Cathedral of Saint John the Divine went to that priest and urged him to come into the Episcopal Church. (Though I knew the dean slightly, this information came from him through a mutual friend.) The dean had arranged for the priest to lead a very comfortable life if he would become an Episcopalian. The priest declined the offer, "sadly," my informant said. When we heard this story we felt sorry for that priest. What a terrible hold Rome has on her priests! we thought. Yet a memory from my youth would not go away: these Catholics are *serious* about their religion.

Earlier I spoke of my first visit to a Catholic church, the cathedral in Tsingtao, China. The second Catholic church I visited was Saint Patrick's Cathedral in New York. I had no desire to go, but friends from out of town wanted to see it. One of our friends from college was a seminarian at Yale Divinity School. His mother and ten-year-old brother came from Oklahoma to visit Tom. When they came to New York for sightseeing, they invited Ruth and me to join them. I knew nothing of the Blessed Sacrament or the tabernacle or the sanctuary lamp. A guide showed us part of the cathedral. At one point he took us deep into the cathedral where he said a number of cardinals were buried. When he pointed out their tombs, Tom's little brother, an ardent baseball fan, asked his mother in a stage whisper, "Mom, does he mean the St. Louis Cardinals?"

When we were living at Union, it housed the Russian Orthodox Seminary of Saint Vladimir. Saint Vladimir's had its own faculty, almost all laymen, headed by Father Georges Florovsky. He was perhaps the pre-eminent Eastern theologian of the twentieth century. We Protestant seminarians had no contact with the Russian faculty and seminarians except to sit occasionally at table with them in the refectory. Father Florovsky was an impressive figure, even though I knew nothing then of his fame as a theologian. Many times I saw him striding through the halls, a tall man, heavily bearded, in flowing black robes, with what we called his "headdress" which made him appear to be seven feet tall.

These Russian Orthodox men and seminarians represented a different world to us Protestants. We had some rudimentary knowledge of their beliefs, which were quite different from ours. We recognized that we were also separated from them by deep cultural and ethnic differences. And yet we felt comfortable in their presence. Indeed, we were glad they shared our accommodations. They were Christians, like us. Best of all, they were *not* "Roman." And so, deep down, we knew they were our allies.

(Years later, I read that a nineteenth-century author, Joseph de Maistre, had declared "every non-Catholic church is 'protestant.'" The distinction often made between heretical groups [Protestants] and schismatic groups [separated Eastern Churches] is only verbal. "Every Christian who rejects *communion* with the Holy Father is a Protestant or soon will be." Why, De Maistre asked, do Protestants never bother to write books attacking the Greek or the Russian or the Nestorian or the Syrian churches, all of which hold doctrines that Protestants despise? The Russian Church, for example, believes in the Real Presence, all seven Catholic sacraments, intercession of the saints, veneration of images, and so forth. Though Protestantism abhors these doctrines, "if it encounters any of these in a church separated from Rome, it takes no offense at them. . . . Russia is separated from the Holy See: that is sufficient for it to be seen as a brother, a fellow Protestant." More succinctly, "All enemies of Rome are friends."[4])

Married couples occupied the first three floors of Hastings Hall, a large dormitory for men at Union. Ruth and I lived on the third floor. One of Saint Vladimir's faculty, a layman, also lived on the third floor. On each floor there were two large bathrooms, one for each gender. None of us had more than a nodding acquaintance with the Russian professor. Occasionally we met him in the hall or in the bathroom at night as he (always hastily, it seemed to me) prepared for bed.

One of my seminary friends, Bob, often said that two of his greatest pleasures were long hot showers and smoking his pipe. One day he told me he had discovered a way to enjoy them simultaneously. The three shower stalls in the men's bathroom were large, about five feet square, each with a five-inch ledge at the entrance inside of which the shower curtain hung. Bob had reasoned that before he entered the stall he could adjust the water temperature, light up his pipe, lay it on the ledge just outside the shower curtain, stretch out in the stall with his head on the ledge, let the shower curtain drape over his neck, retrieve his pipe, and puff away while relaxing under the soothing flow of hot water.

Late one night Bob was lying in the shower, head sticking out beneath the shower curtain, smoking his pipe, eyes closed. No one else was in the bathroom. The Russian professor (who was nearsighted) came into the bathroom without his glasses. To his horror, he thought he saw a decapitated head lying on the ledge, eyes closed, a pipe clutched in its teeth. He screamed, rushed into the hall and began spouting Russian at the students who came out of their rooms. He kept pointing to the bathroom. Finally, one of the

---

4   Quoted by Hans Urs Von Balthasar, *The Office of Peter and the Structure of the Church* (San Francisco: Ignatius Press, 1986), 80-81.

seminarians went in and found Bob still lying in the shower, eyes wide open, asking, "What's going on out there?" Another seminarian led the professor back into the bathroom. He showed him that the head he had seen was well-attached to a seminarian.

In the years before Vatican II, many Protestants saw Catholicism as a threat to their religious liberty. My first alert to this concern came during a summer course on U.S. Protestant history at Union Seminary in 1947. It was taught by William Warren Sweet, a visiting professor from the University of Chicago. At one point he expounded on the threat Roman Catholicism poses to the liberty of other Christians. He held up a book titled *Catholic Principles of Politics*. The book declares, he said, that once Catholics become a majority in a nation they are bound by the Church's teaching to restrict the religious liberty of non-Catholics. This dire warning stuck with me.

The book in question has gone through many editions. I have searched the edition that was current in 1947. Here is the only passage I can find that is similar to what the professor read to us:

> It is true, indeed, that some zealots and bigots will continue to attack the Church because they fear that some five thousand years hence the United States may become overwhelmingly Catholic and may then restrict the freedom of non-Catholics. [Now note the authors' response to this charge.] *Nevertheless, we cannot yield up the principles of eternal unchangeable truth in order to avoid the enmity of such unreasonable persons* [emphasis added]. Moreover, it would be a futile policy, for they would not think us sincere.[5]

Does the second sentence of this quotation admit the truth of the charge reported in the first sentence? Even if this were a Catholic opinion in 1947, it could not be held today. Vatican II has made it clear that "the right to religious freedom has its foundation in the very dignity of the human person as this dignity is known through the revealed word of God and by reason itself."[6] The "zealots and bigots"—and the seminarians at Union in 1947—need have no fear the Catholic Church will ever restrict or destroy their religious freedom.

My thinking about Catholicism received several jolts that summer. I took a course called Devotional Theology (Catholics would call it "spirituality"). It was taught by a visiting professor, Douglas Steere, an eminent Quaker theologian. He gave us a bibliography of perhaps one hundred fifty books and urged us to read as much as we could. I spent two long days in the library,

---

5   John A. Ryan and Francis J. Boland, *Catholic Principles of Politics* (New York: Macmillan, 1947), 320-321.
6   Vatican II, *Declaration on Religious Liberty*, 2.

sampling and reading. On the third day I asked him for an appointment. In his office I told him that I found his lectures helpful and that I was deeply interested in the subject.

"But," I said, "I have a real problem with your bibliography. The authors of all these books are Catholics. I'm Protestant. I don't want to learn from Catholics; I want to learn from Protestants how to pray more effectively."

Dr. Steere smiled gently.

"I'm sorry to say that in four hundred years Protestantism has not developed a literature on prayer," he said. "All of us have to learn from the Catholics how to pray."

That ended the conversation. I walked slowly from his office. The man widely regarded as this country's leading Protestant authority on "devotional theology" had learned from Catholics how to pray, and now he was telling me I had to do the same. Learn from *Catholics*?

A few days later, one of the young women in the class brought a friend, a Catholic nun. At the outset of his lecture Dr. Steere said he wanted to illustrate a point by quoting Bernard of Clairvaux. As he said this, he smiled at the nun. On hearing the name of Bernard she smiled and seemed to settle more comfortably in her seat. Immediately I felt a thrill of rapport with her. After all, I thought, there *is* much we have in common with Catholics. It's a shame our points of agreement are sadly obscured. In the realm of prayer and mysticism, I felt spiritual kinship with the great Catholic men and women of prayer.

But as quickly as it came, that thrill of rapport left me. "Suddenly [I noted in my journal that night] I remembered Catholic intolerance, its rugged determination to overcome other religions—'religions of error'—and was sobered by the realization that this nun would not smile at the name of some great Protestant religionist. Regretfully, I saw the barriers of religious differences rise again to their usually formidable heights." But then came the thought that this woman and her Church are not the only ones who have constructed those barriers. "I feel sadly as though some of my own handiwork were involved."

As for the nun herself, "I began to feel slightly uncomfortable as I looked at her in her stiff black garb. I wondered, 'Is she a *woman*?'" My discomfort was heightened by the suspicion that perhaps an ascetic streak in my own nature "was saying 'amen' to her garb and all that it signified. I have not yet been able to make my peace with the absolute ethic of Jesus Christ." Was it possible that by her way of life she had done just that? Then there were those memories of being impressed with the seriousness of the religious commitment of the nuns I recalled from my youth.

In my pilgrimage that was an eventful summer. I almost reached a parting of the ways from the Disciples of Christ and its founder, Alexander Campbell. Early in my days at Union I studied a book by an English theologian, a member of my denomination. He portrayed Campbell as distinctly "high church." He laid great emphasis on Campbell's practice of celebrating the Lord's Supper every Sunday. He even found in Campbell's Calvinism some evidence of a "high" doctrine of the Supper. By then I was being drawn to a more "churchly" position.

I was delighted with what this writer said about Campbell. I thought that perhaps this new interpretation was correct, and that as a Disciples minister I could help bring these facts to the fore. Reading that book gave me a new lease on denominational life. The author visited Union and lectured to Disciples of Christ students along the lines of his book. I was thrilled.

Then in a tutorial session I undertook a detailed study of Campbell's writings in a magazine, *The Millennial Harbinger*, that he edited for many years. After three weeks of study and note taking, I realized the English interpreter of Campbell had indulged in wishful thinking. Campbell's millenarianism was obvious even in the title of his magazine. I found almost nothing of the "high church" themes I had been told were there. (The English writer obviously had read Campbell while living in the shadow of the Church of England.) My days in the denomination Campbell founded were numbered.

By the beginning of the next year I knew I was being drawn to the Episcopal Church. I expressed my leanings to the pastor of the Disciples church where I served as a seminarian. He thought my leanings would pass and prevailed upon me to accept ordination in the Disciples of Christ that spring. Three ministers and two elders conducted the service. The elders asked three questions to which I responded affirmatively.

"Do you, Ray Ryland, reaffirm your faith in Jesus Christ and your loyalty to Him as your Lord and Savior, and will you strive to show forth His Spirit in all your life and ministry?

"Do you promise to be diligent in your study of the Scriptures, prayerful in your attitude toward God, gentle, patient and faithful in your ministrations to the people, friendly in your relations with other Christians and in your feelings and actions toward all God's children?"

"Will you make it the supreme aim of your life to proclaim the Gospel of Jesus Christ in word and deed, to be instant in season and out of season, and so to live and teach as to try to save yourself and those that see and hear you?"

While I knelt, the ministers and elders laid hands on me, and solemnly set me apart "for the work of a Christian teacher and minister."

For the text of my ordination sermon I selected Jeremiah 1:9–10. "The task of the preaching ministry is as broad as human need, as deep as the lowest reaches of human sin, as high as God's promises to men," I began. All this is "fully comprehended" in Jeremiah's call to be a prophet. I went on to outline what, in my discernment, it means to be called as a servant of God. At that point in my life I thought the die was cast: I would be a Disciples minister.

But the die was still rolling. In the midst of the doctrinal bedlam at Union Ruth and I began to hear what we thought was a voice of theological sanity.

Prayerfully, we began to answer its call.

CHAPTER NINE

DISCOVERING ANGLICANISM

My concern for the unity of all non-Catholic Christians continued to grow. Union was the nerve center of ecumenism in those days. No other American institution had so many faculty and alumni taking prominent roles in ecumenism, both in the U.S. and on the world scene. We were accustomed to seeing world leaders of the ecumenical movement in our refectory and hearing them lecture to overflow audiences. Union's famous library housed the largest collection of ecumenical materials in this country. I often browsed there. This for me was where the action was.

In the summer of 1947 I studied the historical antecedents of the modern ecumenical movement in tutorial work under the guidance of Dr. John T. McNeill, a leading authority on the subject. His book *Unitive Protestantism* documented the yearning for, and attempts at, Christian unity on the part of all the leading reformers. The book was a reappraisal of the Reformation, intending to show that Protestantism has been truly "catholic" in the best sense of the term.[1] He told me that though he regarded *Unitive Protestantism* as the best of his several books, it had sold only a few hundred copies. The plates for the book had been destroyed when the publisher had consolidated with another firm. (Years later the book was reprinted.)

Dr. McNeill told me he believed the most significant accomplishment of the Reformation was the changes it wrought in local parishes, providing worship in which communicants could participate. Now I would have to disagree with this dry old Scotsman whom I highly respected. The chief effect of the Reformation, in my opinion, was the exaltation—dare I say

---

1   All non-Catholic traditions, East as well as West, in their reconstructions, make this claim.

apotheosis?—of subjectivity. (More than fifty years later I had the privilege of becoming acquainted with Walter Hooper, a former Anglican priest who was biographer and literary executor of C.S. Lewis. I met him after Mass at Saint Aloysius Church in Oxford, England, about a year after he was received into the Church. When I congratulated him on having become Catholic, his first words were a joyful exclamation: "Oh, to be delivered from Anglican subjectivity!")

There was great excitement at Union Seminary in the fall of 1948. Scores of our faculty, students, and alumni had taken part that summer in the formation of the World Council of Churches at Amsterdam. The Council and its beginnings were the subject of animated conversation in and out of the classrooms. We reveled in the anecdotes related to us by our professors who had been at Amsterdam. We were especially fascinated by what Reinhold Niebuhr had to say. He was a favorite of Union students, and a world-famous Protestant theologian.

We expected the World Council would be a mighty force for Christian unity. At that time we gave little or no thought to the inclusion of the Catholic Church in our ecumenical yearnings. I cannot recall what specific things we thought the World Council of Churches would accomplish. We were simply convinced it would do great things for pan-Protestant unity.

In my study of the ecumenical movement I became increasingly aware of the prominent roles played by Anglican theologians and church leaders. One of the members of the Edinburgh Missionary Conference in 1910 was an Episcopal bishop, Charles H. Brent, a missionary bishop in the Philippines. During the conference he conceived the idea of a similar conference that would discuss doctrinal issues dividing Christians. Primarily at his instigation, the General Convention of the Episcopal Church issued a call that same year for a world conference to study matters of faith and order. After long delay, due partly to World War I, the first faith and order conference was held in Lausanne, Switzerland, in 1927. The Faith and Order Movement became one of the main tributaries to the World Council of Churches.[2]

---

2   Bishop Brent is commonly regarded as the father of the Faith and Order Movement. In an unpublished dissertation on the history and theology of the Southern Baptist aloofness from the ecumenical movement, I argued that this honor belongs not to Bishop Brent but to a Southern Baptist pastor from Louisville. In 1889, twenty-one years before Bishop Brent's call, Thomas Treadwell Eaton, as editor of the state Baptist paper, had issued a similar call. The following year, on his initiative, the Southern Baptist Convention passed three resolutions implementing Eaton's proposal. The Convention's call to the other denominations fell on deaf ears and after a few years was dropped from the Southern Baptist agenda. The terms Eaton proposed anticipated the form the Faith and Order Movement eventually took more clearly than had Bishop Brent's proposals. If Bishop Brent continues to be known as the father of Faith and Order, then Thomas Treadwell Eaton should be honored as its grandfather. (*My Darling From the Lions": A Catholic Looks at the Southern Baptists*, unpublished Ph.D. dissertation, Marquette University, 1969, pp 69ff.)

A widely respected leader in the ecumenical movement was William Temple, Archbishop of Canterbury from 1942 to 1944. He was a well-known philosopher whose untimely end was widely mourned in the Protestant world. Several of our faculty who had known him well venerated his memory. I became acquainted with his thought through his Gifford lectures entitled "Nature, Man, and God." It was one of the texts in a philosophy of religion course I took. I thought it the most well-written philosophy book I had read.

My susceptibility to the Anglican apologetic was growing. In 1947 I had written a research paper on the Christological formulations of the first four ecumenical councils. By then I had parted with the illusion that the "primitive" church could be "restored." (I would now say "reconstructed.") In the introduction to that paper I wrote, "The 'quest of the historical Jesus' cannot be concluded with the Gospels if one is seeking wider understanding of the founder of Christianity. Jesus Christ is a figure in all subsequent history who must be taken into account." Those Christians so much nearer the time of the Incarnation had "established the norms for all succeeding Christology that claimed to be orthodox." (By now I was almost ready to accept the Anglican claim that the "subsequent history" should be limited to the first five centuries.)

The content of this paper reflected the wide reading I had done in the summer of 1946 at Harvard Divinity School. Except for one reference, all my sources were Protestant. My paper gives no indication of the central role of the papacy in those early councils. It does acknowledge the importance (though not the decisive character) of Leo's Tome for the fourth council.

In my first year at Union I came under the influence of Cyril Richardson, an Anglican priest who taught church history and liturgy. He was what I would call a moderate Anglo-Catholic. In a couple of courses with him I began to learn about the Anglican tradition. I felt strongly drawn to it. Here was a tradition that offered the continuity for which I had yearned for years. The term "apostolic succession" began to make sense to me. Through the succession of Episcopal and Anglican bishops I could be in continuity with the early Church. That succession guaranteed the "catholicity" of Anglicanism. The liturgy (a superb example of Elizabethan English) provides what some Anglicans called "a living continuity" with antiquity.

Anglicanism offered what her apologists called the best of the Church when she was at her best, the first five centuries when she hammered out her Christology. Therefore, all issues of doctrine and liturgy and discipline and ecclesial structure would be determined by reference to "this golden period as to a tribunal without appeal."[3] The threefold formula of authority for Anglican

3   B.H.G. Wormald, quoted by H.R. McAdoo, *The Spirit of Anglicanism: A Survey of Anglican Theological Method in the Seventeenth Century* (New York: Charles Scribner's Sons, 1965), 317.

theology is Scripture, tradition, and reason. Jeremy Taylor, a founding father of Anglican theological method, taught that "Scripture, tradition, councils, and Fathers are the evidence in a question, but reason is the judge."[4] This reliance on reason I had never found in the denomination of my youth. It was refreshing and appealing.

I learned from the Anglican sources I read that Anglicanism is a "bridge" church, combining the best features of Protestantism and Catholicism while rejecting the excesses of both. It offered the *via media*, the "middle way"— not as a compromise but as a comprehensive, reconciling way between Catholicism and the Reformation. Comprehensiveness is one of the chief claims of Anglicanism. It prides itself on encompassing widely varying, oftentimes contradictory, beliefs.

This and much more I eagerly absorbed from classes and from reading. I communicated much of it to my wife, who was equally drawn to it. We agreed we should become Episcopalians. So while working as a seminarian in the Disciples of Christ church, I began taking instruction under Sam Shoemaker in his parish, Calvary Church, in downtown Manhattan. I told the pastor of the Disciples church what my intentions were. He did little to dissuade me, apparently realizing my decision was firm. The service in which I was confirmed was only the third time I had worshipped in an Episcopal church. My wife was not free to take instruction when I did because of her work as a nursery school teacher. She was received into the Episcopal Church the following year.

Not long after entering the Episcopal Church, I realized there had been a change in my attitude toward my professional future. From the beginning of my call to the ministry I had been ambitious. As I often wrote in my journal, I was determined to become "very successful" in the ministry. That meant becoming the minister (they would say "occupying the pulpit") of a prominent Disciples of Christ church in some fairly large city. (I had several prospects in mind.)

Now I discovered to my surprise that this ambition had vanished. When I thought about the future, I knew I could be happy serving a small Episcopal parish in some out-of-the-way place. The reason for the change was my belief that now I was part of a tradition with deep roots in the past. I no longer felt the need to justify my calling as a minister by achieving prominence in my denomination. (This sense of rootedness, at least in the first five centuries, was a slight foretaste of what I would experience upon being received into the Catholic Church. Only as a Catholic can one be rooted in the whole Christian past.)

---

4   Quoted by McAdoo, *op. cit.,* 74.

I graduated from Union with a master of divinity degree in 1948. That summer we worked at a mental hospital in Manteno, Illinois, Ruth in the occupational therapy division of the hospital, I as a chaplain intern in a clinical training program. The program was designed to train seminarians in pastoral counseling. We worked with the patients, shared in hospital staff conferences and spent long hours in theological seminars with the director of the program.

The following summer I worked in the clinical training program at Saint Elizabeth's Hospital in Washington, DC. In both sessions of the program the theological atmosphere was essentially the Unitarianism I had shed after coming to Union, and quite antinomian in its moral outlook. I rejected both.

The following academic year I was a doctoral candidate in Columbia's religion and psychology course of study. Continuing my interest in counseling, I took a number of night courses in a psychiatric institute in midtown Manhattan.

By the spring of 1949 we had decided that I should drop the doctoral program at Columbia and enroll in an Episcopal seminary to better become acquainted with the Episcopal ethos. Though there was an Episcopal seminary in New York, we chose Virginia Theological Seminary in Alexandria, Virginia, largely at the urging of Sam Shoemaker. That meant I had to pass up an invitation to do research for Dr. McNeill in his work as a contributor to the standard history of the ecumenical movement edited by Ruth Rouse and Stephen Neill.

Before we left New York, Ruth received her master's degree in early childhood development from Columbia Teachers College. A friend and I went to her graduation, which was held in the open between Columbia's two main libraries. The only seats available were almost two city blocks from the stage. At my friend's suggestion, we went across Broadway to a bar and watched the proceedings on television. Afterward, Ruth chided me good-naturedly for having gone off to drink while she was graduating.

Upon our move to Alexandria, we found that many of the students at Virginia Theological Seminary were married. We were housed with other families in Parkfairfax, an attractive condominium complex near the seminary. Those young families were reproducing at such a rate that the seminarians referred to the complex as "Rabbit Hill." To help support us, Ruth secured a position in the office of Parkfairfax. I enrolled as a special student, taking the courses that seemed most beneficial.

That summer I again worked as a chaplain intern in clinical training, this time at Saint Elizabeth's Hospital in the District. We followed a series of articles in the local paper about strange phenomena connected with a teen-age boy in a Maryland suburb of DC. Having done some reading in the literature on demon possession, I recognized the reported events as classic evidence of demon possession. According to the newspaper, the parents tried in vain everything they could think of to help the boy.

The family's minister, a Lutheran, testified that he had spent a night with the boy in his room and had witnessed things flying through the air and the boy's bed being suddenly propelled across the room. At the lunch table in Saint Elizabeth's Hospital, I listened to some of the younger psychiatrists excitedly discussing the case. One of them knew a psychiatrist who had examined the boy and had arrived at a diagnosis; I forget the term used. (No matter—the psychiatrist had no cure.) Nothing seemed to help. Then the news reports suddenly stopped.

Somewhat later a Catholic priest who had been called in by the family was reported to have said, "They should have called us in the first place." When I read that I was indignant. "Same old Catholic arrogance," I muttered. Years later I read that the boy had been taken to a Jesuit retreat center in St. Louis. Through a long process of exorcism he was cleansed of possession. The best-selling book and blockbuster movie *The Exorcist* were based on this case.

Virginia Theological Seminary was then the largest and best-known "low-church" seminary of the Episcopal Church. My background, acquired under Cyril Richardson's tutelage, was definitely "high church," though I did not yet classify myself as an Anglo-Catholic. I had begun to incorporate the "branch theory" into my thinking about the church.

This theory seems to have been propounded originally by an Anglican clergyman, William Palmer, in his *Treatise on the Church of Christ* in 1838.[5] It was enthusiastically taken up and expanded and expounded by the Tractarians of the nineteenth century, of whom Blessed John Henry Newman was the most famous spokesman.

According to the branch theory, the one true Church of Christ is now divided into three separated branches: Roman Catholic, Eastern Orthodox, and Anglican. Each is fully "catholic," fully independent of the others. Each has full authority not only in matters of inner discipline but also in matters of liturgy and even of doctrine. Its adherents recognized that none of the Church fathers had ever envisioned the Church thus divided. This state of affairs had

---

5 Palmer subsequently decided to enter the Eastern Orthodox Church. In Saint Petersburg and in Moscow he was told he had valid Baptism; he could be received and given Confirmation if in the presence of a priest he would renounce the errors of Protestantism. In Constantinople he was told he would have to be baptized. He regarded a second Baptism as sacrilegious. But he knew that if went back to Russia to be received, he would still be a heathen according to Greek Orthodox Church. He wanted to join what he thought of as the universal Orthodox Church, not simply a national church. He had discovered there is no such entity as the universal Orthodox Church, but only a series of independent and in some cases conflicting national churches. Finally he became a member of the universal Church by entering the Roman Catholic Church.

been brought about by circumstances that developed after the patristic period. Consciously or not, the theory was designed to rationalize the existence of the national church established in England by the Reformation.

After his conversion to Catholicism, Newman pointed out the basic absurdity (not to say the unhistorical basis) of the branch theory. How, he asked, can one speak or even think of one kingdom that is divided into three separate, totally independent parts? The question never occurred to me until years later in my pilgrimage. As an Episcopal seminarian I clung to the theory. It received little attention from the faculty and students at Virginia Theological Seminary, but I nurtured it in private.

The course of training at the seminary focused on the parish ministry. I found a pastoral emphasis throughout the curriculum. I had never encountered this orientation before. As one Anglican author expressed it, Roman Catholics and Orthodox emphasize their ministers' role as priests; Lutherans and Calvinists emphasize their ministers' role as preachers; Anglicans emphasize their ministers' role as pastors. We were constantly reminded of our obligation to visit our parishioners in their homes, to share in their joys as well as their sorrows, to let them make us members of their families. (Following this advice would do much to alleviate the loneliness that afflicts many Catholic priests.)

Before leaving New York, I had secured permission from my Episcopal bishop to transfer to the Episcopal diocese of Washington, DC. The bishop there was Angus Dun, a former seminary professor, for whom I developed deep respect and affection. During my year at the Virginia seminary I worked in Saint Margaret's Church in the District. Bishop Dun ordained me in the National Cathedral to the diaconate in mid-1950 and to the priesthood at the end of the year. After ordination, for two years I served as associate rector of Saint Margaret's. The rector was Malcolm Marshall, himself a graduate of Union Theological Seminary. He was a splendid mentor and friend.

My work in mental hospitals had led me to believe I should be a mental hospital chaplain. At that time the main Protestant organization for training seminarians and certifying clergy in pastoral counsel mandated that any chaplain must himself undergo psychotherapy. The reasoning was that through therapy he could better understand himself and help others. To carry out this requirement, I secured a list of several psychiatrists from the Protestant chaplain of Saint Elizabeth's. I interviewed several of them. I told them why I wanted to go into psychotherapy. I also told them that I was a Christian, a clergyman, and that I had neither time nor energy to work with someone who had problems with regard to Christianity. I said the person I worked with would have to understand and accept my theological vocabulary.

The third man I interviewed seemed amenable to my requirements. He greatly reduced his fees so that we could afford them on my modest salary. I worked with that psychiatrist for eight or nine months, three times a week. (After beginning therapy with him, I learned from another person that the psychiatrist was the brother of a then-famous American novelist.)

Through those months of psychotherapy I learned much about my reactions to life and some of the possible sources of those ways of reacting. When I stopped going to the psychiatrist, I told Ruth psychotherapy had done at least one thing for me: It had made me much more keenly aware of my need of a personal Savior.

In the second year of my tenure at Saint Margaret's Church, I spent six weeks as a fellow of the College of Preachers at the National Cathedral in Washington. The College of Preachers was a center for continuing education of clergy. They came in groups of several dozen for a week's training. Several times a year, two or three Episcopal clergy from around the country were invited to become fellows, taking up residence at the College. They were allowed to devise their own program of study for a six-week term. Though the program had been in operation for a number of years, I was the first from the Episcopal diocese of Washington and the youngest priest (in terms of years of ministry) ever invited to be a fellow. Ruth's mother came from Texas to stay with her during that time. Occasionally Ruth, her mother, and our first child, Risa (then nine months old), would visit me at the College.

I spent my entire time studying Saint Augustine's work, especially his *De Trinitate*, taking voluminous notes and pondering the saint's thought. During that period of six weeks, a thought popped repeatedly into my mind. "If Saint Augustine were to come to DC today, where would he go to church?" Instantly came the clear answer: "He would go to a Roman Catholic church, of course."[6] Though the question made me uneasy, I banished it from mind. I can see now that the recurrence of this question and answer was another wakeup call from the Holy Spirit. Had I been more responsive to His call, I would have become a Catholic much sooner.

In the summer of 1952, I became rector of Trinity Episcopal Church in the District of Columbia. It was (by Episcopal standards) a medium-sized parish, with about six hundred families. The church itself is rather small but exquisite English Gothic, all stone and massive wood on the inside, with

---

6   In a letter in 1849 to someone who later converted, Newman stated what was to him "the overbearingly convincing proof" that the Church of Rome is the true Church. "Were Saint Athanasius and Saint Ambrose in London now, they would go to worship, not to Saint Paul's [Anglican] Cathedral, but to Warwick Street or Moor Fields. This my own reading of history has made to me an axiom, and it converted me, though I cannot of course communicate the force of it to another." Quoted by Stanley L. Jaki, *Newman to Converts: An Existential Ecclesiology* (Pickney, MI: Real View Books, 2001), 167.

brilliant Tiffany windows. More than fifty years after leaving that parish I remember fondly a window in the sanctuary featuring Saint Augustine and Saint Ambrose in song. According to legend, once in unison prayer spontaneously they began singing (and thereby composing) the Te Deum Laudamus. Because the Te Deum is my favorite of all hymns, that window was and still is dear to me.

That summer when we drove to Quebec with our 15-month-old daughter, we were surprised to see so many roadside shrines in the province. Some were elaborate, some primitive. But all bespoke the Roman Catholic presence to us. We visited the shrine of Saint Anne de Beaupres, a great center of healing. We wondered at the mountain of crutches and prosthetic devices at the rear of the church left behind by persons who had been healed. Yet we took no time to worship in the shrine. One of the prayer cards we picked up gave us a negative impression of the shrine. The prayer addressed to Saint Anne said, in effect, "I've come a long way to get healed, a lot of people know I'm here, and if I don't get healed it is not going to look good for you."

One small incident at a motel in Quebec made a lasting impression us. We were sitting at the edge of the pool. There was no one in the pool. A boy, thirteen or fourteen years old, came to the pool and walked out on the diving board. I don't think he had noticed us. Testing the resiliency of the board, he paused briefly, made the Sign of the Cross, and dived. That gesture, made by a boy unaware we were watching, caught our attention. We assumed the boy was Catholic. What was it about being Catholic that led this lad to invoke the Blessed Trinity before he dived into the pool?

As my wife and I studied Anglo-Catholic sources, more and more we thought of ourselves as Anglo-Catholics. When I first learned that Catholics refer to the Blessed Virgin as the "Mother of God," I thought it was the zenith of idolatry. When I studied the Council of Ephesus (AD 431) at Union Seminary, my sources chose not to mention that the immediate occasion for the third council was the refusal of the bishop of Constantinople to use the term *theotokos*, Mother of God. Nor did they explain that the purpose of the term is to safeguard the reality of the Incarnation.

(Here was an early glimmer of recognition that the Anglican appeal to the first four councils is not selective only in limiting the appeal to those councils. It is also selective in what it chooses to accept of those councils' decrees. Later I found the same problem in Eastern Orthodox thought. More on this later.)

Fairly early in my Episcopal days I learned that Catholics (and, imitating them, some Anglo-Catholics) genuflected when in reciting the Nicene Creed they said the words "was born of the Virgin Mary and became man." Being convinced like most Protestants that Catholics worship the Blessed Virgin, I assumed they genuflected at the mention of her name. This was distasteful to me; another indication of Catholic idolatry, I thought. Only later, and I think from Anglo-Catholic sources, did I learn the genuflection was made to honor the Incarnation, not the Virgin.

While we were serving at Trinity Church we saw a movie titled *Detective Story*. It starred Burt Lancaster as a hard-bitten gumshoe. At the end of the movie, as one of the characters lay dying on the floor, he made an act of contrition. I had scarcely heard of an act of contrition, but Ruth and I were impressed by the spectacle of a dying man taking the time to express sorrow for his sins. I thought that if I were in that condition I would have been too busy trying to stay alive to think about contrition. After the movie, we discussed that scene with Protestant friends who had accompanied us. They were not impressed as we were.

One question repeatedly came up in our inquirers' classes at Trinity. When we discussed the Episcopal Church's doctrines (such as it had), invariably someone would ask, "And what does Rome say about this?" I chided the inquirers who raised this question: "What do we care about what Rome teaches?" In some instances I did not know enough about Catholic teaching to give an accurate answer. But the fact that they wondered what Rome taught was significant. (Protestants look to Rome for direction in doctrinal matters far more than is commonly realized. But more on this later as well.)

But let's face it. Some of those questioners wanted to be assured that what they were learning was not what Catholics believe.

During the four years we served at Trinity, our second daughter, Erica, and our first son, Christopher, were born. Our parish summer vacation Bible school was in session when Christopher was born. Immediately after his birth I called from the hospital and asked the director of the Bible school to share the good news with the children and ask for their prayers of thanksgiving.

A few days later one of the parents told us her nine-year-old daughter had come home from Bible school bursting with the good news that the Rylands had a baby boy. "His name is Crucifer," she said.

"Nancy, are you sure that's the baby's name?" the mother asked.

Nancy hesitated. "No, his name is . . . Lucifer."

"You ask again tomorrow," her mother said.

The next day Nancy brought home the correct name for our new son.

CHAPTER TEN

MORE WAKEUP CALLS

In Lent of 1955, one of my funeral services involved an interment some distance away in Maryland. I rode in the hearse with the local funeral director, who was Catholic. As we drove, our conversation turned to the subject of fasting. I did little fasting in those days, save for Good Friday, when I abstained from food and water until sundown. (This was rather challenging, since at the three-hour Good Friday service I preached nine fifteen-minute sermons.) The funeral director spoke rather casually of the fasting regimen he and his wife observed in obedience to the Church's rules. I was astonished at the rigor of this mortification. It was a different world of Lenten observance he described. Again came the thought that Catholicism is serious business.

My feeling about the Catholic Church in those years was epitomized by a phrase used by George Mackay Brown, a twentieth-century Scottish poet and convert to Catholicism: "supernatural dread."[1] I never failed to notice a Catholic church if I came near one, but I wanted to keep it at a safe distance.

Had I been more attuned to the prompting of the Spirit, my supernatural dread of the Church could have been a warning to me that her claims might be true. From boyhood Blessed John Henry Newman was taught that Rome is the Antichrist. After he banished it from his mind, the notion lingered in his imagination. One of his biographers tells us, "When he finally got free of it, he did not dismiss it as nonsense; it seemed to him a real, but dark, shadow of the truth. The Catholic Church was a mystery and had a power over the human imagination no other thing on earth had; if it did not look like Christ,

---

1   Quoted by Joseph Pearce, *Literary Converts* (San Francisco: Ignatius Press, 1999), 428.

it must look like Satan."[2] Unlike any other institution, the Catholic Church is supernatural. I sensed that, but in my ignorance I dreaded it.

And yet even then I yearned unconsciously for closer relationship with the Church. When the dogma of the bodily assumption of the Blessed Virgin was promulgated in 1950, I felt true sorrow. "Another barrier," I thought, even though I had little hope of unity between Rome and the Church of England or with any other non-Catholic group.

While a student at Union Seminary, I began reading assigned portions of Gregory Dix's book, *Shape of the Liturgy*.[3] Dix was an Anglican Benedictine monk of Nashdom Abbey, an Anglo-Catholic liturgist of encyclopedic knowledge. In my years at Trinity Church I read his book avidly. Of all the Anglo-Catholic literature I read, Dix's book influenced my thinking the most.

From Dix's book I learned the Catholic doctrine of Eucharistic Sacrifice. With keen interest I studied his information about anamnesis, which we translate as "memorial" or "in remembrance of." He explained that the Greek word and its Hebrew background denote a calling into the present of an event from the past, complete with all its original power.

Thenceforth I had to believe that Jesus Christ is truly present in the Eucharist. Reading Dix's book drilled into my mind the necessity of apostolic succession for a valid Eucharist—and beyond that, for the fullness of the faith. (Consequently, when late in my pilgrimage I began to have doubts about the validity of the Anglican succession, those doubts put my whole Anglican position in jeopardy.)

Studying Dix's book convinced me of a necessary presupposition of the "branch theory," namely that all "branches" of the one Catholic Church are in schism. "The eucharist of a group or society which repudiates or is repudiated by the catholic whole is thereby defective, however holy its members and however 'valid' the orders of its ministers." Our Lord's words (Matthew 5:24), says Dix, "'Leave there thy gift before the altar, and go thy way; first be reconciled to thy brother and then come and offer thy gift'—holds true of churches as well as individuals."[4] I took comfort from the thought that the Roman Catholic Church itself is also in schism.

In the early 1950s I became interested in Christian healing, primarily through reading the works of Agnes Sanford. The wife of an Episcopal priest, she was exceptionally gifted with the power of God's healing and wrote and lectured persuasively about that power. Perhaps more than any other person she was responsible for the mid-century revival of interest in healing in Protestant

2   Meriol Trevor, *Newman: The Pillar of the Cloud* (Garden City, NY: Doubleday and Co., Inc. 1962), vol. 2, 335.
3   Westminster, UK: Dacre Press, 1945.
4   *Ibid*, 272.

churches, and also among some Catholics. I attended a week's conference on healing that she and her husband conducted in Whitinsville, Massachusetts, for Episcopal clergy. With renewed interest I studied the Gospel accounts of Jesus' healing ministry.

Not long after that conference, early one Saturday morning I received a call from a stranger asking me to come to a local hospital. Her niece was near death from an explosion. The lady called me because she knew her niece had visited our church a few weeks earlier. While driving to the hospital I prayed earnestly for guidance in ministering to this young woman and her aunt. At the hospital I learned that the young woman, a nurse, had attempted to commit suicide by turning on the gas jets of the stove in her kitchen. When the room filled with gas, the inevitable spark caused an explosion that blew a large hole in the wall of the massive stone building in which she lived. (Later that morning I saw a picture of the damage and a story about the suicide attempt in the *Washington Post.*)

Her aunt, her closest relative, had been summoned from Philadelphia during the night. The aunt explained that her niece's bodily functions had stopped. She was badly burned, especially about the face. Two neurosurgeons had examined her and reported massive brain damage such that if she lived, she would have at best what they called a "vegetable" existence. The aunt urged me to pray that her niece would soon die a merciful death.

To my own surprise, I heard myself confidently assuring the aunt I believed God wanted her niece to be healed. She obviously did not agree but did not argue the point. I spent half an hour at the bedside, praying for an outpouring of God's healing power, both physical and spiritual.

The next day, after my morning services, I went back to the hospital. Her aunt said her niece was still hanging on, but the prognosis was unchanged. On Monday morning when I visited her she was conscious and the bandages that had covered her face were removed. There were only slight traces of burns. We began talking about the healing of her despair that had led to her attempted suicide. I saw her again on Tuesday, when she was much improved. On Wednesday she was transferred to a psychiatric hospital for observation.

I visited her there a number of times. Two weeks later she was discharged. Her physical healing was complete, but her spiritual healing took more time. Years later, after leaving Washington I heard from her. She was happily married, with two children, and at peace with our Lord.

Like many people, I find it harder to pray for my own healing than to pray for the healing of others. For years I had been a smoker. (In an earlier chapter I spoke of my failures to keep promises to stop smoking.) Several times while serving as rector of Trinity Church I had stopped smoking. Each time I gained ten pounds in a week from snacking to compensate for the craving for nicotine. Each time I resumed smoking I lost those pounds. But each time I stopped I relied only on my personal resolve. It never sufficed.

Late one night in my study I felt "smoked out." It had been a long day and I had smoked rather heavily. I sat back in my chair at my desk and said to myself, "I have got to stop smoking!" In those days I knew of no clear evidence of a link between smoking and cancer. Yet I knew it was physically harmful. I knew also that smoking was a spiritual crutch for me. In times of stress, instead of calling on the name of the Lord, I reached into my shirt pocket for a cigarette.

That night, without thinking, I suddenly went down on my knees and began praying: "God, I've got to stop smoking. I promise you I will never smoke again. But you've got to help me keep that promise." Instantly I was shocked by what I had just said. "What have I done? A promise to God?" I had made that promise many times when I was in the navy and never kept it. But now I took that promise far more seriously. I could say only, "God help me!" and go to bed.

The next morning when I awoke, as usual I thought of a cigarette. But what a change! The thought of smoking was repulsive to me. From that moment on I never had a desire to smoke again, was never tempted to smoke. Overnight I had been healed of addiction to nicotine. No nibbling between meals, either; I did not gain a pound.

Like most ministers and priests, frequently at odd times I received calls for help.

Once in the middle of the night I was called to the bedside of a parishioner who was dying in a local hospital. When I arrived, I met her daughter, a Catholic nun, who was there. Though I knew the mother, she had not told me she had a daughter who was a religious. The daughter was polite but distant. I realize now how she must have wanted to have a Catholic priest with her mother at the end. She said she believed God was calling her mother home, so she was praying for a peaceful passage and death. I told her I wanted to pray for her mother to be healed. There was no argument over this, but it was obvious to both of us that we were praying opposing prayers. For half an hour we stood on opposite sides of her mother's bed, praying silently. I was not called—or lacked the courage—to pray aloud in the nun's presence. As I prayed, I wondered if an Episcopal prayer could prevail over a Catholic prayer. My answer came, I thought, a few hours after I left the hospital. The woman died.

It has been noted that often ex-Catholics seem to find something lacking in the Protestant churches they join. I sensed this in a number of the several dozen former Roman Catholics whom I received into the Episcopal Church. They did not seem completely comfortable in the Episcopal Church. I thought they must still have some roots in the Catholic Church. I reacted to this with irritation and of course some defensiveness. My thought was, "They ought to be glad they're not Catholics anymore." Yet it did trouble me that none had left the Catholic Church because they found the whole truth of Christ in the Episcopal Church. Their reasons for becoming Episcopalian were subjective, mostly centering on divorce and re-marriage.

In the spring of 1956, a group of laymen from Beaumont, Texas, visited me at Trinity Church. They were a search committee seeking a new vicar for their mission church, Saint Stephen's, that had been founded three years earlier. I never knew how they learned about me. They were attractive and eloquent in presenting the challenge of joining them in their very young congregation. I thanked them for coming but felt no inclination to accept their invitation to visit their church. My family was comfortably settled in our beautiful rectory. I was serving a fairly large and responsive congregation. My wife and I were extremely fond of living in the District. But I promised to pray about their invitation.

Beaumont is only a hundred miles from Galveston Island in the Gulf of Mexico, where my wife was raised. During our visits with her family there we had resolved that we never would choose to live on the Gulf coast amid the mosquitoes and the humidity. For a few days after the delegation from Beaumont left I dutifully prayed to be led in responding appropriately to this new opportunity. I thought God must surely want us to stay at Trinity.

But in my prayers I could not get the answer I expected (and wanted). Instead, I sensed a growing conviction that I must accept the invitation to visit the mission in Beaumont. By that time Ruth was carrying our fourth child, Timothy. At the invitation of that parish, Ruth and I went to Beaumont and spent a couple of days meeting with the church vestry and other members of the congregation. I began to believe God was leading us to accept that call. After our return to Washington, the belief became conviction. Ruth concurred, but neither of us wanted to leave Washington.

My bishop was annoyed when I told him I had been called to a new mission in Texas. He said in a letter that I had a "very bright future" in the Episcopal Church but implied that future would be clouded—if not ob-scured—by my leaving his diocese. He was right. Yet neither he nor I could know that my future in the Episcopal Church would end in seven years.

In a long evening conference with leaders of Saint Stephen's, I had given clear outlines of the kind of ministry I would carry on if I were to accept the invitation to become vicar. ("Vicar" because the parish was not yet self-supporting. A year or two after we went there it did become a self-supporting parish and I became its "rector.") My presentation was couched in Anglo-Catholic terms. Everyone present declared his or her approval of my proposal.

Yet when I began my ministry there some months later, I encountered widespread opposition. It seemed that either those laymen had not understood what I told them before coming to Beaumont or they had changed their minds about what they wanted. Key leaders made it clear that they were digging in their heels and would staunchly oppose a number of the programs I had proposed.

The real problem was that most of them had never dealt on a pastoral level with a card-carrying, enthusiastic Anglo-Catholic like me. They were almost all "low-church," ardently Protestant, folk. They had a full supply of anti-Catholic prejudice. Somehow they had simply not heard what I told them about myself before coming to Beaumont. In my efforts to minister to recalcitrant parishioners the Holy Spirit taught me much about praying for one's "enemies."

Purely as an act of will, I began earnestly praying for those most hostile to my ministry. God did not change their minds, but he certainly changed my attitude from resentment to compassion. Before I left the parish three years later, the Holy Spirit had given me deep respect and even affection for those who had been my most stubborn critics. In most cases my feelings were not reciprocated. But that was their problem, not mine.

C.S. Lewis was even then highly regarded by persons from a wide variety of Christian traditions, including Roman Catholics. I had begun reading his works in the early 1950s after my first rector introduced me to them. Lewis greatly enriched my understanding of what he called "mere Christianity." We nurtured all our children on his seven-volume Narnian Chronicles. (Twenty years later as a professor of theology at the University of San Diego, I taught several courses on Lewis' writings.) A number of converts have testified that reading Lewis helped bring them into the Catholic Church. I am not aware that his writings had that direct effect on us.

The question is often asked, "Why did C.S. Lewis not become a Catholic?"

Joseph Pearce gives his answer in *C.S. Lewis and the Catholic Church*.[5] It was prejudice that prevented Lewis from becoming Catholic. Lewis was raised in Belfast and was nurtured by an old Irish nurse. Years before Pearce's book appeared, Walter Hooper, Lewis' personal secretary and literary executor,

---

5   San Francisco: Ignatius Press, 2003. A similar answer, though not nearly so well documented, had been given by Christopher Derrick, in *C.S. Lewis and the Church of Rome* (San Francisco: Ignatius Press, 1981).

differed with Christopher Derrick (See footnote below). In conversation, Mr. Hooper told me that Mr. Lewis remained an Anglican because he was convinced that was where God wanted him to be. I assume that what Hooper says is correct.

But I think Pearce and Derrick are also correct. Mr. Lewis' belief about where God wanted him to be must have been greatly bolstered by his ignorance of, and prejudice against, the Church. Mr. Hooper, who reverences Lewis' memory, once told us that despite Lewis' vast range of knowledge, he had only slight knowledge of Roman Catholicism.

Thomas Merton's account of his conversion, *Seven Storey Mountain*, was for months a bestseller while we were at Union Seminary. Ruth read it at the time, but I did not read it until when we were living in Texas. As I read it I experienced a yearning to be a Roman Catholic, but the yearning was vague and short-lived. I urged two parishioners, dear friends of ours, to read it, and they were greatly inspired by it. (Years later they, too, came into the Church.)

When I was rector of Trinity Church in Washington, my wife and I had read Dorothy L. Sayers's *Introductory Papers on Dante*.[6] We agreed the book was well written and informative. I think both of us found our Anglo-Catholicism strengthened by reading this book by a well-known Anglo-Catholic. During our years in Beaumont I dipped back into the book. I reacted with irritation to Miss Sayers's use of the term *Church*. Repeatedly she refers to what the "Church" teaches. I said to myself, "What 'Church' is she talking about?" Her comments reflected what the Roman Catholic Church teaches. "But," I thought, "she's not a Roman Catholic. There's no 'Church' that teaches what she sets forth except the Roman Catholic Church. The Church she belongs to, the Church of England, certainly does not teach what she says the 'Church' teaches." Then briefly came the thought, "There's no such thing as 'Anglo-Catholic Church.'" I hurriedly banished it from my mind.

These thoughts were yet another wakeup call from the Holy Spirit, another "ringing of the bell," to use Maurice Baring's phrase; another call from Home. But not until five years later did I answer the call.

On still another occasion, the bell rang clearly but I quickly closed my ears again.

In the early fall of 1958, I returned to Trinity Church in Washington to solemnize the wedding vows of a dear young friend and former parishioner there. In packing for the trip I tossed in my briefcase a book I had recently received from a bookseller in England. The title was *Anglican Orders*. The author was unknown to me, but as an Anglo-Catholic I read everything I could find that argued for the validity of Anglican orders. After the wedding

---

6   New York: Harper and Brothers, 1954.

in Washington I went to New York City to visit my former associate at Trinity. Returning by train to Washington late one night, I settled back to read and enjoy what I assumed was another defense of Anglican orders.

To my horror, I discovered that the author was Jesuit and he was lucidly defending the Catholic Church's rejection of the Anglican succession. My alarm increased steadily as I read. Suddenly, after reading about thirty pages of the book, I slammed the book shut on the seat and exclaimed aloud, "Dammit! He's right!" (Begging the reader's pardon for the profanity.) I saw my whole Anglo-Catholic system, my whole faith in that system, crumble before my eyes. I was devastated. I dared not think further. I closed my eyes and sought oblivion in sleep. I never looked at the book again; in fact, I threw it away. Nor did I tell my wife about my having read into the book until after we became Catholics.

As I reflect on my repeated rejections of calls from the Holy Spirit, I remind myself of a baseball pitcher. Before he throws the ball, the pitcher will stare at the catcher for a signal indicating the kind of pitch to be thrown. He shakes his head at each signal until he sees one he agrees with, and then he nods, winds, and delivers. The Holy Spirit was giving me signals calling me home to Rome, and I kept shaking Him off.

Somewhat later I had a bout with what Episcopalians call "Roman fever." I became very discouraged by harsh criticism of my Anglo-Catholicism. At one point I became so exasperated with opposition to my beliefs I told Ruth I was going to leave the Episcopal Church and join the Catholic Church. As a layman there I would be free from all this criticism. The Catholic grass on the other side of the fence seemed incomparably greener than the dry, low-church grass on my side. In her typically sensible manner, Ruth said my reason for wanting to make the change was immature. She said if I became a Catholic for that reason she would not join me, nor would the children. I knew she was right. My Roman fever dropped to Episcopal normal within the hour.

And yet I yearned for some contact with the Catholic Church, even if only through brief conversation with a priest. On impulse I called the office of a local Catholic church and asked for an appointment with the priest. The church building complex dwarfed our little parish. I introduced myself and said I wanted to ask him about some point of Catholic doctrine. I cannot remember what point I had seized upon as excuse for coming to him. He was polite and answered my question.

On reflection, the incident reminds me of the two disciples of John the Baptist. They began walking after Jesus when John declared Him to be the Lamb of God. Jesus asked what they wanted, and they asked where He

Grandparents Ben and Matty's family farm, Crescent, Oklahoma, 1905

Mother and infant Ray   Freshman year in college

Wedding photograph

Risa's baptism

Family of 3 in Parkfairfax

Family of 7 in Oklahoma City

NASSAU airplanes

NASSAU

In front of
Royal Hawaiian Hotel

Reinhold Niebuhr

Thomas Merton

Episcopal ordination, 1950

Ray and choir at Trinity

The cycling parson

Ordination to the permanent diaconate

Ordination to the priesthood, 1983

Entire family except for Amalia

was staying. I think the disciples were simply curious about Jesus. When He asked them what they wanted, I think they blurted out, "Rabbi, where are you staying?" (John 1:37). In my brief conversation with the priest I sensed he was somewhat reserved. Perhaps that was because he could tell I was not being honest with him about my reason for coming to his office. But since I couldn't say—indeed, I did not know—exactly why I had come, it was just as well that I left after a brief time.

Because I made my pastoral rounds on a bicycle, I became known in the community and was featured in the local paper as the "cycling parson." One day the "cycling parson" stopped cycling abruptly—too abruptly. Already late for dinner, I was hurrying home at rush hour, pedaling almost as fast as I could along a street that was then a national highway through Beaumont. A stream of cars overtook me on my left. On my right was the curb, a foot high because of the heavy rains that often drench that area. I bent over my handlebars with effort and focused on the pavement directly in front of me.

Just then an oncoming car made a left turn to enter a motel parking lot on my right. As the driver started to cross the lane in which I was riding, he saw that I was headed straight for him. Instead of pulling into the parking lot, he froze, sitting with his car in my lane and staring at me. I looked up. There was the car, directly in my path, ten or fifteen yards ahead. I could veer neither right nor left. I gripped the handbrakes tightly and closed my eyes as I hit the side of the stopped car. The impact badly bent and shortened my bicycle frame and threw me on top of the car, splitting open my chin. I was dazed. The driver was very apologetic, as indeed he should have been.

"What can I do?" he asked.

"You can take me home," I said. My bicycle fit easily into the back seat of his car, and he drove me home.

My wife was serving dinner to the children when I walked into the kitchen, holding my handkerchief over my chin. All eyes widened. "What happened?" she demanded.

"Honey, I had a little accident." I took away the handkerchief.

"You sure did!" she said. The split was clear to the bone. She called a doctor, one of our parishioners, to meet me at the emergency room of the nearest hospital. I drove my car there and let him sew up the gash.

Days later, another parishioner, a close friend, had the bicycle repaired for me. He took delight in telling members of the parish what he found in the saddlebag of the bike after the accident. He embellished the story, with a twinkle, saying I was carrying the previous Sunday's collection. That was not true. He also reported—and this was true—he found a book in the saddlebag titled *Sight Without Glasses*.

Despite the unsympathetic attitude of some leaders in the parish, the Holy Spirit blessed our labors in that part of his vineyard. The mission became a parish. Our numbers grew steadily. The level of giving on the part of the parishioners rose markedly. Proclaiming an Anglo-Catholic faith at every opportunity, I thought of myself as raising the sights of my people. (Notice I say "an Anglo-Catholic faith," not "*the* Anglo-Catholic faith." The latter does not exist. Each Anglo-Catholic decides what constitutes his "Catholicism."). In our years in Beaumont, God blessed us with the birth of our fourth child— our second son, Timothy.

And then God called us to another part of his vineyard.

CHAPTER ELEVEN

WANING ANGLO-CATHOLICISM

That new vineyard was Casady Episcopal School, a K–12 school in Oklahoma City. I was called there as chaplain of the lower and middle schools. We moved to Oklahoma City in the summer of 1959. As a native of the state, I was pleased to live there again and to have our children near my parents in the same city. The school had no living quarters for a chaplain, so we had to buy a home.

Casady School was and is an academically excellent school. It has splendid facilities, small classes, stiff entrance requirements, and a demanding curriculum. It was also expensive. Our four children attended Casady by virtue of the tuition remission I received as a faculty member. As chaplain I conducted chapel services each morning and taught classes in Bible for the lower and middle schools. The atmosphere in the school and in the diocese was much more friendly to my Anglo-Catholic outlook. I became known among students and faculty as "Father" Ryland.

As I gave instruction in Bible and basic doctrine to the lower school classes, my third-grade daughter, Erica, created a slight problem. In class she began calling me "Father Daddy." At first I liked it as an affectionate term. But soon her classmates began calling me "Father Daddy." I had to ask Erica to drop the "Daddy" part.

I also joined the staff of the Episcopal Cathedral, Saint Paul's, as a part-time assistant. In addition to conducting Sunday services, I taught an adult course during the week. The course provided a group of several dozen people with their first systematic introduction to Anglo-Catholicism. The dean of the cathedral and his associate were not Anglo-Catholics, but they tolerated what I was teaching. When the dean resigned abruptly and the associate went to another parish, I became acting dean of the cathedral for several months.

One of the patrons of Casady School and an occasional worshipper at Saint Paul's Cathedral became a benefactor in several respects. As a young man just out of college, Frank had inherited a fortune when his father died in a private plane crash. At the time Frank had been taking instruction to become a Catholic. In his bereavement he asked to be received into the Church. Since Frank came from a prominent family, the pastor, Monsignor John O'Connor (who will be introduced later), thought that if he received Frank, the Church would be criticized for taking advantage of his bereavement. On his bishop's advice, Monsignor O'Connor asked Frank to wait a few months. For Frank, the time of decision had passed. He never became a Catholic.

He attended a series of lectures on Anglo-Catholic themes I gave at the Episcopal cathedral. He embraced the opinions I offered (at that time I did not realize they were only my opinions!), and we became good friends. We had a common interest in Casady School; he was a board member and generous benefactor of the school. It was controlled by "low-church" administrators with many of whose policies he and I strongly disagreed. We had many long conversations in his office downtown and on several auto trips we took together.

I learned much about the Catholic ethos from Frank. He would not listen to criticism of the Catholic Church, which he always referred to as "Holy Mother Church." He thought hymn singing was inherently Protestant. He never sang. Instead, when the cathedral congregation sang a hymn, he fingered the rosary in his coat pocket. His obvious love for the Catholic Church gradually eroded much of my remaining prejudices. In particular, through his frequent references to her, I began a devotion to the Blessed Virgin. Under his influence I started praying the Rosary regularly (but never openly) my last two years in the Episcopal Church. He also gave me a monastic diurnal that I tried to use but found too confusing.

Frank supplemented our meager income as chaplain at Casady School. He also underwrote my summers of study at the University of the South in Sewanee, Tennessee—and all so graciously one would have thought we were doing him a great favor by allowing him to help us. He organized a local chapter of the Confraternity of the Blessed Sacrament, an Anglo-Catholic devotional group. (For a substantial sum he made me a life member without telling me beforehand.) We organized a group of a dozen or so Episcopalians who were attracted to Anglo-Catholicism. For months we met each week in his palatial home, where I lectured on the Anglo-Catholic version of Christianity.

For Anglo-Catholics, Cardinal Newman (as we knew him then) is always a puzzle. "How could he have deserted us?" we wondered. In one of my lectures for the Confraternity, I told the story of Newman attending evensong (evening prayer) at Saint Paul's (Anglican) Cathedral in London after he became a Catholic. He was reported to have left the cathedral with tears in his eyes. I explained this as a sign of his sorrow for having left the Anglican Church. Of course, in making this statement I ignored all he had written after his conversion about the Anglican Church.

(Twenty-five years later my wife and I attended a conference of former Episcopal clergy who had been received into the Church and ordained with dispensation from celibacy. Archbishop—later Cardinal—Bernard Law convened the conference. There he celebrated for the first time the Anglican-use liturgy that had been authorized for congregations of Episcopalians that enter the Catholic Church corporately. The liturgy incorporates the Catholic Church's four Eucharistic prayers into the Prayer Book service. As the liturgy ended and worshipers were praying, my wife burst into tears. Later she explained she was crying not in sorrow for having left the Episcopal Church but from sadness that such liturgical beauty, and all that is good and ennobling in the Anglican tradition, cannot be brought back into the Church where it belongs. It was then we both thought we understood Newman's tears.)

Our eventual decision to become Roman Catholic was a great disappointment to Frank, though he graciously respected our decision. After becoming Catholic, I met with him two or three times and urged him to come into the Church. I reminded him that his beliefs were almost entirely Catholic. Each time he said somewhat sadly, "Keep praying for me, Father." I did. He was still in the Episcopal Church when he died a few years ago. *Requiescat in pace.*

During my tenure at the Episcopal cathedral in Oklahoma City, our fifth child and third son, Mark, was born. At that time Queen Elizabeth was also pregnant with her youngest child. Many in our congregation, anglophile to the core like most Episcopalians, closely followed the news about the Queen's pregnancy. Some members spoke good-naturedly of a race between the queen and my wife to be first to deliver. Then came the news the Queen had borne a son.

The next Sunday morning, while making parish announcements, I thanked the congregation for their solicitude for my wife's pregnancy and conceded that the queen had won the race. Meanwhile, I said, in our house we're all singing hymn No. 576. Then I casually went on to other announcements. As I expected, many people thumbed through their hymnals and grinned at me when they found No. 576: "Come Labor On."

In our later years as Episcopalians, my wife and I encountered animosity on the part of some when we spoke in favor of celibacy for clergy. We said, "Rome doesn't have much going for her, but she does have one thing right: celibacy." We did not understand the theology of priestly celibacy, but we saw the practical advantages in it. The wives and children of some of my colleagues were bitter because they felt neglected in favor of persons whom their husbands or their fathers were trying to serve. Though my ministry brought similar pressures on my family, by God's grace we stayed closely knit.

One evening in the home of cathedral parishioners, the conversation turned to the subject of non-Catholics who marry Catholics. Talk focused on the non-Catholics being required to promise to raise the couple's children in the Church. An Episcopal clergyman present said he had told an Episcopal lady who had made these promises to ignore them. He assured her they did not bind her. My wife and I took issue, not from sympathy for Rome but from principles of moral rectitude. We said she had made solemn promises; she was obligated to keep them. The other clergyman became almost apoplectic, so to spare our hosts embarrassment we tried to change the subject.

Catholics are generally unaware of the strange impressions non-Catholics have about Catholicism. One day I took two of our sons' school blazers to the neighborhood cleaners. Noticing that one blazer had a button missing, I asked the manager to let me look for a match in his box of miscellaneous buttons. I picked up a blazer button with a motto on it and read it aloud: "*Nostra spes est deus.*" Then, again aloud, I absent-mindedly translated it: "Our hope is God."

At that the manager reached for the button. "You wouldn't want that," he said. "It's a Catholic button!"

"What do you mean by 'a Catholic button'?" I asked.

"Didn't you just say that Latin means 'Our pope is God'?" he replied.

The notion that Catholics intend to take over the country by force of arms has long had currency among Protestants. One of our Episcopal friends once told us that on his way to and from elementary school for years he had passed a local Catholic church. Often he would glance up at the third floor of the rectory and say to himself, "I guess that's where they keep the guns"—the guns, he had been told, that the Catholics would use some day against Protestants.

Oklahoma had long been an overwhelmingly Democratic state. Yet in the 1960 presidential campaign, feeling against John Kennedy ran high because he was Catholic. During the campaign a group of Southern Baptist ministers publicly challenged the pastor of a downtown Catholic church to let them search the church and rectory for firearms. Wisely, the pastor made no public response.

(A few years after we had entered the Church and I had become a member of the Knights of Columbus, in the presence of Protestant friends I always referred to the Knights meeting hall as "our armory." This brought questioning looks to people's faces. I never explained that I was joking.)

My most enthusiastic days as an Anglo-Catholic came during my first two years at Casady School. More than a century earlier, as an Anglo-Catholic, Newman had expressed the heady sense of destiny that filled my thoughts: "I had supreme confidence in our cause; we were upholding that primitive Christianity which was delivered for all time by the early teachers of the Church, and which was registered and attested in the Anglican formularies and by the Anglican divines. That ancient religion had well nigh faded away out of the land . . . and it must be restored."[1]

I subscribed wholeheartedly to the Anglican appeal to antiquity, the first four- or five hundred years of the church's history, "when the Church was at the best."[2] This assumed that the closer in time a writer was to the time the New Testament scriptures were written, the more likely it would be that he interpreted those scriptures correctly. (This assumption ignores the fact that heresies plagued the Church from apostolic times.)

Some seventeenth-century Anglicans wrote expansively about the Anglican *via media*. It remained for Newman to give the theory its classical expression. In my halcyon years as an Anglo-Catholic, I absorbed and enthusiastically taught that true Anglicanism holds a mediating position among the chief traditions of Christianity: Rome, the Reformation churches, and the Eastern Orthodox churches. By this I understood that Anglicanism preserves all that is true in each of the main traditions without perpetuating their errors. I held firmly to the "branch theory," insisting on the catholicity of Anglicanism and defending my orders as valid Catholic orders.[3]

All this and more I believed. I believed it because I wanted it to be true. Like other Anglo-Catholics, I continually grasped at straws, so to speak, to bolster the faith I professed. I read widely in Anglo-Catholic literature, always looking for more arguments to sustain what I was teaching others. God

---

1   John Henry Cardinal Newman, *Apologia Pro Vita Sua,* ed. David J. DeLaura (New York: W.W. Norton and Company, 1968), 47.

2   William Laud, quoted by H. R. McAdoo, *The Spirit of Anglicanism: A Survey of Anglican Theological Method in the Seventeenth Century* (New York: Scribner, 1965), 10.

3   A convert from Anglo-Catholicism has pointed out the appalling consequences of believing that the Church of England and her branches have valid orders. That would mean that "vast numbers of her bishops and priests are consecrating the bread and wine in the Holy Communion to be the true Body and Blood of Christ without believing that they are doing so, that they are offering the Sacrifice of the Mass without intending to do so, and that they possess the gift of priestly absolution but never exercise it." It would also mean that "bishops who have no intention of ordaining sacrificing priests can by means of the Anglican ordinal confer a sacrificing priesthood on men who have no intention of receiving it." He concludes, "To believe that is to believe in magic...." See Selden Peabody Delany, *Why Rome* (New York: The Dial Press, 1930), 223f.

forgive me, at times I even had a disdainful attitude toward Protestants. At the same time, like all the Anglo-Catholic clergy I knew, I was self-conscious and therefore defensive in the presence of Catholic priests. Defensive because I knew they and their Church denied my precious "branch theory."

My eagerness to believe I was Catholic filtered out the truth when I encountered it.

Early in our years in Beaumont there appeared a volume of essays on the thought of Reinhold Niebuhr.[4] The book contained twenty essays, to each of which Niebuhr wrote a response. The list of contributors reads like a who's who among contemporary Protestant theologians and philosophers. When I was studying at Union Theological Seminary, Niebuhr was an exciting, inspiring figure. His classroom lectures were stimulating. For most of us seminarians, he was our knight in shining armor.

Though I bought the book when it appeared, I did not read it until after we had moved to Oklahoma City. A Catholic, Gustave Weigel, S.J., a personal friend of Niebuhr's, had written one of the essays. Because I considered myself also to be a Catholic, I eagerly read and re-read Weigel's chapter. The title was captivating: "Authority in Theology."

"Ah, now we get down to brass tacks," I told myself. I paid little attention to the other essays but did study Niebuhr's response to Weigel's criticism.

Weigel made a number of technical philosophical criticisms of Niebuhr's thought. He pointed out that Niebuhr's philosophy of naturalistic empiricism shapes all his religious thought: "[H]is [Niebuhr's] point of departure is epistemological not religious."[5] (I recalled that beginning with Luther, Protestant theologians have scorned philosophy while unconsciously adopting current philosophical fads. Despite historic Protestant disdain for philosophy, it is impossible to think apart from philosophic assumptions. If the assumptions are unrecognized, they can be even more misleading.)

At the root of all theological discussion is the issue of authority. Repeatedly in his writings (and in our classroom lectures), Niebuhr accused the Catholic Church of arrogance. In his response to Weigel's criticism, Niebuhr granted that the Catholic Church "has always preserved some substance of the Gospel truth" despite "the corruptions which are consequent upon its collective arrogance." Protestants may envy the unity of the Catholic Church, said Niebuhr, and recognize it has been a source of grace to many individuals. But they could never accept the Catholic attempt "to lift a historic institution into a trans-historic reality, making the claim of speaking for God, of being

---

4   Charles W. Kegley and Robert W. Bretall, eds., *Reinhold Niebuhr: His Religious, Social, and Political Thought* (New York: Macmillan Company, 1956).
5   *Ibid.*, 373.

privy to the divine will, and of dispensing the divine grace. That claim is in our opinion a very great heresy."[6] Niebuhr's underlying philosophy denied the possibility of any absolutes in history.

Niebuhr's entire thought, Weigel declared, is a reconstruction of the reconstruction attempted by the Protestant Reformation. Weigel declared, "If a man speaks to me of God in order to tell me what God is and what he wills, in piety and awe for the unseen God I must ask of that man: In whose name and by what authority do you speak? The question of authority simply cannot be evaded. To my question the Catholic Church gives a religious answer." Niebuhr's "only authority . . . is that of [himself,] a fallible searcher for the truth of God."[7]

In the final analysis, Niebuhr's charge that the Catholic Church is arrogant forces us to make a choice: Either Niebuhr or the Catholic Church is arrogant. Who has the better claim to authority? In my mind I pronounced judgment: "The Catholic Church, of course—all branches of the Catholic Church."

Niebuhr met the issue of authority with a series of question-begging phrases that I underlined: "All who have become Christian will find their own convictions formed by the witness of the whole Christian Church through the ages, beginning with the witness of Scripture, including, of course the Scripture which gives us the witness of the Church before the Church; namely, Israel. A responsible theologian, as distinguished from an irresponsible speculator, will think and live within the discipline of this Church, though he will feel free to correct what seem to him to be errors of the past."[8]

I was jubilant. As an Anglo-Catholic I took every word Weigel wrote about "the Catholic Church" as applying to my Anglican branch of the Catholic Church. I called Weigel's essay a "devastating criticism" of Niebuhr's whole theology. A magnificent vindication of "our" Catholic heritage!

Not until late in my pilgrimage did I realize that Weigel's penetrating analysis of the Niebuhrian reconstruction of the Gospel applies with equal force to the Anglo-Catholic reconstruction. For that, I gradually realized, is exactly what Anglo-Catholicism is: a reconstruction, a Protestant project with a Catholic veneer.

The story is told of an executioner during the French Revolution who was so skilled with the guillotine that a victim didn't know he had been beheaded until he tried to sneeze. Father Weigel had beheaded my Anglo-Catholicism, but only years later did I try to sneeze. Chalk up another wakeup call to the Holy Spirit. I slept through this one, too.

---

6   *Ibid.*, 444-445.
7   *Ibid.*, 376.
8   *Ibid.*, 445.

Thanks to our benefactor Frank, we spent three consecutive summers in Sewanee, Tennessee, where I was enrolled in the graduate school of theology at Saint Luke's Seminary. Sewanee is the home of the University of the South. Or perhaps I should say, the University of the South *is* Sewanee. Located on top of a mountain in southern Tennessee, it is an ideal setting for a family vacation.

Our first summer there I learned from a Saint Luke's seminarian that it was possible to visit with Thomas Merton at the Abbey of Gethsemane in Kentucky. In response to many requests, the abbot had agreed to let Father Louis (Thomas Merton's religious name) meet with groups on Sunday afternoons and on Monday mornings until lunchtime. Sometimes dozens of people came to be with him. I called the abbey to make a reservation. On a Sunday morning I made the five-hour drive from Sewanee to Gethsemane.

When I arrived in early afternoon, the guestmaster greeted me warmly and led me to pleasant accommodations in the guesthouse, next door to the chapel. He said no one else had yet come to meet with Father Louis. I assumed more would arrive that night. In later afternoon, Father Louis came to the guesthouse to welcome me, and we chatted for ten or fifteen minutes. I was amazed and delighted by his graciousness. Here was I, a total stranger, come to take up his valuable time just to get acquainted and ask him questions. He made me feel he was genuinely pleased I had come.

That night the dinner for guests was plain but tasty. I especially liked the cheese we were served. When I mentioned it later to Father Louis, he said that when a monk is sick in the infirmary he is allowed to have some of the cheese, not otherwise. The monks' diet was vegetarian. "But," Father Louis said rather ruefully, patting his tummy, "I can still gain weight on it."

I spent the long Sunday evening browsing in the extensive library of the guesthouse. I finally settled on a book with an intriguing title, which I cannot now remember. It turned out to be an Anglican's account of his conversion to Catholicism. I thought, "Do I want to read this?" But then I sat down and read most of it. Interesting, I said, if the author couldn't stand fast in his Anglo-Catholic faith. Then about one in the morning I went to bed.

Shortly after two I was awakened by music. It was rather faint, filtered from the chapel through the walls of the guesthouse. It was literally unearthly. I had never heard a sound like it. When only half awake I asked myself, "Is it . . . ? Have I . . . ?" Then awakening fully, I told myself, "No, I haven't died and gone to heaven."

I lay wide awake, listening to the chanting until it stopped. As I later learned, I had been listening to the voices of about one hundred fifty monks well-trained in Gregorian chant, praying the early morning office.

That morning I went to the balcony of the chapel, where a few guests were seated to observe or pray with the Mass being offered. The chapel is a long, tall, rather narrow structure. From my seat I could see all the monks in choir. I was deeply moved by the beauty of the chant. I had never heard Gregorian chant at any length, and certainly none sung like what I was hearing. During the chanting the monks appeared informal, standing and leaning back on their upraised seats, making that heavenly music seem effortless.

After breakfast, Father Louis came to meet me at the guesthouse. To my astonishment, I learned that I had him all to myself. My initial thought was, "But can he spare all this time for just one person?" Father Louis's warm greeting dispelled my misgiving. We spent the morning mostly in the garden, walking, sitting, talking—talking. I thanked him for the moving account of his pilgrimage in *Seven Storey Mountain*. He asked at length about my background and my family. Father Louis was articulate, lighthearted, often quite humorous. I asked many questions about Catholic doctrine. His answers were simple and clear.

Father Louis gave no impression he was trying to interest me in becoming Catholic. I now think that was wise. Writing to a non-Catholic friend who later entered the Church, Flannery O'Connor said, "I did not want you to think I was trying to stuff the Church down your throat. This is a peculiar thing—I have the one-fold one-shepherd instinct as strong as any, to see somebody I know out of the Church is a grief to me, it's to want him in with great urgency. At the same time, the Church can't be put forward by anybody but God and one is apt to do great damage by trying; consequently Catholics may seem very remiss, almost lethargic, about coming forward with the Faith."[9]

Without realizing it, at Gethsemane Abbey I was testing the waters of Catholicism. I still believed I was "Catholic." Being with Father Louis did me a great service: It evaporated my remaining prejudices and apprehensions about the Catholic Church. Yet at that time I did not think about becoming a Roman Catholic. I still had the volume on the Spirit's call to the Church turned down completely.

From what I had read about Father Louis, not from anything he said, I knew he was an extremely busy man: training novices, writing, translating, carrying on voluminous correspondence with many persons at home and abroad, working in the fields—to say nothing of the rigorous schedule of prayer and meditation that was the heart of his monastic vocation. Yet at each moment of our hours together he seemed totally relaxed. It was as if he hadn't a

---

9   Flannery O'Connor, *The Habit of Being: Letters*, edited and with an introduction by Sally Fitzgerald (New York: Noonday Press, 1999), 134.

thing in the world to do but sit or walk and talk with me. He was an excellent listener, drawing me out, never giving the impression (as many of us often do in conversation) of simply waiting as I spoke to take his turn in speaking.

He asked a number of questions about the Episcopal Church. In his youth he had contact with the Episcopal Church through his father. From his autobiography I knew the outlines of his life. Only in response to a direct question would he speak of anything he had done or places he had been.

Before we parted company at noon, he led me to the bookstore and autographed a gift copy of two of his books. I regret I had neither the presence of mind nor the knowledge of Catholic customs to kneel before him and ask his blessing. We shook hands with a warm greeting and parted. For five hours on the drive back to Sewanee I savored almost each moment of our time together. At one point during the trip I realized I was grinning and had been for much of the trip. I was thinking about Father Louis's humor, about his self-deprecating remarks. I told myself, "I have been in the presence of holiness." And I thanked God for the privilege.

The following summer, when we returned to Sewanee, I arranged to visit Father Louis again. And again, no one else came that weekend to see him. As in my earlier visit, we chatted a while later Sunday afternoon. The next morning I observed (I use the term advisedly) Mass from the chapel balcony, again marveling at the beauty of the chant. The monks sang as though directed by a skilled choirmaster, but there appeared to be none.

We spent Monday morning in surroundings different from those of the previous summer. Father Louis had long wanted a hermitage in the woods for secluded time of prayer. Evidently he had mentioned this to a person or persons who had visited him. Later someone had contacted the abbot to tell him that arrangements had been made for building Father Louis's hermitage. The funds had been raised and an architect had drawn up plans. ("All steel and glass," Father Louis said with a grin.) A working party of college students was scheduled to come to the abbey and build the hermitage under professional direction.

Father Louis said the abbot was not going to have a bunch of college students running around the place. "If you're going to have a hermitage," he told Father Louis, "we'll build it." And so the monks did.

On Monday morning, Father Louis drove me in a Jeep through the woods to the hermitage. It was a plain oblong cinder block structure with a room clear across the back and two rooms half that length in front. A porch ran the length of the front. The hermitage was sparsely furnished. One room was for sleeping, one for prayer and writing, one with primitive kitchen facilities.

For three hours we sat on the front porch in old but comfortable rocking chairs, talking animatedly and gazing down a slight slope of clearing in the woods. Father Louis's friend, the author John Howard Griffin, who was a skilled photographer, had been teaching Father Louis the finer points of photography and had given him some equipment. He spoke at length about photography as an exciting art form, but he did not show me any pictures he had taken.

Our conversation turned to current events. (This was 1961.) Father Louis said he was drawn to pacifism and had written several recent articles on peace and war. He said he had been writing as many as he could because he sensed the abbot was not pleased by one of his monks being so involved in temporal affairs.

"I think he's going to tell me to stop writing these articles," he said with a mischievous grin, "so I wanted to get as many in print as I could before I have to stop."

I had brought a movie camera on this trip. While we were at the hermitage, I focused the camera for several minutes on Father Louis as we talked and slowly moved about the clearing around the hermitage. When the film was developed later—I still have it—I was chagrined to discover I had shot a double exposure. (Impossible, of course, with modern digital video cameras.) I had filmed Father Louis over footage taken of our ten-year-old daughter, Risa, dancing alone in a wide circle. The film shows a smiling Father Louis with our daughter apparently dancing circles around him. I think it would make him laugh.

Back at the monastery, he took me to the bookstore and autographed a couple of his books. One was Hans Küng's early book, *The Council, Reform and Reunion*, written in Küng's orthodox years. Father Louis praised it. I enjoyed reading it a few days afterward. (Thirty years later I was clearing out my office at the University of San Diego. When I took this book from the shelf, I wondered why I had kept it so long. Opening the cover I discovered why. It was the copy Father Louis had given me.)

As I drove down the lane from the abbey to the highway, a young monk driving a very large tractor at break-neck speed overtook me. I caught a glimpse of a handsome young man, bareheaded, his short hair flapping in the wind. He was on his way to the fields. A wave of his hand, a broad smile as he glanced back over his shoulder—it was my last contact with that beloved abbey. On the drive back to Sewanee, my thoughts were similar to those after I left Gethsemane the previous summer. But there was more: sadness in my heart. I cannot explain it, but somehow I knew I would never see Father Louis again.

In the course of that second visit I mentioned a book of collects taken from the various prayer books of the Church of England and her transplanted branches. Father Louis said he would like to see a copy. Shortly after my return to Sewanee I mailed him the book of collects. He wrote promptly in reply: "Dear Father Ryland, I am most grateful for the book of collects. It is really beautiful and I will use it with the novices to show them what a collect ought to sound like in English. Many thanks and a happy feast on the 15th. You will remain in my prayers. Very cordially in Xt, (signed) Tom Merton."

At the time I did not know what feast he meant. He was referring of course to the Feast of the Assumption. Did he see farther into my future than I did?

In 1968, Father Louis was electrocuted by faulty wiring in his room while in Bangkok attending a conference on Buddhism. Since his death, numerous dissenting Catholics have tried to claim him for their own. Some have asserted he was about to become a Zen Buddhist. Whatever Merton scholars may make of him, the Thomas Merton I knew was an enthusiastic, loyal Catholic. I shall always be deeply grateful to Father Louis for having gently led me to the threshold of the Catholic Church—and enabling me to see a bit more clearly the treasures within. *Requiescat in pace.*

Nevertheless, in 1961, I was still an Anglo-Catholic.

CHAPTER TWELVE

HOME AT LAST!

Another person whom God used to open my mind to Catholic truth was Mildred. She was a maiden lady who for thirty years had operated Saint Thomas More Book Store in Oklahoma City. She knew the faith and she knew her authors. The store's shelves were filled with the best of Catholic literature, with no room for the dissenters whose poisonous works were beginning to be widely published. As one of her regular customers, I became one of her friends. She never spoke to me about coming into the Church. She did direct my attention to first this book and then the other, assuring me that I would find them interesting. She was shrewd in her perceptions of persons, I gradually learned. I think Mildred knew before I did that I would become a Catholic.

(About seven years after we came into the Church, when I had begun teaching at the University of San Diego, Mildred visited us with a proposition. She said she wanted to retire from the bookstore. If my wife and I would return to Oklahoma City and take charge of the store, she would sell the entire stock to us for one dollar. Mind you, this was a large bookstore. We were moved and honored by her proposal, but after praying about it, we had to tell her we believed God intended us to stay at the university.)

In those days—and in previous decades—there was tension between the "low church" and the "high church" clergy and members. For the "low churchmen" the Episcopal Church was a Protestant church with a rich liturgical tradition. The "high churchmen" generally held to the branch theory and adopted certain Roman Catholic practices. Many of them, like me, contended that there are seven sacraments (not two, as the prayer book says) in the Anglican tradition. A few high-church parishes had tabernacles for their reserved sacrament. Occasional parishes even offered what they believed to be benediction of the Blessed Sacrament. The high-church brethren called the low churchmen "Prots" (short for Protestants). In turn, the low churchmen called the high churchmen "spikes," "papists," and "Romanists."

The Episcopal high-church-low-church tension was well illustrated in my relationship with a leading scholar and liturgist. He was dean of the summer school of theology at Saint Luke's Seminary, where I studied three consecutive summers. I admired his scholarship but sensed he was rather formal in our contacts. I thought it was because I was high church.

His negative attitude became clear in the summer of 1962. For one of his courses I wrote a long review of a book on Peter by the distinguished Protestant theologian Oscar Cullmann.[1] In contrast to almost all Protestant thinkers, Cullmann agreed with what the Catholic Church teaches about Peter and the commission given to him by Christ. But Cullmann argued that the commission was personal to Peter, that it was intended by Christ only to get the Church going, and that it was not passed on to Peter's successors.

Studying this book was another milestone in my journey home. It convinced me that Christ had indeed founded his Church on Peter the Rock. I did not say this in my paper. I did argue, however, that Cullmann had passed a point of no return in conceding Rome's claims. I gave my reasons for saying that, in effect, Cullmann had cut his own Protestant ground from beneath him.

The dean of the summer program wrote a long, harsh criticism of my paper, accusing me of being "dogmatic," saying my paper was negative and unacceptable. He gave me a grade of B-, but I think the tone of his remarks indicated he had an "F" in mind.

(Five years later in 1967, four years after we were received into the Church, we again spent a summer in Sewanee. I was completing research for my Ph.D. dissertation and needed to work in Southern Baptist headquarters in Nashville. I made a courtesy call on the dean, who evidently had heard I had become a Roman Catholic. His attitude toward me was the opposite of what it had been in my Episcopal years. He was warm, ingratiating, animated in our conversation. Why the change? I am convinced it was because as a Roman Catholic I was no longer trying to make over the Episcopal Church he loved into a carbon copy of the Catholic Church. This, I think, is the basis of low-church resentment against Anglo-Catholics. Now I know the low churchmen were justified in their criticisms.)

---

1   Oscar Cullmann, *Peter: Disciple, Apostle, Martyr: A Historical and Theological Essay*, trans. Floyd V. Filson (New York: Meidian Books, Inc., 1958).

The issue of the New Testament canon figured more and more largely in my thinking. Alexander Campbell, the founder of the denomination in which I was raised, the Disciples of Christ, assumed he could read the Bible quite apart from human tradition. All fundamentalists hold to this belief. Campbell expressed the belief by saying he would read his Bible (by which he meant the New Testament) as though it had just fallen into his hands from heaven. In my seminary training I gradually learned his Bible had fallen into his hands from the early Church. Though my professors never drew the necessary conclusion, they and the books I read made it clear that the canon of the New Testament had been sifted from a large collection of writings. I was never taught the exact nature of that sifting process.

After I entered the Episcopal ministry, I began to draw some conclusions from what I had learned about the canon. The fact that it was established by conciliar decree in AD 397 fit well with the Anglican claim to be bound by the Church of the first four centuries. But gradually I began to ponder why twenty-seven books had been selected out of many dozens of writings that claimed to be apostolic. I began to realize that the Church's *tradition* was the criterion for judging early Church writings. The question was, "Does this document or does it not accurately reflect what the Church teaches? If it does, it's in; if it doesn't, it's out." I gradually saw that the New Testament that I took as the inspired Word of God was a compendium of Catholic teaching.

Then came the hard question—hard for a man who was resisting the tugging of the Holy Spirit. If the Catholic Church is wrong on so many issues, how could she have been right in what she taught, and in what she enshrined, in Sacred Scripture? And, the question continued, if she proclaimed the truth in those early centuries—as I had to admit she did—then why would I say she no longer proclaims the truth?

Another biblical question also involved the canon of the Old Testament. Catholic Bibles contain six books, plus some additional chapters in Daniel, not found in Protestant Bibles. Thinking back on biblical training in four Protestant seminaries, I cannot recall a single instance in which the origin of this difference was discussed. As in all other matters where Protestants differ from Catholics, it was simply taken for granted that the Catholics were wrong, *quod erat demonstrandum*. But the truth began to dawn on me: The longer Catholic canon is that of the Septuagint, the Hebrew Bible translated into Greek by about 150 BC.

In chapter 3 I wrote about having spent months aboard ship studying the Old Testament under the guidance of a book recommended by my chaplain. Not until my years as chaplain of Casady School did I go back to earlier sections of the book I had ignored. There I read "the Septuagint Greek Bible

(LXX) was the Old Testament of the Christian Church from the beginning."[2] I began to realize the longer canon—the *Roman Catholic* canon!—was the Bible of Jesus and of Saint Paul.

Where did the shorter Protestant canon originate? It was Martin Luther's creation. Because he did not like certain teachings found in the longer canon, he decreed that he and his followers would adopt the Jewish canon that did not contain the books offensive to him. The Catholic Church defined the canon only in the sixteenth century, at the Council of Trent. She had not acted earlier because, prior to Martin Luther, the canon had not been questioned.[3]

The chinks in my Anglo-Catholic armor began to widen.

We Anglo-Catholics constantly grasped at doctrinal and historical straws in an effort to find support for our beliefs. In those days I often felt resentment at being stranded by my own church. Why *didn't* the formularies of my own church support the Anglo-Catholic position? In conflict with our low-church counterparts, we were always at a disadvantage.

Gradually I began to realize that I had stranded myself by taking on beliefs that have no basis in the Anglican tradition. (In one of Blessed John Henry Newman's letters to a convert, he details some of the beliefs held by Edward Pusey and John Keble, the two leading Anglo-Catholics after Newman's departure from Anglicanism. He challenged anyone to find some of these men's cherished beliefs in any of their Anglican predecessors.[4]) Slowly my Anglo-Catholic system of faith began to appear more and more the product of a Protestant attempt to use Catholic building blocks for a doctrinal structure.

On reflection I saw that, at first, I had loved the Anglican tradition for what I thought she was. As my Anglo-Catholicism unfolded, more and more I loved her for what I thought I—and others like me—could make of her. I began seeing my attitude as being like that of a woman who marries a man to reform him according to her specifications (or a man marrying a woman with the same intent). Not a sound basis for marriage.

The cacophony of conflicting doctrinal and moral views in Protestantism was becoming unendurable. All agreed that God has revealed Himself in Christ. *What* has God revealed? *What* has God promised? *What* does God expect of us? *Where* do we turn? Gradually I realized what later as a Catholic I found in Newman: "A revelation is not given, if there be no authority to decide what it is that is given."[5]

---

2   Robert H. Pfeiffer, *Introduction to the Old Testament* (New York: Harper and Rowe, 1948), 69.

3   Except by Saint Jerome, who under the influence of Jewish scholars with whom he worked in Palestine, urged the Church to adopt the Jewish canon. Pfeiffer seems to make much of Jerome's opinion. But after all, Jerome was only one individual member of the Church.

4   Stanley L. Jaki, *Newman to Converts: An Existential Ecclesiology* (Pinckney, MI: Real View Books, 2001), 383.

5   John Henry Cardinal Newman, *An Essay on the Development of Doctrine*, foreword by Ian Ker (Notre Dame, IN: University of Notre Dame Press, 1989), 89.

I became more devoted to the Blessed Virgin and to praying the Rosary (in private, of course). I began going to confession to another Anglo-Catholic priest. I tried to teach my people about the Holy Sacrifice of the Mass (which until then I believed I was commissioned to offer). I began to invoke some of the saints. All of this led me farther away from the Episcopal Church.

Numbers 35 gives detailed instructions about establishing "six cities of refuge" among the chosen people. Persons who committed unintentional homicide could find sanctuary in those cities, so long as they remained there. On reflection I realize now that for us Anglo-Catholics, the Eastern Orthodox churches were our theoretical cities of refuge. I say *theoretical* because we never fled to them. On more than one occasion it appeared the Episcopal General Convention was about to adopt policies inimical to Anglo-Catholic beliefs. Each time prominent Anglo-Catholics declared that if the Convention did so decide, they and many others would go to Orthodoxy. Each time the General Convention did adopt those policies. Each time the Anglo-Catholics stayed where they were.

Still, we sought solace in the very existence of the separated Eastern churches. We reasoned that since Rome acknowledges the validity of Eastern Orthodox sacraments, then it admits the Orthodox churches are "Catholic." (As a Catholic I learned that Rome does acknowledge the validity of Eastern Orthodox sacraments, but Rome does *not* recognize the separated Eastern churches as Catholic.) So, we said, here is living evidence that one can be a Catholic without being Roman. What's true of the Orthodox must be true of us Anglo-Catholics: Catholics but not Roman Catholics.

In 1961, my wife and I began to look with interest toward Orthodoxy. We had begun to realize our reading and discussion and prayers were gradually sawing off the limb of the branch theory on which we sat. Providentially (we thought), an opportunity for me to study Eastern Orthodoxy arose that summer in the graduate school of theology in Sewanee. Dr. Glanville Downey, a distinguished scholar from Dumbarton Oaks, taught an introductory course in Eastern Orthodoxy. (Dumbarton Oaks is Harvard's Byzantine Center in the District of Columbia.) Dr. Downey's course reflected his appreciation and love for the Orthodox tradition. As I shared my reading and the lectures with my wife, we began to think, "Maybe this is it!" (By *it* we meant our ultimate church home.)

But we searched Orthodoxy in vain for what we knew was essential: a solution to the problem of authority in doctrine and morals. Though the separated Eastern churches have kept much of the ancient Catholic faith, we could not find evidence of a living magisterial authority beyond the Orthodox appeal to "tradition." As Anglo-Catholics we appealed to our own version of tradition, but we were divided among ourselves as to what the tradition is and what it means for our lives today.

We began to see dimly that the Orthodox appeal to the first seven centuries as normative is much like the Anglican normative appeal to the first five centuries. As Anglicans we said, in effect, "We have the faith of the Church of the first *four* ecumenical councils, and we have not changed that faith." Now we listened to Orthodox writers who said, in effect, "We have the faith of the Church of the first *seven* ecumenical councils, and we have not changed that faith."

But even assuming both claims to be true, one must ask this question. What would you say about an adult contemporary who proudly announces, "I have the same faith, the same understanding of the faith, I had when we were five"? Or "when we were eight"? Ruth and I were gradually recognizing what is now perfectly clear. What growth in understanding of the faith is to an individual, development of doctrine is to the Church. Both are necessary. But how is legitimate development of doctrine to be distinguished from deformation of doctrine? We found no answer in the Orthodox tradition.

Nor did we find in Orthodoxy any solution to the continuing problem of Christian disunity. The Eastern Orthodox churches have a common faith but no discernible unity among them. In the U.S. alone there are over three dozen separate Orthodox jurisdictions, some of which are not in communion with some of the others. We found no structure by which the various Eastern churches can speak and respond as a whole to challenges facing them. We also noted the essentially ethnic nature of each of the Eastern churches. And so what we had long thought of as a "city of refuge" for us Anglo-Catholics turned out to be a mirage.

We were taking our last long look at Anglo-Catholicism. The whole edifice rests on the assumption that Anglo-Catholic orders are valid Catholic orders. We knew that the English Church had maintained an episcopal succession from the days of Henry VIII's break with the papacy. We also knew that in 1896 the Catholic Church had declared those episcopal orders "absolutely null and utterly void" because of defect of intention.

Like all Anglo-Catholics, we tried to take comfort from the 1897 rebuttal made by the archbishops of Canterbury and York on their own authority. They declared that the English Church had always intended to ordain its ministers to offer the Holy Sacrifice, and therefore the ordinations were valid Catholic ordinations. But we also knew that those two archbishops spoke purely as individuals; they had no canonical authority to speak for their denomination. (More about this in chapter 15.)

In mid-1962, my wife and I finally realized there was only one alternative to the doctrinal chaos in which we had lived so long as Protestants. Somewhat reluctantly we began reading Catholic literature. We found Karl Adam's *Spirit of Catholicism* particularly helpful, especially with regard to understanding papal authority. When Thomas Merton realized he was being gradually led toward the Trappists, he regarded himself as headed "true north."[6] Now Ruth and I believed we were headed the same.

I must confess that when I saw the Catholic handwriting on the wall, I was downcast. First of all, if I left the Episcopal ministry, I would have no job. I had no other means of supporting my family. We had no savings. We had no Catholic friends. The Catholic ethos was a strange, unexplored, at times forbidding world to us. I had no desire to be a Roman Catholic. I had found joy and satisfaction in serving as an Episcopal priest. My work as chaplain at Casady School was interesting and challenging. All our good friends were Episcopalians. Though our income was modest, it was adequate. The retirement program of the Episcopal Church was quite generous. For these and other reasons I had no desire to leave the Episcopal Church. But I knew I could not stay.

Recently I read in one of Newman's letters to his sister Jemima a description of his situation as he saw himself being drawn to the Church. It is presumptuous to speak of our pilgrimage in the same breath with which I speak of Newman's conversion. Yet I will presume to quote him because he expressed so well what on our own small scale we were undergoing at this stage of our pilgrimage. "I have a good name with many; I am deliberately sacrificing it. . . . I am distressing all I love, unsettling all I have instructed or aided. I am going to those whom I do not know, and of whom I expect very little. I am making myself an outcast, and that at my age. [About the same as ours when we came into the Church.] Oh what can it be but a stern necessity which causes this?"[7]

(I can see now there were two other dimensions to my sorrow at the thought of having to become Roman Catholic. More about those in the next chapter.)

And yet there was peace. The "stern necessity" simplified our lives. The quest for the fullness of Christ's truth was coming to its end. With regard to Catholic doctrines—especially those most troublesome to Protestants (the papacy and mariology)—we no longer thought of what we *could* believe. Having recognized the Church for what she claims to be, we now saw all her teaching is what we *should* believe.

---

6   Thomas Merton, *The Seven Storey Mountain,* 50th ann. ed. (New York: Harcourt Brace and Co., 1998), Part 3, Ch. 2.

7   Stanley L. Jaki, *Newman to Converts: An Existential Ecclesiology* (Pinckney, MI: Real View Books, 2001), 40.

By grace we began living out the truth Newman expressed in a letter to a man who later became a convert: "Everyone who joins the Church must come in the spirit of a child to a Mother—not to criticize anything, but to accept." Stanley Jaki's comment on Newman's observation is simple and direct: "To have this spirit was the only way of coming to the Church."[8]

That summer while we were at Sewanee, we had as guests the family of an Anglo-Catholic priest with whom I had worked in a couple of parishes. With him I had previously dropped hints about our interest in Rome. Early in his visit he asked me point-blank if I were going to Rome. I hedged in my answer, but I think he realized we were going to become Roman Catholics.

Not long ago we read a poem applicable to our situation in 1962. Maurice Baring wrote it after his conversion to the Church in 1909:

> One day I heard a whisper: "Wherefore wait?
> Why longer in a separated porch?
> Why nurse the flicker of a severed torch?
> The fire is there, ablaze beyond the gate.
> Why tremble, foolish soul? Why hesitate?"[9]

Yet we had to wait while I completed my contract as chaplain for the coming school year. Newman described his last years as an Anglican as a time of "tedious decline."[10] By contrast, my last year as an Episcopalian was the happiest, most peaceful year of my life in the Episcopal Church. This was not due simply to the fact that my wife and I were excited at the prospect of becoming Roman Catholics. It was also due to the fact that in my mind I let the Episcopal Church be what she is, a Protestant church with a rich liturgical tradition. I stopped trying to make it over into a small copy of Rome. I felt at peace with my low-church colleagues, whose criticisms of Anglo-Catholicism I now realized were valid. I taught a confirmation class in the school, adhering strictly to the Book of Common Prayer and traditional Anglican teaching (so far as that could be ascertained).

In 1961 and 1962, I assisted on Sundays in an Episcopal church in Shawnee, Oklahoma, forty miles east of Oklahoma City. The drive there took me past Saint Gregory's Benedictine Abbey, toward which I always glanced while driving by. I was vaguely attracted to the place, but I tried to ignore it.

By 1963 I was assisting in a parish in Oklahoma City. One day early that year I had occasion to return to the Shawnee parish in which I had been

---

8   *Ibid.*, 166.
9   Quoted by Joseph Pearce, *Wisdom and Innocence* (San Francisco: Ignatius Press, 1996), 262.
10 Newman, *Apologia, op. cit.,* 121.

an assistant. On my return trip to Oklahoma City, as I neared Saint Gregory's Abbey entrance, on an impulse I turned down the lane leading to the Abbey. I realized I had suddenly decided to seek instruction in the Catholic faith.

When the porter answered the door, I said I wanted to talk to a priest. He first summoned Father Augustine, who taught languages in Saint Gregory's Junior College. He welcomed me graciously, but when I told him the purpose of my call, he said I should talk to Father Denis. Father Denis was chairman of the theology department in the junior college, a brilliant, no-nonsense man who quickly put me at ease. After a brief conversation, we agreed that Ruth and I should come to the abbey one evening a week for instruction. On the drive home, I drew many deep breaths as I thought about the step I had taken. When I could talk to Ruth away from the children, I told her what I had done. She was surprised and pleased.

In those days my intention to become Roman Catholic would have been a considerable embarrassment to Casady School. Ruth and I had to keep our trips to the abbey a secret, both from the children and from my parents who lived not far away. Once a week we simply "went out" for an evening while my mother stayed with the children. Later in the course of our instruction Ruth's mother came for an extended visit, so she cared for the children during our weekly absences.

On the drive to and from the abbey we thought and talked of little other than what we were learning and what we were about to do. It was an exciting time, but a time of apprehension. Every married Protestant clergyman who is drawn to the Church has to face the question "How will I provide for my family?"

We continued our intensive reading of Catholic literature. With Father Denis, we set a goal of Pentecost for being received into the Church. The reception would take place in Christ the King Church, which would be our parish. Soon after our instruction began, Father Denis put us in touch with Monsignor John Connor, pastor of Our Lady's Cathedral in Oklahoma City. He quickly became a valued friend and benefactor to our family. He told us that when he was a young man he had planned to go to Saint Louis University to earn a doctorate in education. Just before his departure, the bishop unexpectedly asked him to become acting pastor of the cathedral, assuring Monsignor Connor that he would name a replacement and release him within six months.

"And that," he said, with a smile, "was forty years ago. I'm still here. And the bishop is long gone." We soon learned Monsignor Connor was a beloved and widely respected priest and pastor. A number of diocesan priests, including one who became bishop of a neighboring diocese, had discerned their vocations under his wise direction.

Monsignor Connor had a wry sense of humor. He was devoted to his dog, which had been his inseparable companion for many years. The dog accompanied him on his pastoral errands, sitting up proudly in the back seat of the car. Once after Monsignor had called on us, we followed him to his car and waved to the dog.

"That dog," said Monsignor Connor, "is quite remarkable. He is the only son of a bitch in Oklahoma who has a monsignor for a chauffeur."

The first Mass we attended was an Easter Vigil service at Saint Patrick's Church in Oklahoma City in 1963. I wore civilian clothes and hoped no one there would recognize me. Strangers though we were, both to that community and to the liturgy itself, that vigil service was the most deeply moving experience of worship we had ever known. Missalettes clutched in our hands, we tried to keep up with each step in the liturgy. We listened intently to the long list of Scripture readings. Never had we heard so much Scripture in one service. And then—when the choir and congregation began singing the Gloria, when many people began bringing in a small mountain of flowers to fill the sanctuary, when the church was brilliantly lighted for the first time—then we knew we were present at, though not yet sharing in, the heavenly banquet. Any doubt we might have had about our call to enter the Church was resolved that night.

I have said we found peace in the latter stages of our pilgrimage. There was still some apprehension, especially on my part as head of the family. I faced a deadline for making our decision known. I had to notify the Episcopal bishop and the administrators at Casady School. After that, we would have no income. I was prepared to dig ditches, but at that point no one was offering me a shovel. The Holy Spirit led us up to a stone wall. For a time He let our noses rest against it. Ruth and I repeatedly told one another that God never leads people down blind alleys; that God was calling us into the Church and therefore He would provide a way.

For years I had been using Anglo-Catholic materials to catechize our children. In that last of our Episcopal years I gave them the Catholic doctrine I was learning. At one session, a few months before we were received into the Church, our ten-year-old daughter, Erica, announced to her siblings and me, "When I grow up, I'm going to be a *real* Catholic. I'm going to be a *Roman* Catholic." I could only say, "God bless you, sweetie; I hope you will."

We knew our children could not keep secret the news of our becoming Roman Catholics, so we did not tell them until two days before we were received. The two girls cried. Risa, who was twelve, cried because I would not be a priest any more. Erica cried because she loved Casady School and now must leave it. The three boys, Chris, Tim, and Mark—ages nine, six and three, respectively—were silent.

Our parents were not silent. When we informed them of our decision, they were astonished and grieved. When we told Ruth's mother we were going to become Catholics, her anguished response was, "How can you go into that darkness, once you have known the light?" We were not offended. We realized that in years gone by, the mere thought of becoming Catholic would have caused us even greater distress than our announcement caused her.

Years later I read G. K. Chesterton's words about conversion and darkness and light.

> The outsiders stand by and see, or think they see, the convert entering with bowed head a sort of small temple which they are convinced is fitted up inside like a prison, if not a torture-chamber. But all they really know about it is that he has passed through a door. They do not know that he has not gone into the inner darkness, but out into the broad daylight. It is he who is, in the beautiful and beatific sense of the word, an outsider.[11]

(Over the years Ruth's mother was reconciled to our being Catholic. In fact, she said she enjoyed going to Mass with us during her visits. Her only regret was that she could not receive Communion. My parents had become Episcopalians after Ruth and I did. They kept saying they could not understand our decision. A year or so later, when our family was living in Milwaukee, I challenged them to take a course of instruction and find out why we had entered the Church. They accepted my challenge, took instruction from a faithful priest at Our Lady's Cathedral, and were led to become Catholics.)

On the eve of Pentecost 1963, Ruth and I and our five children were received into the Catholic Church at Christ the King parish. Father Denis, assisted by Monsignor Connor, received us. The pastor of the parish was also present. Ruth and I and our three older children each made a life confession. Father Denis was sponsor for each of us, and he drafted a couple of his lay friends to be present as sponsors.

As I mentioned earlier, I had been baptized at the age of nine in the Disciples of Christ church by trine immersion. There should have been no doubt about the validity of my baptism. As an Episcopal clergyman I had baptized each of our five children. In each case I knew the form and intention

---

11 G.K. Chesterton, "The World Inside Out," in *G.K. Chesterton: Collected Works*, vol. 3 (San Francisco: Ignatius Press, 1990), 107.

were correct. Yet I insisted on conditional baptism for all of us except my wife. She had been baptized as an infant in the cathedral in San Antonio but had never had any further contact with the Catholic Church until the time of our reception. The priests agreed to the conditional baptisms.[12] I wanted every possible vestige of doubt to be erased, and I also wanted us to have Catholic baptismal certificates.

We walked out of that church Roman Catholics. My joy amounted almost to a daze. How I wish now I had known then G.K. Chesterton's poem written immediately after he was received into the Church. The closing stanza expresses so well what I then felt.

> The sages have a hundred maps to give
> That trace their crawling cosmos like a tree,
> They rattle reason out through many a sieve
> That stores the sand and lets the gold go free:
> And all these things are less than dust to me
> Because my name is Lazarus and I live.

The following day, Pentecost, five of us received the Body, Blood, Soul, and Divinity of our Lord Jesus Christ for the first time. An indescribable blessing! The next day Bishop Victor Reed confirmed three of us in his private chapel. As we sat waiting for him to lead us to his chapel, our six-year-old, Tim, suddenly crawled far back under a large sofa and refused to come out. It was unusual behavior for him, especially in public. When the bishop came to greet us I was still on my hands and knees trying to pull him out. With a smile the bishop waited patiently until Tim could be extricated. Then we went to the chapel for the confirmation. Such was our joy that afterward a contrite Tim received only a fatherly hug.

---

12 Under similar circumstances, this would not be allowed today. Only in my case would conditional baptism be possible, because I have no record of my baptism as a child.

Part 2
BEING CATHOLIC

CHAPTER THIRTEEN

TOWARD HOLY ORDERS

Until just a few weeks before I resigned from the Episcopal ministry, I had no employment. I had talked with several Catholic businessmen but had not found a job. Our Benedictine priest benefactor and friend came to our rescue. Father Denis persuaded the abbot of his monastery to crowd into their tight budget allowance for a part-time teaching assignment for me. Then he canvassed some of his friends and raised enough money to enable me to teach full time in the theology department at Saint Gregory's Abbey in Shawnee, Oklahoma. Our family is forever grateful to that community for its material and spiritual assistance. During that year while I commuted the forty miles from our home, I managed to review Latin grammar thoroughly.

Through friends a grant became available in 1964, sufficient to support our family for two years. Together with scholarships I was able to complete course work for a doctorate in religious studies at Marquette University. It was then the only Catholic university offering doctoral studies for laymen. For a dissertation topic I chose to study the Southern Baptist movement. It was then (as now) the largest single Protestant denomination in the country, and the only major ecumenical holdout. No one—not even a Southern Baptist scholar—had ever done a thorough study of its historical reasons for remaining aloof from ecumenical involvement. Marquette even allowed me to secure the services of a Southern Baptist scholar from Texas, James Leo Garrett, as my major adviser. I completed the dissertation three years later, while working for the Oklahoma diocese as director of an ecumenical center in Oklahoma City.

Earlier in a footnote I noted that my research for the dissertation showed the Southern Baptist Convention to be the true pioneer of modern non-Catholic ecumenism in this country. My adviser and others were intrigued. I was invited to give a lecture in the summer of 1969 at an executive meeting of the Baptist World Alliance in Baden bei Wien, near Vienna, Austria. I would be guest lecturer in the Alliance's newly formed Commission for Cooperative Christianity. That would make me the first Catholic ever to have addressed the Baptist Alliance. Only one other non-Baptist, a Mennonite scholar, was on the same program. At my adviser's request, a wealthy Southern Baptist layman gave my wife and me a three-week tour of central Europe, with the Alliance meeting in the middle of our jaunt.

Up to that time there had been no official interchange between the Vatican and the Baptist World Alliance. At my request, then-Monsignor Bernard Law asked Cardinal Johannes Willebrands, head of the Vatican's ecumenical secretariat, for a greeting for me to take to the Baptist World Alliance. Very soon a gracious answer to my request came from Rome:

> To the commission for Cooperative Christianity of the World Baptist Alliance:
>
> In recent years the mysterious bounty of Providence has happily accustomed us to the frequent setting up of landmarks in ecumenical progress. Yet I have special pleasure and a special sense of significance in extending warm greetings to this first Meeting of the world Baptist Alliance's new Commission for Cooperative Christianity.
>
> One substantial reason for this significance is the singular courtesy the Commission has shown in inviting serious dissertation on the genius of the Southern Baptist movement from a Roman Catholic scholar who has made this field his own. Patient, impartial and sympathetic study of other traditions is of the essence of ecumenical progress, and that a Roman Catholic should have earned the confidence of your Commission is a most happy omen for the future development of Baptist-Roman Catholic relations and discussions. I warmly wish every success and blessing to the Vienna meeting."
>
> (Signed) John Cardinal Willebrands
> (Dated) Rome, July 14, 1969

The Cardinal's letter was warmly received, and a gracious response was immediately voted unanimously.

At the end of that meeting, the executive secretary of the Alliance rejoiced with me over the letter and the Alliance executive committee's response. Seven years before the Vatican had inquired informally if it should invite the Alliance to send representatives to the Second Vatican Council. The secretary said that members of the Alliance outside the United States wanted to reply in the affirmative. Southern Baptist members, however, objected. They declared that if the Alliance accepted an invitation, the Southern Baptist Convention would withdraw from the Alliance, thereby dissolving it. So the Alliance declined the invitation to Vatican II. Now, said the secretary, see how the executive committee has responded to the Cardinal's outreach. "What great changes God has made in a few years," he said.

In the early 1970s, the bishops' ecumenical committee inaugurated a series of dialogues with representative Southern Baptist leaders and theologians. It was my privilege to share in the first four of these dialogues. In 1970, Baylor University celebrated the 125th anniversary of its founding with a symposium on "Baptists in American Culture." I was invited to read a paper, again the only Catholic on the program. My lecture was titled "Southern Baptist-Roman Catholic Dialogue: What Catholics Need to Hear." It focused on a few Baptist themes that Catholics could ponder in better understanding the Baptist movement. When it came my turn to read a paper, I called the assembly's notice to an interesting—one might say Freudian—typographical error in the printed program. The title I had submitted was "Southern Baptist-Roman Catholic Dialogue: What Catholics Need to Hear." The program billed my lecture as "Southern Baptist-Roman Catholic Dialogue: What Catholics Need to *Learn*."

In 1969, our family moved to San Diego, where I taught religious studies at the University of San Diego until 1991. In the fall of 1970, while teaching full time, I began a four-year course of study at night in the university's school of law. A month later I was ordained to the permanent diaconate, and began working on weekends in a local parish.

When the possibility of being ordained to the permanent diaconate arose, I discussed it with Bishop John Quinn, then auxiliary bishop in San Diego. My question concerned the adjective *permanent*. If ever the opportunity to apply for dispensation from celibacy and ordination to the priesthood should arise, would my status as permanent deacon disqualify me? He assured me that would pose no obstacle. Because I had a doctorate in theology and had been teaching for a number of years, I was not required to undertake further study for diaconal ordination. Busy years, indeed! In 1975, I was admitted to the California Bar, intending to practice law full time after retiring from the university.

To pick up the trail I followed to ordination, it is necessary to go back to 1963. I had talked with Bishop Victor Reed of Oklahoma City before he received us into the Church. He knew I believed I had a continuing vocation to ordained ministry even as I became a Catholic. At the same time, I saw no possibility of securing dispensation from the rule of celibacy. Upon his return from the first session of Vatican II, the bishop told me he had inquired about the possibility of his ordaining me with the dispensation. He was told the Vatican would not grant such permission to individual bishops. The request would have to come from the national conference level. I kept praying for a miracle.

In 1966, as director of an ecumenical center in Oklahoma City, through phone conversations I became acquainted with Monsignor Bernard Law, executive secretary of the bishops' ecumenical committee. He lent a sympathetic ear to my desire to serve in the priesthood. The following year I visited him in his office in Washington. He suggested I talk with Bishop Joseph Bernardin, secretary of the bishops' conference, and called for an appointment. The bishop was about to leave for National Airport. At his invitation Monsignor Law and I rode with him in a cab to the airport. He, too, was sympathetic to my belief I had a continuing vocation to ordained ministry.

Upon my return to Oklahoma City, I conferred with Bishop Reed. On his recommendation I wrote to Bishop Bernardin. I requested him to ask Cardinal John Dearden, then president of the bishops' conference, if he were willing to bring before the conference the issue of dispensation and ordination of former Episcopal clergy like myself. Bishop Bernardin promptly filled my request, and came back with a "no" from the cardinal. But we kept praying.

In the late 1970s, I met then-Bishop Law at an ecumenical workshop in Tulsa. He told me the bishops' conference had appointed a committee to discuss allowing former Episcopal clergy to apply for dispensation and ordination. The trouble was, he said, that some viewed this proposal as an opening wedge for optional celibacy. The committee did not want to give that false signal.

Meanwhile, negotiations behind the scenes were ongoing.[1] The bishops began receiving such a large volume of inquiries like mine they decided to ask Vatican permission to establish a program enabling qualified clergy converts to apply for dispensation from celibacy and ordination. That permission was given. In 1980 Archbishop John Quinn, then president of the bishops' conference, announced the formation of the Pastoral Provision, with Bishop Law in charge as Ecclesiastical Delegate. The following year guidelines were issued for applicants.

At that time I had begun to ease into law practice, planning to go full time in a few years. Now I cast all those plans aside. They could wait! Or

---

1 Details are given in Fr. Jack D. Barker, "A History of the Pastoral Provision For Roman Catholics," in Stephen E. Cavanaugh, ed., *Anglicans and the Roman Catholic Church* (San Francisco: Ignatius Press, 2011), 3–26.

even be forgotten! The day the guidelines were announced I began work on the required dossier, which was extensive. At the same time I contracted the worst case of flu in my life. From a Friday through a Sunday I worked on my application. I could type for no longer than half an hour, then had to go back to bed for an hour. By Monday morning I had completed the application. I took it directly to my local bishop, Leo Maher. Since he and I had already discussed this matter at length, he immediately forwarded my application and his recommendation to Bishop Law's office.

One requirement for the application was to trace the episcopal lineage of the bishop who ordained me. Father James Parker, Bishop Law's assistant for the Provision, called to tell me his records showed some Old Catholic bishops had taken part in the episcopal succession in which I was ordained. He asked if he could change my application to a request for conditional ordination. I readily agreed but said I thought the Old Catholic strain would not have given me valid orders. Nor did the Congregation for the Doctrine of the Faith so rule. It ignored the question of conditional ordination.

Thirteen months later, I came home from the university to find a message from Bishop Maher. His secretary had asked me to call his private number if I received his message after his office closed. I knew he must have something important to say. He did. He had just received permission to ordain me with dispensation from celibacy, subject to the examination process of the Pastoral Provision.

Great was the thanksgiving in our home that afternoon! Then that evening we attended a Mass for ordination of five young deacons. In the light of my impending ordination, that was the most moving ordination service I had ever attended.

Afterward, I told my wife that as those men lay prostrate during the litany, I knew what must have been filling their minds. Each one must have been thinking how unworthy he was to receive the inestimable privilege of serving Christ as one of his priests.

"It will be different when I'm ordained," I told my wife. "There'll be *two* of us who know how unworthy I am." She smiled back, "Yes, that's true."

A few months later I took seven written—in those days, typed—examinations in the San Diego chancery. The Scripture examination called for me to evaluate one sentence from a volume of the published proceedings of Lutheran-Catholic ecumenical dialogues. Fortunately, I had read the volume but thought this a strange question for a comprehensive Scripture examination. The sentence in question was a consensus statement about the role of Peter. It was equivocal. I attacked it with vigor. I could not type fast enough to keep up with the Scripture quotations that flooded my mind. When I finished I said to myself, "I know I aced that one."

Several weeks later I went to Washington, DC, to take my oral examinations. I joined a company of eight or ten former Episcopal clergy who had come for the same purpose. All of my examinations seemed to go well. I felt especially elated after my Scripture exam, given by the same scholar who had prepared the question for the written examination. At the end of the day, each of us went singly before the examining committee to receive their verdict. When I walked into the room, the chairman said, "Dr. Ryland, you failed the Scripture exam. You will have to take it again."

So great was my shock that I was unable to speak. Literally dumbfounded, I nodded my head and left the room. I was dazed. How could this be? Then suddenly I thought, "Now I've got to go back home and tell my wife and children I flunked Scripture! Yes, and I'll have to tell Bishop Maher—and maybe even worse, tell all my colleagues in the religious studies department!" I was devastated. Saint Therese of Lisieux repeatedly declared we learn humility only by being humiliated, but that afternoon I was not ready for that lesson. I had planned to visit my second daughter in New York after the examining process, so I went directly to the station and boarded a train.

I could think of nothing but my failure. About halfway between Washington and New York a thought suddenly came to me. I know who wrote that sentence I was supposed to "evaluate"—the same man who gave me the exam! Though convinced of the soundness of my answer to his question, I realized I had trod very heavily on his scholarly toes. He had given no hint of this in his oral exam. He had asked a number of straightforward questions about the Gospels and the epistles and had seemed satisfied with my ready answers. So I failed the written exam—supposedly intended to test my knowledge of Scripture—because I strongly disagreed with his opinion on one point!

This struck me as grossly unfair. The next day I wrote a long, strong letter of protest to him, to the committee, and to Bishop Law.

As soon as I could see Bishop Maher after returning to San Diego, I gave him the bad news. Though in a dozen years I had had many conversations with him about a number of controversial subjects, I had never seen him angry. He was this time.

"Forget the examination process," he said. "I'll ordain you anyway!" Then, as he cooled a bit, he reflected on the fact that he *had* promised to follow that process. So he said he would demand that a different scholar examine me. Bishop Law readily arranged for another examiner, a Jesuit scholar in Berkeley. A few weeks later I took his written exam, then went to his office for the oral exam. When I walked into his office, he said jovially, "You passed! Let's chat." And we did.

The ordination was celebrated on February 12, 1983, in Saint Mary Magdalene Church, where I had been serving as a permanent deacon. The cantor and my two younger sons sang a moving song about priesthood that Tim, the elder of the two, had written. Present were all of our children, our first grandchild, my youngest son's fiancée, and my mother. (My father had died a dozen years before.) Before his final blessing, the bishop did something unusual. He asked me if I would like to say a few words to the congregation. Surprised but pleased, I accepted his invitation.

I thanked the bishop for his generous encouragement and support. I explained that our first grandchild had been due to be born later that month. However, I said, when she heard about her grandfather's ordination, she said to herself, "I can't miss that!" So she came into the world two weeks early. I added, "Now you can not only call me 'Father'; you can also call me 'Grandfather.'"

In the recessional my family preceded me. As they filed out of the front pew, I asked my daughter-in-law who had the baby in her arms, "May I carry her?" Without a word she handed Catherine to me. As I walked out I held the baby aloft. After Mass one of my friends said, "I could hold back the tears until you started waving that baby around."

The following day I baptized her, and a few months later solemnized the wedding vows of my youngest son and his wife.

In the summer of 1990, my wife and I spent a couple of months in Oxford, studying and sightseeing in the United Kingdom and on the continent. A friend who had once lived in an Anglican seminary put me in touch with the seminary, which rented flats while students were on vacation ("on holiday," as the British say.) In our correspondence the administration had assumed I was an Episcopal priest, but when I arrived and identified myself, all were gracious and hospitable.

We had just settled in our flat when I went to one of the libraries to return a book. I was carrying an umbrella for shelter from the light rain. Crossing a street and trying to dodge an errant cyclist, I caught my right foot behind the rear tire of a parked car and crashed to the pavement.

I made no effort to stand up; I knew I had seriously injured myself. Soon a crowd gathered and someone called an ambulance. While waiting for the ambulance, various persons tried to cheer me with light conversation. They knew of course they were talking to a Yank.

"So, you came to see England?" one man asked as I lay there flat on my back in the drizzle.

"Yes, but not from this angle," I said.

Suddenly a thought struck me, and I started laughing. The crowd must have thought I had become hysterical. My thought was, "Here I am lying on Keble Avenue, down the street from Keble College, with a library book entitled *The Ambiguity of Anglo-Catholicism*. [Keble was a prominent Anglo-Catholic leader of the Tractarian movement who did not follow Newman into the Church.] And I've 'poped.' The Anglo-Catholic curse has struck me down!"

The ambulance took me to John Radcliffe Hospital, the university's medical school. My left hip was broken. After a wait of nine hours, I was finally taken into surgery (what they called "the theater") and the damage was repaired. Later I learned that hospital is a world-famous center for orthopedic surgery. People come from other countries for surgery there. I comforted myself with the thought that at least I had picked the right place to break a hip.

My hospitalization lasted eight days. When my wife was not at my side, I read Ian Ker's magisterial biography of Cardinal Newman,[2] which she brought me. It is a long book. I read it slowly, admiringly, even lovingly. My thoughts were continually on and with the cardinal. Though I cannot recall having specifically asked his prayers for healing, I believe I had the benefit of his intercession. I know I had the benefit of prayers of family and countless friends back in the States.

This belief was confirmed six weeks later when I went to the hospital for my final x-ray before being discharged. When the surgeon met with me, x-ray print in hand, he said, "I can't find the fracture." There was no trace of a break, though the plate and screws were plainly visible. A month later in San Diego my doctor ordered another x-ray. When he studied it he said (and I recall his exact words), "You have had a most remarkable healing." Indeed; never a moment's discomfort in all these years.

When I was able to walk with crutches, we visited Littlemore, the stable Newman converted into a kind of monastery after he left Oxford. With several like-minded friends, he lived there until shortly after he was received into the Church. Littlemore is a small museum of Newmania. I was privileged to stand at the desk at which he stood when he wrote *An Essay on the Development of Christian Doctrine*. Our guide took us into the chapel where Newman and his friends celebrated Holy Communion according to the Book of Common Prayer. I went to a priedieu near the altar and knelt to pray. After praying a sentence or two, I suddenly realized I was praying half-aloud the opening collect of the Prayer Book service. I had not prayed or thought of that prayer for about twenty-five years. I completed the prayer, judging it entirely appropriate for that setting.

---

2   Ian Ker, *John Henry Newman: A Biography* (Oxford: Oxford University Press, 1988).

Two years later we returned to Oxford for a couple of months. We took a train to Birmingham to visit Newman's Oratory there. When we were admitted to the entrance, a young man apologized that there was no one to show us around. Before I could respond, my wife spoke up, rather indignantly, "We've come all the way from San Diego, California, and we want to see Cardinal Newman's quarters!"

The man excused himself and returned soon with a priest of the Oratory. He took us to Newman's study, where we stayed forty-five minutes while he talked with us about Newman. The Oratorians had tried to keep the study as it was when Newman died. In one corner was a very small altar where Newman offered Mass. His cardinal's wide-brimmed hat was near the altar. The spacious shelves were lined with books. We took none of them down, but did touch quite a number of them, plus some objects on Newman's desk. Holy ground, indeed. In 1995, on another visit to England, when we visited Newman's grave, his study was no longer open to the public.

In 1991, I reached the mandatory retirement age for faculty members. The University of San Diego, like so many other Catholic colleges, had become quite secularized during my twenty-two years there. A handful of us faculty and staff members had vainly tried to stem the tide. I told my wife I wanted to teach at least one year in a truly *Catholic* college. For years I had heard and read that Franciscan University of Steubenville, Ohio, is faithfully Catholic throughout. I wrote to the president, Father Michael Scanlan, T.O.R., and asked if I could teach part-time for a year and carry on some research. He promptly invited me to come.

When we went to Steubenville in 1991, I had been serving as a priest for eight years. Only at Franciscan University did I learn the meaning of the fraternity of priests. Periodically, the president would gather all the priests—faculty, staff, graduate students—at the Holy Spirit monastery for an evening to discuss campus ministry. No matter what position he might hold on the campus, every priest was regarded as a campus minister. Each time we met, I looked around a circle of two dozen or more priests and marveled at the unity that bound us. Here were priests from Asia, Africa, Latin America, Europe, and of course from this country. Here were Franciscan friars, other religious, and diocesan priests. Here were priests of widely divergent cultural backgrounds, differing personalities, yet united in our loyalty to our Lord and to His Church and to His vicar, the pope. We were truly brothers in Christ, good friends from the moment we met. What a blessing, this fraternity of priests!

At the end of the first year I was invited to spend another year, and the same at the end of the second year. After a third year at the university, my wife and I realized we either had to return to our home in San Diego or move to Steubenville. In prayer we discerned a call to return to San Diego. There I worked as chaplain and part-time apologist with Catholic Answers. Then in 1998 we were led to move permanently to Steubenville. For several years I served on the adjunct faculty in the graduate program in theology at Franciscan University.

In 1993 during our temporary stay in Steubenville, it was my privilege to share in the founding of a significant apostolate, the Coming Home Network International. Like so many clergy converts, Marcus Grodi, a former Presbyterian minister, had known loneliness in his pilgrimage. He determined to organize a network that would give aid and comfort to non-Catholic clergy who were looking toward the Catholic Church. He and his wife, along with Dr. Scott Hahn and his wife, and my wife and me, hosted a meeting at Franciscan University for several ministers who were on their pilgrimage to the Church.

A few years later, Marcus initiated a weekly program on the Eternal Word Television Network, "The Journey Home," with hour-long interviews of clergy converts. This program reaches millions of viewers in North America and Europe. More than two thousand non-Catholic clergy from over a hundred non-Catholic traditions have contacted the Coming Home Network International, which offers counsel and resources and puts them in touch with others of their former tradition who are coming into the Church. The number of new inquirers grows weekly. Close to a thousand of these inquirers are now within the Church's communion.

These clergy converts and their families endure great hardship in order to be received into the Church. They give up their employment, their retirement, many or most of their friends. Some have even been rejected by their parents and siblings. They struggle to find means of supporting their families. But having found the pearl of great price, they leave all to follow Christ's call into His Church. They are a faithful, devout and growing leaven the Holy Spirit continues to bring into the Church.

Growing into old age, I am continually grateful for the opportunities for service the Spirit brings. I am privileged to offer Mass weekly for two local religious orders and to concelebrate in a local parish. I continue to write for several Catholic publications, to serve on the boards of two international Catholic apostolates, and to offer spiritual direction to several persons. Our lives are greatly blessed by our five children, twenty-two grandchildren, and three great grandchildren as of this writing. All the while, my wife and I strive to become more and more fully possessed by the Truth into which the Holy Spirit has led us.

CHAPTER FOURTEEN

REFLECTIONS ON PILGRIMAGE

The story of a pilgrimage is the story of a lifetime. Although my call to ministry came to me in a Protestant denomination, I see now that it was the beginning of my call to enter the Church. Much of my understanding of my pilgrimage has unfolded as I look back on the journey. Many things I apprehended dimly as a pilgrim have become clear to me in my years in the Catholic Church. Hearing and reading the experiences of other pilgrims has also helped me to see more clearly the path along which I was led.

My original motivation for entering the ministry was to "help people," though I had little idea about the help I wanted to give, or even could give. My long hours with Chaplain Smith aboard the Nassau lifted my sights. He led me to believe that the task of the minister is to find the truth and share it with the people he serves. He never mentioned—nor did I give thought to—the question of how we will *know* the truth; how we can be certain the "truth" we find *is* the truth.

When I became a Trinitarian at Union Theological Seminary, I came into personal relationship with Jesus Christ who *is* "the way and the truth and the life" (Jn. 14:6). But I still had no secure guidance in exploring the truth of Christ, in applying the truth of Christ to my life or to the lives of those whom I would serve in ministry.

From early childhood I joyfully sang in my Protestant church the hymn, "More About Jesus."

More about Jesus I would know,
More of his grace to others show;
More of his saving fullness see,
More of his love who died for me.

More about Jesus let me learn,
More of his holy will discern;
Spirit of God, my teacher be,
Showing the things of Christ to me.

It was that yearning that is now being fulfilled in my life in the Catholic Church.

After Blessed John Henry Newman, Ronald Knox is perhaps the most distinguished convert from Anglicanism. In a sermon preached on the centenary of Newman's 1845 conversion, Knox said of Newman: "Truth stood before him, fully embodied, and he gave way. I say then that Newman was, as in a measure all converts are, a witness to truth . . . The convert sees truth, as truth is represented proverbially, naked. And I say that his witness to truth is all-important in our time."[1] In a letter to a prospective convert, Newman wrote, "I feel more and more as regards myself that the *fact* that I have become what I am is a preaching—that my presence is an exhortation. The sight of a convert is the most cogent and withal the most silent and subduing of arguments."[2]

The term *convert*, according to the National Conference of Catholic Bishops' rules for the catechumenate, should never be used for baptized Christians received into the Church. It must be used only for unbaptized persons who enter the Church through Baptism.[3] This reflects a continuing concern in the Statutes about something called "ecumenical sensibilities," which the Statutes never define. I respectfully disagree with this approach.

For the present, ignore the fact that for twenty centuries Catholics have used the term *convert* for all non-Christian and non-Catholic persons who become Catholics. Put aside the fact that each one of the great many converts I know is proud to bear the title. There's a deeper reason for using this term to designate non-Catholic Christians who come into the Church. I can explain that reason in terms of my own experience, which is described early in chapter 16.

Since becoming a Catholic, I have worked with a large number of persons seeking to be received into full communion with the Church. There are countless aspects of Catholicism that might be attractive to a non-Catholic. Yet I insist that there is only one basic and enduring reason for becoming Roman Catholic: one has to become convinced that what the Catholic Church

---

1   Quoted by Stanley Jaki, *Newman to Converts* (Pinckney, MI: Real View Books, 2001), 469.
2   Quoted by Jaki, *ibid.*, 158.
3   Appendix III, "National Statutes For the Catechumenate," section 2, in International Commission on English in the Liturgy and Bishops' Committee on the Liturgy, *Rite of Christian Initiation of Adults* (Washington, DC: United States Catholic Conference, 1988).

teaches about herself is true.[4] That is to say, one must be convinced that she is the one true Church established by Jesus Christ. One must be convinced that Jesus Christ has entrusted her with the fullness of truth and means of grace. One must be convinced that Christ has authorized her to teach authoritatively in His name. Get all that straight, and everything else falls in place. For the person who comes into the Church for some other reason, trouble lies ahead.

The first permanent deacon ordained in this country in the 1960s had been a clergyman in the Church of England. For a year he was often in church news as he traveled around the country on speaking engagements. Then he announced that he and his wife were going back to the Church of England. He said that he had become a Roman Catholic because he had thought the Catholic Church is the best vehicle for communicating the Gospel today. In his year in the Church he had decided otherwise, so he was returning to Anglicanism.

When I read his announcement, I told myself he had come into the Church for the wrong reason. He had entered the Church on the basis of a prudential judgment: that he could use the Church to proclaim the Gospel. Without knowing what was in his mind, I must assume he never submitted to the Church's authority. He never really *became* a Catholic. His marriage to the Church, in other words, was never consummated.

Earlier I spoke of my brief attack of "Roman fever," which was quickly cured by my wife's common sense. True conversion never springs from a desire to get away from some aspect or teaching of one's tradition. It can come only from the realization that there is so much in the Catholic faith that one can possess only by entering into the Church's communion.

Mature converts are always keenly aware of the shortcomings of the denominations from which they come. Yet they always come with thanksgiving for what the Spirit has given them in their previous church home. In other words, they become converts because of what they did *not* have, rather than because of their dissatisfaction with what they had.

Contrast this with the attitude of ex-Catholics. Those who leave the Church to join some other tradition almost always have reactive, and often bitter, attitudes toward the Church. Is it because they feel guilty for having left the Church and in self-justification want to put the Church in the worst possible light?

---

4   There may be an occasional exception to this rule. Flannery O'Connor, writing to a friend, said one of her cousins, a non-Catholic college professor, had long attended Mass with his wife. When he decided to become a Catholic, "We asked how he got interested and his answer was that the sermons were so horrible, he knew there must be something else there to make the people come . . ." See *The Habit of Being: Letters,* edited and with an introduction by Sally Fitzgerald (New York: Noonday Press, 1999), 348.

The grace received in non-Catholic traditions always comes through the Catholic elements retained in those religious expressions. The *Decree on Ecumenism* of Vatican II says of these elements of Catholic truth to be found in the various denominations, "All of these, which come from Christ *and lead back to him*, belong by right to the one Church of Christ."[5] It follows therefore that grace is given to those outside the Church *not* to enable them to remain outside but to bring them into the Church.

The convert does not bring new spiritual goods to the Church. The Catholic faith is complete in itself. Rather, he often brings new zest for the Church's riches, new ways of making those riches more widely available. Former evangelicals, for example, have much to teach us Catholics about evangelization and about nurturing our people in Sacred Scripture. The positive Christian elements the convert brings with him become new for him in his life in the Church.

This was a vivid experience for my wife and me. New meaning filled so many terms we had used as Episcopalians: *sacrament, sacrifice, reparation, invocation*, and a host of others. As Flannery O'Connor expressed it, "I don't believe the fundamental nature changes, but . . . it's put to a different use when a conversion occurs, and of course it requires vigilance to put it to the proper use."[6]

The opening section of Vatican II's *Declaration on Religious Liberty* declares repeatedly that everyone has a duty to search for the true Church. "All men are bound to seek the truth, especially in what concerns God and his Church and to embrace it and hold on to it as they come to know it" (1). In a letter to a potential convert, Newman reminded him, "Scripture is full of warnings upon the necessity of '*crying after* knowledge.'"[7]

It follows, then, that once a person begins to catch a glimpse of the truth about the Church, he is obligated to pray for the grace to convert. Some potential converts try to close their ears to this call by concentrating their search on the minutiae of the Church's teachings: "Can I accept *this*? Does *that* really make sense to me?" For the person who begins to realize just what the Catholic Church *is*, the issue changes from whether I *can* believe to whether I *ought* to believe. For that person, the question of entering her communion becomes a matter of eternal life and death. In its *Dogmatic Constitution on the Church*, the Second Vatican Council states unequivocally that persons who know what the Church is and yet refuse either to enter her or to remain in her communion "could not be saved" (14).

---

5   Vatican II, *Decree on Ecumenism,* section 3 (emphasis added).

6   O'Connor, *op. cit.,* 184.

7   Quoted by Jaki, *op. cit.,* 241.

Father Martin D'Arcy, distinguished twentieth-century English Jesuit theologian, wrote of the summons that comes to one who recognizes the truth of Catholicism:

> As in some rich design, whether of a cathedral or poem or tapestry, the significance of the parts shines out for the first time when the mind of the onlooker coincides with that of the builder or worker, so the evidence for the truth of the Catholic Church gathers itself up into an irresistible converging mass of evidence. But—and this brings out the point of the word "overwhelming"—the truth thus revealed is a way of life, not a theorem, a way of life which stretches out to limitless spaces, full of promise but also full, as divine truth must be, of mystery; and it imposes itself upon the convert as a duty, as something final and imperative. There is no option possible; the yoke must be worn and the old life with its inner reserve of human planning and self-assurance must be surrendered.[8]

Newman's conversion, Jaki writes, was "sparked, nurtured, and decided by the consideration that if there was a divinely established Church, there had to be a divinely imposed obligation to belong to that same One Church."[9]

A "divinely imposed obligation," yes; my wife and I clearly realized that. Another way of stating the obligation to enter the Church, to use Newman's terminology again, is that of "stern necessity." It is presumptuous to speak of his experience and ours in the same breath, but his description fits our experience. When the stern necessity, the divine obligation could no longer be ignored, we had no Catholic friends. We knew nothing of life in a Catholic parish. I, too, was in my forties. We had no savings. I had no employment. All our friends were Episcopalians, as were my parents. All would be greatly saddened, many deeply resentful. Humanly speaking, we had nothing to gain and much to lose.

Yet the knowledge of the "stern necessity" finally dispelled all doubts or misgivings about any of the Church's teaching. The question was no longer "What *could* I believe?" Now it was "What *should* I believe?" And hard on the heels of the latter question comes the next: "What must I *do*?" The answer was clear: "Come to me in full surrender." True, "the gate is narrow and the way is hard, that leads to life" (Mt. 7:14). But the fact that we had no alternative widened that gate and made the road relatively easy for us.

---

8   *Conversion to the Catholic Church*, p. xxi; quoted by John A. O'Brien, ed., *The Road to Damascus: The Spiritual Pilgrimage of Fifteen Converts to Catholicism* (Garden City, NY: Image Books/Doubleday and Co., Inc., 1956), 220f.

9   Stanley L. Jaki, "Introduction," to John Henry Newman, *Anglican Difficulties* (Pinckney, MI: Real View Books, 2004), xxxviii.

Almost all former Protestant clergymen I have known and worked with have suffered, and many continue to suffer, for having chosen the narrow gate that leads to life. All of them lost their means of employment for which they had prepared for years in graduate school. Severe economic hardship was the lot of many for considerable periods of time. They lost all or almost all of their friends to whom they had ministered. Many of them were ostracized by their families. Some of them had to endure years of strain in their marriages because their spouses were adamantly opposed to becoming Catholic.

Yet—again to look to Newman for insight—"never was any sorrow undergone for Christ, but He repaid it a hundredfold."[10] Out of the suffering of these converts the Holy Spirit has drawn deep loyalty to the Mystical Body of Christ and to its vicar, the Holy Father. Several years ago I shared in a gathering of former Episcopal clergy who have come into the Church. I overheard one man say, "My wife and I have gone through hell to get here [into Catholic communion]. We're not about to become Protestant all over again in the Catholic Church. We're with the pope!" These many hundreds of men—and in most cases, their wives—have become Catholics because they came to realize that what the Church teaches about herself is true. Because they already know Christ as Lord and Savior, they have no alternative but to come into His Church.

Some converts go through what G. K. Chesterton calls "the last phase of real doubt." He says the convert wonders "whether the thing that everybody told him was too bad to be tolerable, is not too good to be true."[11] A younger faculty member at Franciscan University of Steubenville told me he went through exactly that phase. He said that for several years after coming into the Church out of a Baptist background, he did not want to explore the faith more deeply. It all seemed too good to be true, and he feared finding out it *was*. Gradually his fear subsided. He began to study and found that indeed it is *not* too good to be true. Now he is a lay leader in his parish.

I have detailed my long years of vainly seeking in non-Catholic traditions a solution to the problem of authority. Finally, there was only one remaining answer: that of Rome. But the papacy? How could I accept that? Then a benefactor I have mentioned previously, Mildred Stone, the bookstore owner, asked me to read Karl Adam's *The Spirit of Catholicism*. Reading and re-reading his explanation of the role of the papacy brought me into that "last phase of real doubt." It made perfect sense. Was it too good to be true? The Holy Spirit soon led me to realize the truth of what the Church teaches about the papacy, so movingly summarized by Adam.

10 Quoted by Jaki, 169.
11 G.K. Chesterton, "The Real Obstacles," *Collected Works*, vol. 3 (San Francisco: Ignatius Press, 1990), 94.

By grace we began living out the truth of what we *should* believe. As quoted earlier, Newman said, "Every one who joins the Church must come in the spirit of a child to a Mother—not to criticize anything, but to accept."

From the beginning of my superficial acquaintance with the Catholic Church, I had regarded her as the implacable foe of intellectual freedom. In an earlier chapter I recalled my reaction to hearing John Courtney Murray, S.J., lecture at Union Theological Seminary in the late 1940s. I actually felt an absurd compassion for that obviously intelligent man who had to subject his thinking to his Church's direction. By sharp contrast, I regarded myself as intellectually free.

My attempt to remain faithful to what God has revealed in Jesus Christ should have alerted me to a basic fact with regard to revelation in general. Late in my pilgrimage I learned from Newman what then seemed obvious: that the concept of revelation itself presupposes an infallible authority to interpret and preserve that revelation. Without that, who could know what God has revealed? And how or by whom would that truth be preserved for all mankind until the end of time? I believed that Christ had established *one* Church to proclaim the Gospel throughout human history. Now it seems logical to conclude that Christ intended His Church to be the custodian of His revelation. To be, in other words, a Church teaching with His authority.

A few years ago I told the late and revered philosopher, Ralph McInerny, that one of my granddaughters had been admitted to his school. His first words were, "Tell her to come and see me." And she did, with her parents, before she enrolled. He helped her plot a course of study, recommending some courses and instructors, warning her against others. I said he showed her a path through the intellectual landmines, the locations of which he knew well.

Later, on reflection, I realized what Professor McInerny had done for my granddaughter is similar to what the Church does for us by her teaching authority. This recalled an observation in G. K. Chesterton's account of why he had become a Catholic. The Church, he wrote, is the only institution that has been thinking about thinking for two thousand years. She carries and shares with us a map of the mind. By far the larger portion of the map "consists of playgrounds and happy hunting-fields, where the mind may have as much liberty as it likes." The Church's map also marks "any number of intellectual battlefields in which the battle is indefinitely open and undecided." But the Church also marks "certain roads as leading nowhere or leading to destruction, to a blank wall, or to a sheer precipice."[12] The Church is the only "corporate mind in the world that is thus on the watch to prevent minds from going wrong."[13]

---

12 G.K. Chesterton, "Why I Am a Catholic," in *Collected Works*, vol. 3 (San Francisco: Ignatius Press, 1990), 129.
13 *Ibid.*, 130.

At the time our family was received into the Church, we sent a letter to several hundred persons across the country and beyond, giving a summary of our reasons. When he received our letter, my Congregational friend and former mentor, Chaplain Smith, sent a gracious reply. In it he asked my prayers for those who like him choose to "remain in the maelstrom of the Spirit."[14]

Two years later he and I visited briefly in Boston, where I had gone to attend an ecumenical workshop. After the usual exchange of news about our families, Herb said quite seriously, "Ray, what's happening to the Catholic Church?" (This was prior to the last session of the Second Vatican Council.) I asked what his question meant. He reminded me that from the beginning of his ministry, he had studied widely, diligently seeking new and better ways of presenting Christianity. He said he persevered because he always knew that if he lost his way, he could "take station" on the Catholic Church and get back on the right track. (In navy parlance, to take station on another vessel is to follow its same course, with the same speed, and in the same position relative to that vessel.) "Is the Catholic Church starting to change?" he asked. "If she loses her way," he added, "we're all lost."

I told him the Catholic Church always remains on the same steady course, despite the storms she encounters. He seemed reassured. After we parted, I thought again of his letter. While he and I were aboard the Nassau, we spent hundreds of hours in earnest conversation about the faith we shared. Never once had he referred to his reliance on the Catholic Church. Now I could understand his willingness to remain in a tumultuous, even hazardous, ecclesial situation. I think many other non-Catholics "take station" on the Catholic Church.

That same day, in the conference I was attending, at dinner I was seated at a table with six Catholic priests and a Russian Orthodox priest, a well-known biblical scholar. Early in the conversation he called for our attention, and asked, "Hey, guys, what's happening to the Catholic Church?" Before any of us could reply, he said, "Always before, the Catholic Church has been *there*. Of course she was wrong [he couldn't resist the dig], but she was *there*. Is she shifting?" Several of us said to him essentially what I had said to Chaplain Smith earlier. Both the tone and the content of his question bespoke anxiety. I said to myself, "Maybe the Orthodox also 'take station' on the Church more than they will admit."

A year later, a well-known Russian Orthodox theologian, John Meyendorff, spent several hours one afternoon at Marquette University with

---

14 "Maelstrom": "a powerful often violent whirlpool sucking in objects within a given radius." The "maelstrom" my friend Herb chose to remain in is not "of the Spirit," but of "reconstructionism." See chapters 14 and 15 for details.

a small group of us doctoral candidates. He had been an official observer at all sessions of Vatican II. He reminisced in a friendly way and answered many questions.

At one point, with rare candor, he reflected on the difference between the work of Catholic theologians and Orthodox theologians. (We all sat up straighter in our seats when he spoke of us as theologians, neophytes that we were.) He said Catholic theologians can freely go about their work. They know that if they move into error, eventually someone will tap them on the shoulder and call them back on course. (How much this is needed today!) In sharp contrast, when an Orthodox theologian sets out to write, he must try to figure out in advance how his thoughts will affect the rest of theology. "And that's not easy," he said. Even more candidly, he said that sometimes (I would guess often) Orthodox theologians solve their problem by not venturing into particular areas.

On television, millions of us have anxiously watched astronauts on a spacewalk performing tasks outside the vessel. Their lives depend on the integrity of the long tether by which they are secured to their ship. Suppose an astronaut decided he wanted to be free in space and not be hampered, so he cut his tether. He would be free, indeed—free to float aimlessly in space until he perished. For Catholics, the magisterium serves a function somewhat like that of the astronaut's tether. It is only by obedience to the magisterium, by preserving our connection with the magisterium, that we can be assured of remaining within the communion of Christ's one true Church, in harmony with the truth Jesus Christ has entrusted it.

The use of one's reason plays an essential role in one's conversion to Catholicism, simply because one is seeking the truth. Some well-meaning Episcopal friends insisted on ascribing my conversion to a purely emotional *need* for authority. Of course I need authority! Like every other human being, I need the God-given authority without which there is only doctrinal chaos. One's emotions are not absent from the search for truth, but they are hardly decisive. As Chesterton pointed out, "A man who finds his way to Catholicism, out of the tangle of modern culture and complexity, must think harder than he has ever thought in his life."[15]

That was my experience. Not only was there a great deal to learn about Catholicism, there was also a great deal to unlearn: blind prejudices absorbed from a Protestant culture and even more prejudices absorbed from five years in four Protestant seminaries.

---

15 Quoted by Joseph Pearce, *Wisdom and Innocence: A Life of G.K. Chesterton* (San Francisco: Ignatius Press, 1996), 417.

Earlier I spoke of my continuing effort as an Anglo-Catholic to find ways of bolstering the faith I professed. It was an effort beset with anxiety. As soon as we entered the communion of the Catholic Church, all that pressure vanished. The Catholic faith did not depend on my efforts to keep it alive. It is solid, assured. Moreover, submission to the Church's magisterium brought a moral certainty that I had not known before about *all* basic Christian doctrines. That certainty was based no longer on my own study of Scripture and antiquity but on the authority of Christ Himself speaking to me through His Church.

Jaki points out that Newman's sermons when he was Anglican "exude search instead of possession, which only one's assimilation with the full sacramental reality of the Church could deliver." Jaki finds Newman's Anglican sermons "full of angst" but his Catholic sermons "replete with the sense of security."[16] I make this reference because of a clear parallel with my sermons as an Episcopalian and those of my Catholic years. I still have copies of some of the former. I smile as I re-read a lengthy five-part series on "Why I Am an Episcopalian." The content is all argument, some of it strained. In sharp contrast, my sermons as a Catholic are essentially proclamation—again, a reflection of confidence and security in the truth of Jesus Christ.

The grace of infallibility granted by Christ to His Church is not assurance that the Church can ever fully articulate what God has revealed in Christ. Rather, it is the guarantee that when the Church's magisterium does speak in His name, she will be protected from error. It is this protection that brings a deep experience of freedom for the Church's children. Error enslaves; only truth liberates. "If you continue in my word, you are my disciples, and you will know the truth, and the truth will make you free" (Jn. 8:31-32). Again, "if the Son makes you free, you will be free indeed" (Jn. 8:36). Furthermore, says Karl Adam, "the authority of the Church secures the liberty of the individual Christ, by its impersonal and extra-personal character." He goes on to explain that the Church's authority sets the believer free from "the spiritual domination and claims to mediatorship of alleged leading personalities." In other words, the magisterium "sets Christ and the believer in direct contact with each other."[17]

Submission to Christ through His Church's authority has not dimmed the Catholic intellect. In twenty centuries the Catholic Church through her members has challenged the mind of every age. No religious tradition has

---

16 Stanly Jaki, *Newman to Converts*, 494. This difference between Newman's Anglican sermons and his Catholic sermons explains "the appeal of Newman's Anglican sermons to modern minds infected with the view … that search for truth is to be preferred to its possession. No wonder. The emotion of an ongoing search, with no tangible terminus in sight, gives the illusion that one never has to surrender to truth."

17 Karl Adam, *The Spirit of Catholicism* (Steubenville, OH: Franciscan University Press, 1996), 24.

shed Gospel light on such a vast number of subjects as have her sons and daughters. The Catholic Church alone has been able to absorb truth she finds in all cultures without losing her way in the process. And all because of the Holy Spirit working through her magisterium.

In the previous chapter I noted my concern about being able to support my family when we came into the Church. I also said there were a couple of other dimensions to my hesitancy in leaving the Episcopal Church. One was the matter of authority, to which I have so frequently referred. I knew that authority requires obedience. I was still an individualistic Protestant at heart, despite my Anglo-Catholic veneer. As a Protestant I had never submitted to Christ except on my own terms; I had no other. The thought of complete obedience to the Catholic Church frightened me. It was one thing to yearn for authority in general. But when I confronted that authority in a visible institution with a visible head, when I contemplated something called a magisterium composed of a specific pope and thousands of specific bishops, it took my breath away. What would be required of me?

The other reason for my hesitancy in embracing the faith has been well analyzed by G. K. Chesterton. He said that non-Catholics think they feel a sort of claustrophobia when they imagine entering the Church. At one point in my pilgrimage I certainly did. How could I contend with all those rules Catholics have to observe? Now I agree with Chesterton that my real problem was not claustrophobia; it was agoraphobia, what Chesterton calls "a fear of something larger than himself and his tribal traditions."[18] Looking from the outside at the vast reaches of the Church's liturgy and spirituality and doctrine and history, I felt overwhelmed. It seemed too much! I had a good grasp of my little Anglo-Catholic world. After all, I was its creator. But Rome! How could I possibly take it all in?

The answer, of course, is that one can never take it all in. At the beginning of the *Dogmatic Constitution on the Church*, Vatican II spoke of the Church as a "mystery." This is a technical theological term. It does not mean something that has yet to be explained. It refers rather to gift and activity of God that in some degree the human mind can understand but never fully comprehend. And yet out of love for Christ and His Church, one does try. Evelyn Waugh explained the process: "Conversion is like stepping across the chimney piece out of a Looking-Glass world, where everything is an absurd caricature, into the real world God made; and then begins the delicious process of exploring it limitlessly."[19]

---

18 G.K. Chesterton, "The Church and Agoraphobia," *op. cit.,* 451.

19 Quoted by Pearce, *op. cit.,* 277.

Though a convert to Christ and His Church is keenly aware of the shortcomings of the denomination from which he came, the Spirit imparts compassion to him whenever he thinks of his former church home. For a sharp contrast, talk about the Church to former Catholics turned some form of Protestant. As noted before, their attitudes are normally reactive. Or consider this. A number of Episcopal friends have reminded me that whereas I became a Catholic, there are a good many Catholic clergy who become Episcopalians. "So," they say, "this matter of conversion is a two-way street." This fact seems to reassure them in their adherence to the Episcopal Church.

I agree there is two-way traffic between the Catholic Church and various denominations. But I insist they are two entirely different kinds of traffic.

Let me illustrate the contrast with a challenge: Show me one Catholic (priest or religious or lay person) who truly understands his faith; who loyally and lovingly accepts all the Church's teaching; who devoutly practices his faith; and yet who through study and reflection comes to the conclusion that not the Catholic Church but the Episcopal Church (or whatever other denomination) is the one true Church of Jesus Christ; who becomes convinced that only in the Episcopal Church (or in whatever denomination) can he find the fullness of Christ's truth and authority; and who decides on that basis *alone* he must become an Episcopalian (or whatever).

No courage is required to issue this challenge. It is immune to an answer. The challenge sums up the motives of converts *to* the Catholic Church. No Catholic ever left the Church with these motives. Ex-Catholics give a host of reasons why they left, but they are always subjective reasons.

Some years ago there appeared a book called *Finding Home*[20] containing the stories of a dozen or so Catholic priests and lay people who became Episcopalians. The word *truth* did not appear in any of the stories. God was referred to obliquely once or twice. All reasons given were subjective. Several persons wrote that they preferred the Episcopal Church to the Catholic Church because they wanted "more ambiguity" (read "wiggle room") in church teachings regarding sexuality.

Though each convert to the Catholic Church travels a different road, simply because each is unique, the roads (that is, the reasons) are essentially the same. Hillaire Belloc once wrote to a friend, "The Catholic Church is central, and therefore approached at every conceivable angle!"[21] Malcolm Muggeridge characterized his conversion as a "sense of homecoming, of picking up the threads of a lost life, of responding to a bell that has long been ringing [so

---

20 Christopher L. Webber, ed., *Finding Home: Stories of Roman Catholics Entering the Episcopal Church* (Cambridge, MA: Cowley Publications, 1997).
21 Quoted by Pearce, *Wisdom and Innocence*, 272.

true of my adult years before conversion], of finding a place at a table that has long been left vacant."[22]

I look back on my years in the Episcopal Church with fondness and appreciation. The Holy Spirit enriched our lives deeply in those fourteen years. The sonorous, Elizabethan beauty of the liturgy, the dignity of the worship, the 1940 Hymnal that contained many ancient and pre-Reformation Catholic hymns (and which I still use in the Liturgy of the Hours), the emphasis on the pastoral ministry of the clergy—these parts of that heritage remain dear to us.

Shortly after we entered the Church, a friend and former parishioner wrote to ask what I would say about the services of Holy Communion I had offered in my years as an Episcopal priest. Would I, she asked, consider all that of no benefit? I wrote and assured her that Jesus Christ was present to us when we celebrated Holy Communion. It is an undeniable fact, I said, of my—and your—experience. He was present to us because of our faith in Him and our yearning to receive Him. I went on to say that because I did not have Catholic orders, I was not empowered to be the channel by which He would make Himself fully present as He intends. (In Catholic terms, Jesus was present because of our faith—*ex opere operantis*—and not because of the objective efficacy of a Catholic sacrament—*ex opere operato*.)

Anglicans like to refer to their church as a "bridge church" that offers the best of Protestantism and the best of Catholicism, without the errors of each. Long before I realized I was being led to Rome, I sometimes teased my fellow clergy about our being in a bridge church. No one lives on a bridge, I insisted. A bridge is for getting from point A to point B.

In my early Catholic days I was a bit ambivalent about the Anglo-Catholic phase of my pilgrimage. On the one hand, I am grateful for having been led from a "low-church" position to Anglo-Catholicism. I learned to love (my interpretation of) Catholicism and eventually to embrace authentic Catholicism. On the other hand, that involvement in Anglo-Catholicism took me off on a tangent that kept me away from Rome for a time, perhaps years. But it was all part of God's plan.

This prayer of thanksgiving by a convert well expresses what has been in our hearts and minds for almost fifty years.

> For giving me desire,
> An eager thirst, a burning ardent fire,
> A virgin infant flame,
> A love with which into the world I came,
> An inward hidden heavenly love

---

22   Joseph Pearce, *Literary Converts* (San Francisco: Ignatius Press, 1999), 400f.

Which in my soul doth work and move,
And ever ever me inflame
With restless longing, heavenly avarice
That never could be satisfied,
That did incessantly a paradise
Unknown suggest, and something undescribed
Discern, and bear me to it; be
Thy name forever praised by me.[23]

23 Clare Booth Luce, "Under the Fig Tree," in O'Brien, *op. cit.*, p. 197.

CHAPTER FIFTEEN

RETROSPECT:
TERRAINS TRAVERSED (1)

N o one who puts his hand to the plow and looks back is fit for the kingdom of God" (Lk. 9:62). The first chapter recalls an event in which as a ploughboy I learned the literal truth of our Lord's admonition. Yet in evaluating one's pilgrimage, looking back can help. It can give better perspective on life within the communion of the Church.

I have noted that Catholic converts regard their former church homes with compassion and appreciation. Yet only from within Catholic communion can they truly understand the traditions out of which they were led. My retrospection necessarily focuses not only on my Protestant and Anglican roots but also on Eastern Orthodoxy. Though I never shared in the communion of a separated Eastern Church, for several years as an outsider I looked hard, and indeed longingly, at what we call the Orthodox tradition.

This backward glance must first recall the context: what the Catholic Church teaches about the non-Catholic traditions. Then it will unfold a paradigm herein designated as *reconstructionism*.

The context

Through the centuries, various communities have separated themselves from Catholic communion. People brought up in these traditions are not guilty of "the sin of separation." All "who believe in Christ and have been truly baptized are in communion with the Catholic Church even though this communion is imperfect." The Church regards them "with respect and affection as brothers." Indeed, the Church speaks of them as "her sons."[1]

---

1 Vatican II, *Decree on Ecumenism*, 3, 4.

Yet Baptism is "only a beginning" for sharing in "fullness of life in Christ." One acquires fullness of life in Christ by accepting "a complete profession of faith," being incorporated into "the system of salvation" willed by Christ, and "complete ingrafting in eucharistic communion."[2] Blessed John Henry Newman gave this admonition to non-Catholics: "When He gives grace to those outside the Church, it is not to keep them outside but to bring them into it. As He gave grace to Abraham or to Cornelius, not to keep them where they were, but to bring them on where they were not."[3]

The Church recognizes that some of the elements of her life can and do exist outside her visible boundaries: Sacred Scripture, "the life of grace," the theological virtues plus other gifts of the Holy Spirit, and "visible elements." But, the Council reminds us, all these gifts "come from Christ and lead back to Christ" because they "belong by right to the one Church of Christ." The Holy Spirit uses non-Catholic traditions "as means of salvation which derive their efficacy from the very fullness of grace and truth entrusted to the Church." Yet our separated brethren as individuals and as communities "are not blessed with that unity which Jesus Christ wished to bestow" on those who constitute his Mystical Body. They are not blessed with the fullness of Christ's gifts. Why? Because "it is only through Christ's Catholic Church . . . that the fullness of the means of salvation can be obtained."[4]

With regard to the separated Eastern Churches, we should define the term commonly used. There is no such entity as "Eastern Orthodoxy." This is a generic term used to designate the more than a dozen independent national ethnic churches that we commonly call "Orthodox." Furthermore, the term "Eastern Orthodoxy" does not comprehend all the separated Eastern Churches. There are more than thirty million Christians in the East who are separated from Rome but are not part of "Eastern Orthodoxy."

The Second Vatican Council acknowledged that the separated Eastern Churches have retained the apostolic succession and therefore have a valid Eucharist.[5] In fact, therefore, "through the celebration of the Holy Eucharist in each of these Churches, the Church of God is built up and grows in stature."[6] This fact differentiates the situation of the separated Eastern Churches from that of all other non-Catholic traditions.

Aidan Nichols points out that these Eastern Churches *are* in schism from the one true Church because they are not in communion with Rome. But because they have preserved the succession of bishops and a valid Eucharist,

---

2   *Ibid.*, 22.
3   Quoted by Stanley, Jaki, *Newman to Converts,* 176.
4   *Decree on Ecumenism,* 3.
5   Vatican II, *Dogmatic Constitution on the Church,* 15.
6   *Decree on Ecumenism, op. cit.,* 15.

they must not be in total schism. He therefore argues that we should regard them as being in partial schism.[7]

This brief glance at the Church's teaching regarding the separated Eastern Churches concludes with two reminders from the Congregation for the Doctrine of the Faith (CDF). The first, issued in 1992, makes this distinction vis-à-vis communion with Peter's successors:

> Since, however, communion with the universal Church, represent-ed by Peter's successor, is not an external complement to the par-ticular Church, but one of its internal constituents, the situation of those venerable Christian communities [the separated Eastern Churches] also means that their existence as particular Churches is *wounded*.[8]

The second specifies how the term "sister Churches" is properly to be used.

In recent decades, the term *sister Churches* has been used by prelates of separated Eastern Churches designated as "Eastern Orthodox" and by popes Paul VI and John Paul II to refer to the relation of those churches and the Catholic Church. At first glance the term implies equality between those separated churches, taken as a whole, and the Catholic Church. It implies that the separated Eastern Churches collectively called "Eastern Orthodox" have ecclesial reality equal to that of the Catholic Church. This implication contradicts what the Catholic Church teaches about herself.

On June 30, 2000, the CDF issued a document titled "Note on the Expression 'Sister Churches.'" The note specifies that it is permissible to speak of a particular Catholic diocese as *sister* to an Eastern Orthodox diocese. It is never permissible to refer to the Catholic Church herself as sister to a particular church or group of particular churches: "The one, holy, catholic and apostolic Universal Church is not sister but *mother* of all the particular Churches" (sec. 10). "In fact, there is but a single Church"—the Catholic Church (sec. 11).

This, then, is the magisterial context for retrospection on terrains traversed in my (our) pilgrimage. The other context is a fundamental pattern in all non-Catholic Christian traditions.

The paradigm: Reconstructionism

When anyone leaves his family home (the Catholic Church), he has no alternative but to build a home of his own. Naturally he will build according

---

7 Aidan Nichols, O.P., *Rome and the Eastern Churches: A Study in Schism* (Collegeville, MN: Liturgical Press, 1992), 25.

8 CDF, *Letter to The Bishops of the Catholic Church on Some Aspects of the Church Understood as Commu-nion*, 17.

to his own specifications of what a church should be. That is what we call reconstructionism. Every non-Catholic Christian tradition—every tradition not in communion with Rome—is a reconstruction. No matter how much of Catholicism (as in the separated Eastern Churches) or how little (as in Protestantism and Anglicanism) is incorporated into Christian religions, they are all reconstructions. A reconstruction not only serves as a house to live in, it also constitutes a rationalization for having broken with the Catholic Church.

"For no other foundation can anyone lay than that which is laid, which is Jesus Christ" (1 Cor. 3:11). Every reconstructionist would agree with this verse. Every one claims he is building only on Jesus Christ. But Jesus Christ Himself laid a specific foundation that is to endure to the end of time. "And I tell you, you are Peter, and on this rock I will build my church, and the power of death will not prevail against it. I will give you the keys of the kingdom of heaven, and whatever you bind on earth will be bound in heaven, and whatever you loose on earth will be loosed in heaven" (Mt. 16:18–19).

According to Newman, it is quite clear that "the Christianity of history is not Protestantism." This is shown by Protestantism's determination to dispense with "historical Christianity altogether" and to form "a Christianity from the Bible alone."[9] Newman could have added "or from arbitrarily chosen centuries of the Church's history."

His observation applies to reconstructionism, which is the attempt to put some—or almost all—of church history aside in favor of an alternative ecclesiology. Protestants seek to put aside nineteen centuries. Anglicans want to ignore fifteen centuries. Separated Eastern Churches choose to dispense with twelve centuries. To state the fact differently, Jesus promised to lead His Church into all truth (Jn. 16:13). Protestants believe Jesus led His Church into all truth until AD 100. Anglicans believe Jesus led His Church into all truth until 451. The separated Eastern Churches believe Jesus led His Church into all truth until 787.

My wife's and my pilgrimage was a series of attempts to find a home in three different reconstructions. Like all ecclesial reconstructions, they turned out to be houses built on sand, because they were not built on the rock of Peter (Mt. 7:24–27).

As we have just noted, all non-Catholic reconstructions postulate a former "golden age" of the Church. History records countless movements that began with the notion that in a previous age life was at its best. Driven by the belief that things were so much better then, they try to recreate or return to that previous period. The movements always fail. It is impossible to turn back the calendar, to re-create a period or situation of the past.

---

9   John Henry Newman, foreword to *Essay on the Development of Christian Doctrine* by Ian Ker (Notre Dame, IN: University of Notre Dame Press, 1989), 7.

The "golden age" for Christian reconstructionists is the "primitive" Church or "primitive" Christianity. Reconstructionists postulate different time-frames for this allegedly golden age of the Church. For Protestants, it is the Church's first century; for Anglicans, the first five centuries; for separated Easterners, the first eight centuries. This pursuit of an historical will-o-the-wisp, Hugh Ross Williamson tells us, is sometimes spoken of as the "hunt-the-acorn" theory: "When you see a mighty oak, you do not joy in its strength and luxuriant development." Instead, "you start to search for an acorn compatible with that from which it grew and say: 'This is what it *ought* to be like.'"[10]

Newman's eloquent summary of the necessity of development of doctrine refutes the "primitive" mentality with regard to the Church. It deserves to be heard in some fullness.

> It is indeed sometimes said that the stream is clearest near the spring. [Anglican apologists often made this claim.] Whatever use may fairly be made of this image, it does not apply to the history of a philosophy or belief, which on the contrary is more equable, and purer, and stronger, when its bed has become deep, and broad, and full. It necessarily rises out of an existing state of things, and for a time savours of the soil. Its vital element needs disengaging from what is foreign and temporary, and is employed in efforts after freedom which become more vigorous and hopeful as its years increase. Its beginnings are no measure of its capabilities, nor of its scope. At first no one knows what it is, or what it is worth. It remains perhaps for a time quiescent; it tries, as it were, its limbs, and proves the ground under it, and feels its way. From time to time it makes essays which fail, and are in consequence abandoned. It seems in suspense which way to go; it wavers, and at length strikes out in one definite direction. In time it enters upon strange territory; points of controversy alter their bearing; parties rise and fall around it; dangers and hopes appear in new relations; and old principles reappear under new forms. It changes with them in order to remain the same. In a higher world it is otherwise, but here below to live is to change, and to be perfect is to have changed often.[11]

In a more jocular vein, one could recall the wag's claim that the Mississippi River arose from a leaky faucet in northern Minnesota. If that were true, the faucet could give no hint of what the mighty Mississippi becomes.

---

10 Quoted by Joseph Pearce, *Literary Converts*, 353.
11 Newman, *Essay, op. cit.,* 40.

Development of doctrine is to the Church as growth in understanding the faith is to the individual. The reconstructionist groups claim, "We have the faith of the first century (or the faith of the first five or the first eight centuries)." All of them add, "And we have not changed." Earlier we asked, what should we say to the person who proudly announces, "I have the same faith, the same understanding of the faith, we had when we were a year old" or "five years old" or "eight years old"? And not only says it but boasts about it. What would we call this attitude? A case of arrested development. What would we say to this person? "Grow up!"

And so the essence of reconstructionism is discontinuity, a total opposite of Catholic continuity. Stanley Jaki argues persuasively that what he calls the "gist" of Catholicism is continuity. The Catholic Church is the Mystical Body of Christ, which is Christ's supernatural presence on earth. The Church, therefore, is in union with Him who, the Book of Hebrews tells us, is the same yesterday, today, and forever (13:8). The Incarnation, says Jaki, is "the continuity of the eternal Word in a human form, a continuity to last through eternity." The Church is a divinely appointed means for "communicating that continuity to mere men."[12]

Reconstructionism rationalizes its break with Rome by redefining *church* in new terms. The Protestant traditions have rejected any thought of a visible, universal church. Their definitions reduce the church to an invisible institution whose real members are known only to God. The Lutheran Augsburg Confession states that the church is "the congregation of saints, in which the gospel is rightly taught and the sacraments are rightly administered." But who decides what *are* the sacraments? And who decides what is *right* teaching and *right* administration of the sacraments? Luther, of course, and those who follow his teaching.

The Calvinist Heidelberg Catechism asks in question 54, "What believest thou concerning the 'holy catholic church' of Christ?" The answer is that

> the Son of God (a) from the beginning to the end of the world, (b) gathers, defends and preserves (c) to himself by his Spirit and world, (d) out of the whole human race, (e) a church chosen to everlasting life, (f) agreeing in true faith; (g) and that I am and forever shall remain, (h) a living member thereof.

Agreeing in the "true faith," of course, means the Reformed faith. But what *is* that "true faith"? And who determines whether one actually holds that faith?

---

12   Sanley Jaki, *The Gist of Catholicism* (Pinckney, MI: Real View Books, 2007), 17.

Article 39 of the Church of England's *Thirty-Nine-Articles* gives us this definition: "The visible Church of Christ is a congregation of faithful men, in which the pure Word of God is preached, and the sacraments be duly ministered according to Christ's ordinance, in all those things that of necessity are requisite to the same." (Anglo-Catholics in my Episcopal years called the *Articles* "the 40 stripes save one.") Though the word *visible* is used, this is simply another version of the standard Protestant doctrine of an "invisible" church. Like other Protestant definitions, this one is loaded with question-begging phrases: "faithful men," "pure Word of God," "duly ministered," "according to Christ's ordinance," "those things that of necessity are requisite."

The separated Eastern Churches believe the universal church is a federation of ethnic churches, each independent of all the others. This is true both of the dozen or so Churches generically termed "Eastern Orthodox" and of the other separated Eastern Churches. Their federation of "Eastern Orthodox Churches" has no overall structure of authority (more about this key issue in the next chapter); no way for the individual churches to speak in common. In its previously quoted *Some Aspects of the Church Understood As Communion* (sec. 8), the CDF sums up the separated Easterners' ecclesiology: "Thus it is asserted that every particular Church [for most of the Easterners this means "national Church"] is a subject complete in itself, and that the universal Church is the result of a *reciprocal recognition* on the part of the particular Churches." This means in effect that "universal Church" is a concept, not an entity. The CDF's note continues: "This ecclesiological unilateralism . . . impoverishes not only the concept of the universal Church but also that of the particular Church."

Karl Adam points out another characteristic of what we're calling reconstructionism. He reminds us "all non-Catholic bodies originate, not in unconditional affirmation, but in denial and negation, in subtraction and in subjective selection."[13] When reconstructionists focus on a particular "golden age" of the Church, they retain only portions of the Church's tradition of those centuries. Protestants appeal to a New Testament that did not exist in the first century. At that time there was only a large group of documents (a group many times the size of the eventual canon) circulating among the churches. The Church's sifting process was not completed until the late fourth century. But in the first century there was a papacy, there was apostolic succession, there were seven sacraments; these things Protestants ignore. Much the same can be said about Anglicans, who claim to preserve the faith of the first five centuries of the Church.

---

13 Karl Adam, *The Spirit of Catholicism*, 10.

Or take the case of the separated Eastern Churches. We have noted they retain much of the Catholic tradition: a valid episcopate and therefore valid sacraments and much of the Church's doctrine. But in their apologetic (to be discussed in the next chapter), the separated Eastern Churches choose to ignore the power of the papacy given it by Christ. Cut off from Rome, those churches have given up celibacy for their clergy (except for the bishops). In moral matters they have given up the Church's perpetual rule against artificial contraception. They claim to uphold the indissolubility of marriage, yet they allow a person married and divorced three times to retain communion in their churches. Though individual prelates and theologians hold pro-life positions, the separated Easterners have no united stand against abortion.

Consider the innovations of reconstructionism. The first-century Church knew nothing of *sola scriptura*, nothing of an "invisible" Church composed of true believers, nothing of a non-sacramental ministry, nothing of a purely memorial meal called the Lord's Supper, nothing of private interpretation of Scripture. Indeed, as we have noted, the first-century Church knew nothing of the New Testament we have today. The fifth-century Church knew nothing of a national church headed by a sovereign (as in the case of Anglicanism); nothing (again) of the many innovations of Protestantism that the Church of England adopted at the Reformation. The eighth-century Church knew nothing of independent national ethnic churches, nothing of the claim that ecumenical councils themselves are the Church's final authority.

Prelates and scholars of the separated Eastern Churches display an astonishing misunderstanding of history and the papacy. They claim, despite the clear evidence, that not until the fourth century or later did the pope have universal jurisdiction. Papal authority, they say, developed primarily because of the prestige of the city of Rome. It is true, says Fouyas, that in the fourth century the bishops of Rome were sound in the faith. And why? Because they were simply lucky. In all the doctrinal disputes, they just happened to pick the winning side. Therefore—and for no other reason—they were held in unparalleled regard by the rest of the Church.[14] This explanation chooses to ignore the fact that the winning side won only because it was the papal side.

The separated Easterners claim that final authority in the Church rests with the entire episcopate, with no significant role for the bishop of Rome. In their eyes, he is only *primus inter pares* (first among equals). (In the centuries to which the Easterners appeal, the pope was never so regarded.)

A non-Catholic scholar has summarized what the first seven ecumenical councils, to which the Easterners appeal, taught about the divinely given power of the papacy.

---

14 Methodios Fouyas, *Orthodoxy, Roman Catholicism and Anglicanism* (London: Oxford University Press, 1972), 134.

(1) The primacy of the Bishop of Rome. (2) That the Bishop of Rome had that primacy because he was the successor of Saint Peter. (3) That Christ had given headship of the Church to Peter; therefore it was of divine right. (4) That that headship was passed on and was inherited by his successors in the See of Peter. Therefore the Bishops of Rome held their headship de jure divino [by divine right]. (5) The documents of the Councils of Ephesus [431] and Chalcedon [451] [to mention no others] show that these Eastern councils, by promulgating the sentence of Pope Celestine on Nestorius, and the exposition of the Catholic faith set forth in the Tome of Pope Leo the Great, acknowledged the power and right of the Roman Bishop to declare authoritatively to the universal Church what was the Catholic faith."[15]

The ultimate result of all reconstructionism is summarized by Chesterton. He wrote about what happened to the Church of England when Henry VIII broke communion with Rome. Chesterton's insight applies as well to all of Protestantism and even (to a much lesser extent) to the separated Eastern Churches. At the moment when the Church of England "lost touch with Rome, it changed instantly and internally, from top to bottom, in its very substance and the stuff of which it was made. It changed in substance; it did not necessarily change in form or features or externals. It might do the same things, but it could not be the same thing. It might go on saying the same things; but it was not the same thing that was saying them." Chesterton added that some Anglicans call this change (which is continuous) "progress." This, he said, is like saying that "a corpse crawling with worms has an increased vitality; or that a snow-man, slowly turning into a puddle, is purifying itself of its accretions."[16]

One more characteristic of Protestant and Anglican reconstructionism is the sharp contrast between their attitude toward theology and the attitude of the Catholic Church. For Protestants and Anglicans, the church is primarily a vehicle for proclaiming the Gospel. Reformation theologians define the Church in terms of what it proclaims. For them, the "Mystical Body of Christ" is essentially a metaphor. A seminary classmate of mine studied for two years in Europe under the world's then most famous Protestant theologian. My friend told me that the theologian seldom went to church when he was not preaching.

For the Catholic, the Church is herself an essential part of the Gospel. The Mystical Body of Christ is the very life of a Catholic. In Newman's piquant

---

15 E. F. Scott, *The Eastern Churches and the Papacy*, 352; quoted by Selden Peabody Delany, *Why Rome* (New York: The Dial Press, 1930), 191.
16 G.K. Chesterton, *Collected Works*, vol. 3; "The Surrender Upon Sex" (San Francisco: Ignatius Press, 1990), 367f.

terms, Anglican theology (and all Protestant theology, we must add) regards the truth as "entirely objective and detached, . . . sole and unapproachable, as on the Cross or at the Resurrection, with the Church close by, but in the background." The theology of Rome, on the other hand, lies " hidden in the bosom of the Church, clinging to and . . . lost in her embrace." In other words, it is a contrast between Calvary and the Madonna and her child.[17]

---

17   John Henry Newman, *Apologia Pro Vita Sua,* ed. David J. DeLaura (New York: W.W. Norton and Co., 1968), 95.

CHAPTER SIXTEEN

RETROSPECT: TERRAINS TRAVERSED (2)

Protestant reconstructionism

To justify its "denial and negation," its "subtraction and selection" (Karl Adam) in breaking with the Catholic Church, every reconstruction appeals to an authority that is unworkable. Luther (and all Protestants after him) appealed to Scripture alone. But, we must ask, Scripture as interpreted by whom?

Years ago I attended a lecture on Luther given by the late Jaroslav Pelikan, the leading Lutheran scholar of his time. He brought up the issue of subjectivity. Luther, he said, has often been accused of relying entirely on his own interpretation of Scripture. This is not true, Dr. Pelikan said. Luther was simply reporting what God's Word actually means. Furthermore, Luther was willing to change his interpretation of Scripture in the light of a better one. At this point I asked myself, "And who would decide what would be 'a better one'?" I knew the answer: Luther himself. For Luther, the final authority on what Scripture means would always be Luther.

In the question period I asked two questions. Would Dr. Pelikan agree that the heart of Luther's message was his doctrine of justification by faith through grace? Unhesitatingly came the answer, "Yes." Next, was there any instance in which Luther changed that teaching in the light of another and "better" interpretation? Dr. Pelikan paused for three or four seconds, then replied, "No." And thereby he answered my third and unasked question, "Then how can you say that Luther was not relying simply on his own interpretation of Scripture?" In practice, Luther's *sola scriptura* ("scripture alone") was in fact *scriptura secundum Lutherum solum* ("scripture according to Luther alone"). And so it is with all "reformers."

Protestant and Anglican reconstructionists' concept of "reform" is quite different from that of orthodox Catholic reformers. The latter see themselves called by the Spirit to help open the Church to renewed life by recalling her to her true nature. Non-Catholic "reformers" begin by rejecting the communities out of which they arose and starting new communities. Early in his career, Martin Luther stated that, for him, reform was revolution. He would build a new church from the ground up. Writing to a former professor in May 1518, he declared: "My firm belief is that the reform is impossible unless the ecclesiastical laws, the papal regulations, scholastic theology, philosophy and logic as they presently exist are thoroughly uprooted . . . a resolution from which neither your authority, though it is certainly of the greatest weight for me, nor that of any others, can turn me aside." Luther's revolutionary spirit is summed up in the last pamphlet he wrote. These are his words about the pope and cardinals:

> Let them hold a council on the gallows or in Hell with all the demons, so that thunder and lightning would strike them, Hell-fire burn them, the plague, syphilis, epilepsy, scurvy, leprosy, carbuncles and all manner of disease attack them. Whenever I say "Hallowed be Thy Name" I am forced to add "Cursed, damned, dishonored be the name of the Pope."[1]

Yet, tragically, the acts of rejection by non-Catholic "reformers" unleash within their own ranks a virus of perpetual rejection. Just as the reformers (Protestant and Anglican)

> acted against the Catholic Church, so the community founded by them was, in turn, treated by its own children in the like manner. The want of reverence towards father and mother (for such is the Church to us in a spiritual relation) is transmitted from generation to generation; and the wicked spirit, that first raised the son against his father, goes out of the son as soon as he becomes a parent, and in turn, goads his offspring on to wreak bloody vengeance upon him.[2]

Evangelicals, and especially fundamentalists, rely, as they say, on "the pure Word of God." For them, *tradition* is an almost obscene word when

---

1 Quoted by Warren Carroll, *Instaurare*, April, 2007, 7. At the end of the quote, Dr. Carroll asks rhetorically, "Are these the words of a reformer who loves the Church of Christ and wants to purify it and make it better?"

2 Johann Adam Mohler, *Symbolism: Exposition of the Doctrinal Differences Between Catholic and Protestants As Evidenced By Their Symbolical Writing*, trans. James Burton Robertson (New York: The Crossroad Publishing Company, 1997), 437.

used in connection with the Bible. My wife once spoke about Scripture with a fundamentalist friend. Her intention was to help the friend understand the role of tradition with regard to Scripture. She asked, "Why is that you and I both love the Lord, we both try to let the Spirit guide us, and yet we get such different interpretations of certain key passages?" Her friend promptly replied, "Because you don't read it right. If you would put aside all those man-made traditions you get in your church and take just the pure Word of God, you would see what it means." Then she proceeded to give her interpretation of the "pure Word." It turned out to be exactly what the preachers of her denomination held.

For determining Christian truth, *sola scriptura* has never been a workable principle. Indeed, those who most vehemently espouse it have never used it. *Some* tradition inevitably will guide anyone's interpretation of Scripture or any other writing.[3] Under the banner of *sola scriptura* almost thirty-five thousand separate denominations have been formed. The number of new denominations increases by several hundred each year. In none of those proliferating denominations is there an authority that can separate truth from error. When disagreements arise within a denomination, the only solution is to split and reconstruct—again.

Anglican reconstructionism

Though Vatican II's *Decree on Ecumenism* distinguishes Anglicanism from the other Reformation traditions, it is still a distinctly Protestant tradition. It, too, appeals to Scripture as final authority. Starting with Scripture, Anglicanism makes three gratuitous assumptions. The first is that the earliest Christians best understood Scripture because of their nearness to its writing. The second assumption is that what Anglican theologians have decided the Church was in the beginning must be the pattern for all time. The third assumption is that the first five centuries of the Church's history are normative.

In his classic study, *The Spirit of Anglicanism*, H. R. McAdoo insists that setting the limits of the first five centuries is not at all arbitrary. Rather, "this delimiting of dates" is "controlled by the reference back to Scripture and to the period after the apostles."[4] The reasoning is circular. It goes like this: Fixing limits at the close of five centuries is *not* arbitrary because it follows from the reference to Scripture and the early Church. But that reference itself

---

3   In an ecumenical dialogue between Catholic and Southern Baptist representatives, one of the Baptist theologians spoke to me about the issue of tradition with this anecdote. An elderly Southern Baptist preacher snorted in disgust when someone used the word "tradition" in his presence. "Nonsense! We Baptists don't have any traditions!" Then after a pause he added thoughtfully, "We only have certain ways of doing things."

4   New York: Charles Scribner's Sons, 1965, 335.

is arbitrary. Again, part of the reason for the appeal to antiquity is "to discover what the Church of the first centuries was like."[5] In other words, appeal to a criterion to discover what the criterion *is*.

McAdoo quotes from a number of founding fathers of Anglicanism of the sixteenth to the eighteenth centuries regarding an underlying purpose of their method. The appeal to antiquity was an attempt to establish the "identity of [Anglican] doctrine with the early period." Or again, "to show the resemblance between it [the Church of the first five centuries] and the contemporary [Anglican] Church."[6]

Even stronger is McAdoo's statement that "the *raison d'etre* of the use of antiquity as a criterion" was to show "the substantial agreement between the contemporary [Anglican] church and the Church of the first five centuries on what constituted fundamentals."[7] Thus, continuity with the early Church was a deep concern of classical Anglican theologians. In fact, "the appeal to antiquity had as its object to establish this continuity between the teaching and order of the contemporary [Anglican] Church and those of the early Church."[8] Again, this reasoning is circular. It amounts simply to this: Postulate a hypothetical authority, then appeal to it to justify one's present position which in fact is based on that hypothetical authority.

Serious thought about historic Anglicanism raises many questions. The basic flaw in this theological method is the arbitrary assignment of ultimate authority to the first five centuries. Of the many conflicting traditions of those centuries, which will an Anglican theologian choose? And by what criterion or criteria? Who is to decide what the selected traditions have to say about Scripture? And in the light of that commentary, what does Scripture really *mean*? And like all non-Catholic traditions, Anglicanism has no final authority to distinguish between the conflicting (often contradictory) opinions of its scholars and theologians.

Like all Protestant reconstructions, Anglicanism has given rise to many new denominations. Yet it is unique among the ecclesiastical reconstructions in two respects.

The first is this. Anglican apologists, especially those of a high-church persuasion, argue for the continuity of the Church of England with its pre-Reformation history. They claim their church was not the creation of an individual, like Luther or Calvin. The so-called English Reformation, they say, was in fact not a theological but a political series of events. And thereby

5   *Ibid.,* 316.
6   *Loc. cit.*
7   *Loc. cit.,* 345.
8   *Loc. cit.*

they admit, however unwillingly, that the Church of England is a creation of the state. No other denomination was so begun. Since Henry VIII broke with Rome, the Church of England has always been under the ultimate control of the state.

The Church of England and its scattered branches is also unique in this regard. It is the only reconstruction that has harbored and retained within its bounds a further reconstruction of itself. Every denomination has given birth to new reconstructions, but, apart from Anglicanism, those reconstructions ordinarily take the form of new denominations. Yet Anglicanism still contains, more or less loosely, the Anglo-Catholic reconstruction of itself.

Since by virtue of the "branch theory" Anglicans hold that their church is truly "Catholic," they believe their clergy have valid Catholic orders like those of Rome and Eastern Orthodoxy. They claim that Anglicanism offers seven sacraments, not just the two (Baptism and the Lord's Supper) affirmed in the Book of Common Prayer.

In retrospect, I wonder at the fact that in my Anglo-Catholic years I never questioned the word *branch* in "branch theory." Branch of what? If the Catholic Church is "one," how can there be three separate divisions, each of which is equally Catholic? If there are presently three branches of the Catholic Church, where is the trunk? Like Catholics, Anglicans affirm the Nicene Creed's declaration of "one, holy, Catholic, and apostolic Church." "One" Church composed of three separate "branches"? It is nonsense to speak of one kingdom composed of three separate, totally autonomous kingdoms.

Earlier we referred to the matter of Anglican orders. They were declared "utterly null and void" in 1896 by Leo XIII in his encyclical *Apostolicae curae* because of defect of intention. The Anglican archbishops of Canterbury and York jointly made their personal response to Leo's encyclical in 1897. They agreed that defect of intention would have invalidated Anglican orders. But, they declared, Anglican bishops had always intended to ordain priests to offer the Holy Sacrifice. The archbishops neglected to mention what the Anglican bishops had done sixty years earlier. In the 1830s, almost the entire Anglican hierarchy condemned John Henry Newman and his fellow Tractarians for insisting that Anglican bishops *had* ordained their clergy to offer the Holy Sacrifice. (Incidentally, the Church's teaching about Anglican orders was reaffirmed in 1998.)[9]

As I gradually embraced the Anglo-Catholic position, I thought of Newman as the outstanding exponent of Anglo-Catholicism. His two-volume *Via Media* I regarded as the bible of the movement. I treated it like many

9   Cardinal Joseph Ratzinger, for the Congregation for the Doctrine of the Faith, "Commentary on the Concluding Formula of the *Professio Fidei*" (John Paul II, *Ad Tuendam Fidem*, 1998), section 11.

treat *the* Bible: that is, I appealed to *Via Media*, relied on it, but never read it carefully. Like other Anglo-Catholics, I deplored his having succumbed to the lure of Rome. Only after entering the Catholic Church did I look more carefully at *Via Media*. I discovered that in the introduction he admitted that what he espoused was a theory that had never been tried but that he thought was valid. And all my Anglo-Catholic years I thought he (and I and others who followed his Anglican teaching) were the ones who rightly understood what the Anglican Church essentially *is*.

After becoming a Catholic, Newman wrote to an unidentified correspondent about the subjectivity of Anglo-Catholicism. He said that while Anglo-Catholics do hold certain points of doctrine in common with Roman Catholics, they hold them, as he said, "on their own judgment." They do not hold them because the Church of England teaches them; indeed, it does not teach them.[10]

In another letter, Newman detailed beliefs held by Edward Pusey and John Keble, the two leading Anglo-Catholics after Newman's departure. He showed how eclectic were the systems they had devised. Especially in Keble's case, Newman challenged anyone to find some of Keble's cherished beliefs in any of Keble's Anglican predecessors, even back to the time of the English Reformation. Toward the end of my pilgrimage, I realized Newman's charge against Keble's beliefs held true against some of my own. As mentioned earlier, I finally saw myself as Protestant desperately trying to use Catholic building blocks to assemble my own version of Anglo-Catholicism.

I see myself clearly in Newman's reflection on his Anglo-Catholic days after his conversion. He wrote one correspondent that "only when the English Church was not English"—that is, when he could innovate upon her received customs—did he find real joy in being Anglican. He gave as an example of his innovations introducing early communion services at Saint Mary the Virgin in Oxford when he was vicar there.[11]

As noted earlier, one sometimes hears of a woman who married a man to reform him. (Seldom does one hear of the converse). It is a self-centered motivation and a disastrous basis for marriage. I must admit there is an analogy here to my love affair with the Episcopal Church. Originally I loved her for what I thought she was. But as my Anglo-Catholicism unfolded, I more and more loved her for what I thought I—and others like me—could make of her.

A distinguished convert expressed the matter succinctly. Walter Hooper, private secretary and literary executor and biographer of C.S. Lewis, reflected

---

10 Quoted by Jaki, *Newman to Converts*, 383.
11 *Ibid.*, 49.

on his journey from Anglicanism to the Catholic Church: "I had been trying to save the Anglican Church for twenty years [as an Anglo-Catholic]. Then I decided I had to let the Catholic Church save me."[12] This mission of saving the Anglican Church from itself lies at the heart of the Anglo-Catholic movement.

Reflecting on his Anglican years, G.K. Chesterton wrote that "our whole position was a common contradiction; since we were always arguing that England had suffered in a thousand ways from being Protestant, and yet, at the same time, arguing that she had remained Catholic." Once he entered the Church, Chesterton could see that this was "the attempt to remedy a mistake without admitting it."[13]

Newman describes many symptoms of the fact that Anglo-Catholicism is like a foreign object in the body of the Anglican tradition. Writing to a convert, Newman said that "the direction of their [Anglo-Catholics'] holy feelings, views and works, is not *towards* that Church, but *away from* it" whereas in the Catholic Church the saints grow ever more strongly attached to the Church.[14] This was also my experience. My growing devotion to the Blessed Virgin, going to confession, invoking the saints, focusing on Holy Communion as a Sacrifice, all led me more and more away from the Episcopal Church. They were simply "foreign object(s) in the body" of the Episcopal Church reconstruction, which had rejected them.

Separated Eastern Churches Reconstructionism

A consequence of the Eastern Churches' break with Rome is what is known as *caesaro-papism*. The term denotes control of the church by the ruling power of the state. In some instances emperors interfered with the churches' teaching. In many other instances they sought to control the inner life of the churches. Right into modern times the separated Eastern churches have been subject to state control. Russian Orthodoxy, for example, by the admission of its leaders was under the thumb of the Communist party for seventy years. This is the inevitable fate of any so-called national church. The Church of England is another example of a national church controlled in many ways by the state.

The fact of caesaropapism stands out clearly in the Church's early centuries. Though in touch with the leading Eastern prelates, the popes and their ambassadors often had to deal with the Byzantine emperors who exerted control over the Church in the East. The popes tirelessly sought to work even with heretical emperors who were hostile to Rome.

---

12 Interview on "The Journey Home," Eternal Word Television Network, July 11, 2003.
13 "The Case For Complexity," *Collected Works,* vol. 3, 39.
14 Quoted by Jaki, *Newman to Converts*, 177.

In modern times, as James Likoudis points out, caesaropapism has segued into something called *phyletism*.[15] Both have the same result: the domination of the spiritual by the temporal. The word was coined by a pan-Orthodox synod meeting in Constantinople in 1872. The word denotes ethnic-religious discrimination. A separate diocese whose parishes were open only to Bulgarians had been created in the Bulgarian community in Constantinople. The synod condemned, but could not eliminate, this ecclesiastical discrimination. Likoudis explains that the separated Eastern Churches, which were totally independent of one another, "were easily dominated by civil rulers who used the religion of their people to weld a national spirit, just as the Byzantine emperors had done. The unity, apostolicity, and Catholicity of the Church were all submerged that nationality might be made cohesive."

The result has been to deepen the schism into which the separated Eastern Churches have declined. "Nationalism brooks no foreign domination, and this explained in great part the fierce historic opposition to that Western foreigner, the Bishop of Rome, and to reintegration in the Universal Church over which he presided."[16] Lamenting the effects of phyletism in the life of the Eastern Churches, John Meyendorff recognizes that while "our national, ethnic, or cultural commitments" are not in themselves evil, they "constitute real cover for the 'de facto' separatism. They inhibit the missionary spirit, and hide the universal nature of the Church."[17] A Catholic must say there is only one lasting solution to the "separatism" Meyendorff bewails: return to communion with Peter's successors.[18]

Eastern Orthodox apologists claim that by divine intention the structure of the Church is conciliar. They base their case for the authority of councils on the story of the apostolic council at Jerusalem recorded in Acts 15. The Eastern Orthodox version goes like this. A problem arose—whether Gentiles must accept Jewish law, especially circumcision, before becoming Christians. It was brought to a council of the apostles and elders; they made the decision, and the issue was closed. An ecumenical council, the Orthodox say, is by divine intention the ultimate authority for the Church.

This appeal to Acts 15 lifts the passage out of context to prove an extra-scriptural assumption. What actually happened at the Council of Jerusalem

---

15 James Likoudis, *Eastern Orthodoxy and the See of Peter: A Journey Towards Full Communion* (Waite Park, MN: POS, Inc., 2006), 40-43.

16 *Ibid.*, 42f.

17 John Meyendorff, *Catholicity and the Church* (Yonkers, NY: St. Vladimirs Seminary Press, 1983), 140.

18 See Vladimir Soloviev, *The Russian Church and the Papacy*, ed. Ray Ryland (San Diego: Catholic Answers, 2001), 73-85. This eminent Russian Orthodox philosopher-theologian argues eloquently that unless the Russian Church comes back into communion with "the universal Church" (his term for the Catholic Church), it will remain simply an ethnic, national church; in our words, a reconstruction. His insight applies to all the separated Eastern Churches.

provides no basis for the Eastern Orthodox appeal to conciliarism. Turn back to Acts 10. The facts are plain. By sending Peter to the house of Cornelius, God revealed to Peter that Gentiles did not need be circumcised in order to become Christians. Acts 11 tells us that the apostles and others back in Jerusalem were appalled that Peter had been a guest in a Gentile home and had baptized its occupants. However, "when they heard this [Peter's explanation of his divine revelation], they were silenced. And they glorified God" (Acts 11:18).

Now read Acts 15 in its proper context. After much discussion, Peter arose and in the light of the revelation given to him told the council that Jewish requirements could not be laid upon Gentile converts. James, then presiding, retained one requirement: that converts abstain from meat of animals sacrificed to idols. (That was the source of almost all meat offered for sale in markets. In 1 Corinthians 8, Saint Paul ignored James's codicil to the Jerusalem decree. He told the Corinthians they should abstain from meat offered to idols only if it gave offense to another believer.) The council concurred in Peter's decision. But it was his decision, not their concurrence, that settled the issue.

Think about the Eastern Orthodox claim that an ecumenical council is the final authority for the Church. As previously noted, they confine their appeal to the first seven councils, the last being held in the late eighth century. The first question to ask the Eastern Orthodox apologist is, who will convene an ecumenical council? Emperors (with the approval of the reigning pontiff) convened the councils to which Eastern Orthodoxy appeals. The separated Eastern Churches no longer live under an emperor, and they have cut themselves off from the jurisdiction of the pope. No Eastern Orthodox patriarch (not even the ecumenical patriarch of Constantinople) dares summon a council. If he tried, the immediate reaction by other patriarchs would be that he had acted on a presumed, non-existent authority over all the Eastern churches.

Many other unanswered, unanswerable questions confront these advocates of conciliarism. They would agree that individual bishops are not infallible. How would they become infallible simply by gathering in a council? (Unless, that is, they acknowledged the authority of a particular head of all the bishops.) Many bishops in the East had espoused every single heresy that the ecumenical councils—by the authority of the pope—had condemned. Who would decide which bishops had remained faithful and would therefore be entitled to sit and vote in council?

Some Eastern Orthodox theologians doubt they will ever be able to convoke an ecumenical council. Greek theologian Hamilcar Alivisatos states their dilemma in these terms:[19] They can never summon an ecumenical council until they have settled the question of their attitude toward Rome. (This is an admission that the Eastern apologetic has not been approved by their final authority.) They cannot settle their attitude toward Rome without an ecumenical council. Result: stalemate. (My term, not his.) Eastern apologists should also keep this fact in mind. If a council could be convened, and if it included Rome (how else could it claim to be ecumenical?), Catholic bishops would vastly outnumber their Eastern counterparts, and their views presumably would prevail.

Another difficulty of the Eastern Orthodox apologetic for conciliarism is its doctrine of reception. It holds that while an ecumenical council is the ultimate authority, its decrees become binding and infallible only when the whole Church receives them.

The theoretical problem regarding reception is this. How can it be known that the whole Church has accepted a given ecumenical decree? And who makes that determination? One theologian concedes that the answer to this question "is not clearly formulated in Orthodoxy."[20] Another is more forthright: "It is impossible to indicate where and when the acceptance [of dogmas by the Church's consciousness] is accomplished."[21]

The factual problem regarding reception is this. Of the first seven councils, which the Eastern Orthodox claim as their authority, not a single one has been accepted by the whole Church. After each council, groups of churches have gone into schism in protest against the council's actions. If the councils fail to meet this essential Orthodox requirement, how can they be considered final authority?

Or think about the seven ecumenical councils that the Easterners claim to accept. (We have already pointed out that they accept only portions of those conciliar decrees). First, the bishop of Rome had already settled the key issue with which each council dealt (Arianism, Nestorianism, Monophysitism, Monothelitism, Iconoclasm). Conciliar decrees were always concurrences in papal decisions. Second, a council was not regarded as ecumenical and binding until and unless approved by the pope. This is one of the many facts Eastern Orthodox apologists ignore. Third, no ecumenical council has taught that an ecumenical council is the supreme authority for the Church. Fourth, no ecumenical council has had authority and structure for interpreting its own decrees. No ecumenical council has been able to enforce its decrees. Only

---

19 HamilcarAlivisatos, "Is It Possible To Convoke An Ecumenical Council?" *Diakonia*, vol. 4, no. 1 (1969), 26-35.
20 Fouyas, *op. cit,*, 142.
21 Sergius Bulgakov, "Does Orthodoxy Possess an Outward Authority of Dogmatic Infallibility?" *The Christian East*, vol. 7 (1926), 21.

the papacy could and did fulfill the roles of interpretation and enforcement. Finally, the general councils to which separated Easterners appeal were only irregular means for dealing with particular heresies. The Church ordinarily spoke her mind through the papacy and/or councils approved by the pope. Still, the separated Eastern Churches maintain that only what an ecumenical council decrees is binding.

Now consider the key element in their reconstruction, namely conciliarism. As Meyendorff acknowledges, the Eastern Orthodox apologetic, what he calls "the debate" with Roman Catholicism, "actually [did] not [start] until the thirteenth century."[22] In other words, the Eastern Orthodox reconstruction, essentially conciliarism, did not appear until centuries after the Eastern Churches had broken communion with Rome. Like all reconstructions, it is an attempt to rationalize leaving the communion of the Catholic Church.

Alivisatos makes the same admission as Meyendorff. He speaks generically of all the separated churches known as Eastern Orthodox as "our Church." "Our Church," he writes," has never spoken officially, nor made any decree in a synod about the dogmatic position either of the Papal Church nor of the Protestant Churches." This is fact. The reason he gives is not fact: "[S]uch a decision could not have taken place since these Churches appeared only after the seventh ecumenical council in the eighth century."[23]

That is false. His explanation clearly implies that "our Church" (Eastern Orthodoxy) could not hold an ecumenical council after the eighth century. That is true. In any case, the important fact is this. The Eastern Churches' case for conciliarism is an *ad hoc* argument. The entire Eastern Orthodox apologetic, insofar as it contradicts or questions Catholic teaching, is *not* the faith held by the Eastern churches before their break with Rome. It is *not* the faith of the "first eight centuries." It has never been taught by what they claim is their ultimate doctrinal authority. That apologetic necessarily and on its own terms is purely the private opinion of their bishops and theologians.[24]

In 2006, Pope Benedict XVI dropped from his titles the phrase "patriarch of the West" while retaining the titles "vicar of Jesus Christ" and

---

22 John Meyendorff, "Rome and Orthodoxy: Authority or Truth?" Peter J. McCord, ed., *A Pope For All Christians? An Inquiry Into the Role of Peter in the Modern Church* (New York: Paulist Press, 1976), 132.

23 Alivisatos, *op. cit.*, 20.

24 James Likoudis looks at this fact optimistically. "There is great hope for the Reunion of the [separated Eastern] Churches since none of the doctrines rejected or questioned by Orthodox prelates and theologians (and this includes the Catholic doctrine of the Petrine Ministry of the Bishop of Rome) can be said to constitute 'official teaching' binding in conscience on all Eastern Orthodox," since none has been taught by an ecumenical council, the authority by which Eastern Orthodox claim they are bound. (James Likoudis, *Eastern Orthodoxy and the See of Peter: A Journey Towards full Communion* (Waite Park, MN: POS, Inc., 2006), 57f.

"supreme pontiff of the universal church." The bishops of the patriarchate of Constantinople criticized the pope's action. (The separated Eastern churches have long preferred the title "patriarch of the West" because for them it restricts the pope's authority to the Latin Church.) Their secretary said the pope's change in titles is "perceived as implying a universal jurisdiction of the bishop of Rome over the entire church, which is something the Orthodox have never accepted."[25]

The record of history clearly invalidates this claim.[26] Well beyond the time of the first seven ecumenical councils, the universal jurisdiction of the papacy *was* recognized and accepted in the East. Practically all the major heresies that arose in the first eight centuries were Eastern products.[27] The East was prolific in creating heresies but was unable to overcome even one of them without the intervention of papal authority. Every council held in the East independently of papal authority turned out to be heretical, with one exception: the Council of Constantinople in 381 was attended only by Eastern prelates, and it was recognized as ecumenical only because the pope approved it subsequently.

Yet in one sense it is literally true that "the Orthodox" have never accepted the pope's universal jurisdiction. So long as the Eastern churches remained within Catholic communion, they were never known as "Orthodox" or "Eastern Orthodox." They were simply "Eastern." When they broke away from Rome, by the reconstruction they created they gradually became known as "Eastern Orthodoxy." (As pointed out previously, this is an abstraction. There is no "Eastern Orthodox" church. There are only individual, independent, national, ethnic churches corporately designated by the term "Eastern Orthodoxy.")

So for Eastern Orthodox bishops to say the Orthodox have never accepted the pope's universal jurisdiction is like saying the United States of America has never been under the rule of the king of England. When the colonies *were* under British rule, they were not known as "the United States of America." That is what they became after they achieved independence of British rule. "The Orthodox" are what some of the Eastern churches became after they separated from Rome. To press home an important point, before

---

25 *Catholic News Service* (www.catholicnews.com/data/stories/cns/0603382.htm), June 14, 2006.

26 Stanley L. Jaki gives a helpful introduction to the affirmation of papal primacy by early Eastern theologians and prelates in *Eastern Orthodoxy's Witness to Papal Primacy* (Port Huron, MI: Real View Books, 2004).

27 In 668, Pope Vitalian appointed Theodore of Tarsus, a monk, to be archbishop of Canterbury. With no trace of sarcasm, Saint Bede tells us the pope also gave an assistant to the new archbishop, to insure Theodore would not "introduce something contrary to the faith, according to the habit of the Greeks" (John Collorafi and Scott Butler, *Keys Over the World* [Unpublished manuscript]).

those churches became "Orthodox" by breaking with Rome, they were indeed under papal jurisdiction.

A former Protestant minister who converted to the Church told me that in his pilgrimage a Russian Orthodox priest aggressively evangelized him. The priest argued that while Rome claims to be "the Church," in fact Eastern Orthodoxy is "the Church." My friend asked, "How can you say the Eastern Orthodox churches are '*the* Church' when you're not even *one* church?" That, he told me, ended the conversation.

CHAPTER SEVENTEEN

SUBMISSION TO ROME

I treasure a letter from Thomas Merton, the only Catholic to whom we sent our letter announcing our entering the Church. His letter contained wise counsel for converts.

"Dear Ray, I am happy to hear the good news. Blessings, and congratulations. It is not the human element in the Church that is important, so don't be surprised if you run into hardship sometimes.[1] But it is worth it to be in the true Body of Christ and to be fully His and more able to serve Him effectively. Ever in the Spirit, Father M. Louis."[2]

That first winter, after a heavy snowfall, I went to the bishop's office for an appointment. Since he was behind schedule, to pass the time I asked the secretary for a snow shovel to clean the walks leading from the chancery to the streets. The palatial chancery had once been the home of an early Oklahoma City entrepreneur. It was set back some distance from the streets on two sides. One of the streets was a thoroughfare to the downtown area. The residence of my former Episcopal bishop was a few blocks away. As I shoveled, I suddenly laughed aloud. I thought, suppose one of my former clergy colleagues should drive by and see me shoveling the bishop's sidewalk. I could imagine him saying, "Wow! When you submit to Rome, you really have to *submit*!"

---

1 Writing to a friend, a prospective convert, about human weakness in the Church, Flannery O'Connor observed that sometimes "… you have to suffer as much from the Church as for it…." *The Habit of Being: Letters,* edited and with an introduction by Sally Fitzgerald (New York: Noonday Press, 1999), 90.

2 Catholic friends later asked us to share with them the ways in which we had been disillusioned during our two years in the Church. My wife and I looked at each other in astonishment. Almost in unison we said "in no way!" We said we had come into the Church with no illusions, therefore we could not be disillusioned. After two years we could see more clearly the human need for renewal and reform. But, we said, it's still the one true Church of Jesus Christ.

A former parishioner replied graciously to the letter announcing our conversion. Among other things she expressed a deep concern. "I am so afraid in seeking your 'authority' you will lose the gift of freedom which Christ gives us when we live in Him alone." She spoke far more profoundly than she knew. I did lose the "freedom" she had in mind. But I found new and true freedom in Christ by submitting to Rome.[3]

Very shortly after being received into the Church, I realized my personal relation with Jesus Christ had changed radically. As a Protestant, I had accepted Christ on my own terms. I had no other. But as a Catholic, I accepted Jesus Christ as Lord and Savior on *His* terms. I was no longer dependent on my own interpretation of God's Word for guidance and strength. Jesus Christ Himself speaks to me through the guidance of His Church. Jesus Christ comes and gives Himself to me directly in His sacraments. He, the High Priest, presides at all bestowal of sacraments. In the Holy Eucharist, He allows me to join Him in continually re-presenting to the Father His one perfect Sacrifice of Himself. And thereby He continues the unfolding of my salvation and the salvation of the world. My early longing for continuity with Christ and His Church is being fulfilled daily. Despite their human shortcomings, our bishops are direct successors of the apostles and, through them, of Jesus Christ Himself.

A minister in whose church I worked as a seminarian in New York told us of being caught in a traffic jam. At a certain intersection in midtown Manhattan, cars were stacked up, bumper to bumper, for several blocks in each direction. The sidewalks were filled with pedestrians who could not pass except by climbing over the tops of the cars. The minister sat for a long time in a taxi, waiting for the gridlock to clear. He looked out the window at hundreds of grim faces. Suddenly, near the curb he saw a smiling face: a little boy, three or four years in age. The minister wondered why the child was so serene in the confusion and the clamor of dozens and dozens of taxi horns. Then, he said, he realized why. That child was firmly clasping the hand of a man who must have been his father. He had no fears.

The childlike obedience a faithful Catholic gives to the Church is obedience to Christ on Christ's terms. Non-Catholics cannot understand this obedience, just as single persons cannot understand deep marital union. This is an obedience whereby the Catholic "freely and cheerfully submits his own little notions and wishes to the will of Christ expressed in the action of authority." It is obedience "whereby his own small and limited self is enlarged to the measure of the great self of the Church." The Catholic's obedience to the Church is "a profoundly religious act, an absolute devotion to the will of Christ which rules the Church."[4]

---

3   See chapter 13 for development of this theme.
4   Karl Adam, *The Spirit of Catholicism*, 29.

This is how Catholics "take every thought captive to obey Christ" (2 Cor. 10:5). At our best we do not simply practice obedience; we *love* obedience, because we love serving Jesus Christ on His terms. New freedom, and therefore new joy, awaits all who come into the Church.

Some non-Catholic friends ask, "But what about your conscience? Haven't you given up your freedom of conscience? How can it be free when you have to believe what the Church teaches and not what your conscience tells you?"

To answer this question, we must begin by making clear the true nature of the human conscience. Conscience is the faculty whereby we make judgments about moral decisions. The decisions are based on what we know is true. Unless conscience has truth on which to make moral judgments, it is helpless. As an analogy, consider a magnetic compass. If you're lost in a wilderness, a compass can be a lifesaver, but only because there is a magnetic north pole. The compass did not put that magnetic pole in place. If through some catastrophe that north pole should be destroyed, the compass would be useless.

The Catholic Church does insist that one must always follow the dictates of his conscience. With equal vigor the Church requires that a person's conscience must be properly *formed*. That is to say, the conscience must be provided with truth on the basis of which it can draw moral conclusions. The Church is the custodian of truth. Not all truth, but the truth of faith and morals—in other words, the truth by which moral judgments are made. We receive that truth through our intellect and through our will to adhere to it. The conscience has nothing to do with discerning truth. It can only function when the truth is presented to it.

Many times I have heard and read statements by Catholics who claim that what the Church teaches conflicts with what their consciences tell them. Therefore, they say, in order to carry out the Church's command always to follow the dictates of conscience, they must reject a particular teaching. Persons who make this argument misunderstand the role of conscience. My decisions of conscience can never conflict with what the Church teaches. This is because what the Church teaches and what I discern through my conscience operate on two different levels.

Illustrate this fact with a particular example. Drawing infallibly on God's revelation regarding human sexuality and marriage, the Church condemns the use of artificial contraception as a serious sin. Many Catholics dissent. They say their consciences tell them it is morally acceptable to practice artificial contraception.

Now think about what they have done in arriving at their dissent. They have rejected the Church's teaching about human sexuality and marriage and have chosen other teaching that would allow the use of artificial contraception. *Then* they apply their consciences to this *contrary* teaching and conclude that their consciences approve using artificial contraception. Of course their consciences will approve. That's why they chose to believe differently from the Church's teaching about human sexuality and marriage.

But see where the conflict is. The conflict is not between the Church's teaching and their consciences but between what the Church teaches and the contrary doctrine they have chosen to believe. Their consciences had nothing to do with that choice. They made that choice by their intellect and their will. They chose contrary doctrine because they wanted to justify the use of artificial contraception. They having made that choice, their consciences naturally approve the result they sought. (More about dissent in the next chapter.)

Our Lord clearly promised, "If you continue in my word, you are truly my disciples, and you will know the truth, and the truth will make you free" (Jn. (8:31-32). Truth liberates. Error enslaves. "If the son makes you free, you will be free indeed" (Jn. 8:36). We continue in His Word when we faithfully obey His teaching through His Church. All Christians agree Jesus established a Church, though there is wide disagreement about what that Church is. As Blessed John Henry Newman reminded us, if Jesus did establish a Church, it had to be a teaching Church. That is precisely the reason He gave for His Church. He promised to send the Spirit, and "when the Spirit of truth comes, he will guide you into all the truth" (Jn. 16:13).

Had Jesus not established a teaching Church, He would have abandoned His followers to the doctrinal and moral chaos we see in the non-Catholic world. The revelation would soon have been lost in the welter of human opinions. And if He established a teaching Church, He had to endow it with His infallible authority. Otherwise, why bother? As was earlier noted, the very concept of revelation presupposes an infallible authority to receive, interpret, and transmit the truth conveyed in the revelation process. Submitting to that authority, as converts discover, gives a degree of moral certainty about basic Christian doctrines not available to those persons not under that authority.

Through my pilgrimage I have learned that to be Catholic one must make use of his reason. Indeed, a conscientious convert must use his reason far more vigorously than he has ever done before. He must think through the implications of revelation and history as never before. It is through the exercise of his reason that he comes to recognize the truth of the Church's claims about herself. Several professors at Union Theological Seminary cautioned us about the dangers of Catholic theology. Once one accepts Catholic presuppositions, they warned, the whole of Catholic theology logically follows. And so, goes the non-Catholic criticism, Catholics don't think clearly or objectively about the doctrine of their Church.

The inimitable G.K. Chesterton took up the charge that Catholics are not allowed to make use of their reason in matters of doctrine. The truth is, he declared, Catholics think much more about their religion than do non-Catholics. "It is precisely because most non-Catholics do *not* think that they can hold a chaos of contrary notions at once, as that Jesus was good and humble, but falsely boasted of being God; or that God became Man to guide men till the end of time, and then died without giving them a hint of how they were to discover His decision in the first quarrel that might arise."[5]

So far as the use of reason in matters of faith is concerned, for two thousand years the Catholic Church has been exalting the role of reason while pointing out its limitations. No other institution can match this record. Indeed, to refer to a Chestertonian analogy already noted, the Catholic Church carries a map of the mind. That map has been compiled from the vast reservoir of the Church's knowledge. The purpose of the map is to guide the use of reason, to warn travelers against the errors of the past. On this map "all the blind alleys and bad roads [of reason] are clearly marked, all the ways that have been shown to be worthless by the best of all evidence: the evidence of those who have gone down them."[6]

Oscar Wilde, himself a convert near the end of his life, once quipped, "The Catholic Church is for saints and sinners alone. For respectable people the Anglican Church will do." Sometimes people being drawn to Catholicism begin to focus on the sinners in the Church, not the saints. They are puzzled, if not repelled, by reports of human weakness and sin of Church leaders, to say nothing of the sins of Catholic laity.

With regard to sins in the Church, two facts must be kept in mind. First of all, though the Church as the Mystical Body of Christ is herself a divine institution, she is composed of weak, sinful human beings. It was ever so. Immediately after being appointed earthly head of the Church, Saint Peter tried to dissuade our Lord from carrying out His sacrificial mission. The Lord Jesus called Peter a name He never used for another person: Satan. When

---

5   Quoted by Joseph Pearce, *Wisdom and Innocence*, 461.

6   G.K. Chesterton, "Why I Am a Catholic," in *Collected Works*, vol. 3, 129. "The greater part of it [the map] consists of playgrounds and happy hunting-fields, where the mind may have as much liberty as it likes; not to mention any number of intellectual battle-fields in which the battle is indefinitely open and undecided. But it does definitely take the responsibility of marking certain roads as leading nowhere or leading to destruction, to a blank wall or a sheer precipice. By this means, it does prevent men from wasting their time or losing their lives upon paths that have been found futile or disastrous again and again in the past, but which might otherwise entrap travelers again and again in the future. The Church does make herself responsible for warning her people against these. . . . She does dogmatically defend humanity from its worst foes, those hoary and horrible and devouring monsters of the old mistakes."

our Lord was about to be crucified, that same Peter three times denied that he even *knew* Jesus. Another trusted successor of Jesus betrayed Him to the authorities and then in despair took his own life.

To a friend who expressed horror at human weaknesses in the Church, Flannery O'Connor wrote, "[W]hat you seem actually to demand is that the Church put the kingdom of heaven on earth right here now, that the Holy Ghost be translated at once into all flesh." Again, she said, "You are asking that man return at once to the state God created him in, you are leaving out the terrible radical human pride that causes death." She told the friend that to have the Church be what he expected, there would have to be "continuous miraculous meddling of God in human affairs" to prevent sin. This is not God's way with His creation. We can and must pray for the conversion of sinners and healing of the effects of their sin.

But—and this is the second fact to remember—we must not dwell overlong on sin in the Church. We must not be too critical of others. As O'Connor added, we have a responsibility for "not being scandalized." If we dwell on our scandalization, she warned, "you will scandalize others and the guilt for that will belong to you."[7]

Submission to Rome sheds new light on dogma. For Protestants in general, *dogma* is a harsh word, closely associated with the word *dogmatic* in its pejorative sense. They seldom if ever speak of their beliefs as "dogmas." In my Protestant years, I shared this abhorrence of the term. Strictly speaking, Protestant avoidance of the term is correct, since Protestants have no authority that can define doctrines as dogmas. But for them it would be a limiting term, restraining their freedom in Christ to interpret the faith as the Spirit leads them.

Submission to Rome, I discovered, uncovers the true purpose of dogma as a basic tool of the Holy Spirit. Again as so often, Chesterton opened my eyes to the true function of dogma. Using an analogy from mathematics, he refuted the notion that accepting the dogmas of the Church enables a Catholic to avoid the effort of serious thinking about the faith. "Euclid does not save geometricians the trouble of thinking when he insists on absolute definitions and unalterable axioms. On the contrary, he gives them the great trouble of thinking logically." Chesterton added, "The dogma of the Church limits thought about as much as the dogma of the solar system limits physical science."[8]

From a different point of view, in a letter to a friend, O'Connor wrote, "[A] dogma is only a gateway to contemplation and is an instrument of freedom and not of restriction."[9] For the traveler using the Church's map of

7   O'Connor, *op. cit.,* 307-308.
8   Quoted in Joseph Pearce, *Wisdom and Innocence,* 149.
9   O'Connor, *op. cit.,* 92.

the mind, dogmas of the Church loom large as points of reference. Or, to use another previous analogy, the traveler can "take station" on the dogmas and be assured of staying on course to truth.

In pilgrimage from my Protestant background, for twenty years I sought the full truth of Christ. My wife and I found that truth in the Catholic Church, so we submitted to Rome. We began to take possession—in the sense of intellectually grasping—the truth of the Church. Then and only then could we begin to take the necessary and final step. It is well epitomized in a dictum of French archbishop and theologian François Fenelon: once we possess the truth of the Church we must allow that truth to possess us.[10] That is to say, we must begin, by grace, ever more deeply to explore and to live that truth.

Thoughtful readers of this pilgrimage will have wondered at my failure to mention any consciousness of the Blessed Virgin's role in my conversion. I confess I did not often invoke our Blessed Mother's prayers during our pilgrimage. Earlier I noted that in my years in four Protestant seminaries I heard one favorable mention of the Virgin. Ten years later, in my friendship with our Episcopal benefactor in Oklahoma City, his love for the Virgin softened and eventually removed the last traces of my Protestant prejudice. Under his influence I began to pray the Rosary.

In our early years in the Church, the priests of our parish discouraged not only praying the Rosary during the liturgy (as they should have) but also praying the Rosary at all. In our last year as Episcopalians, without telling them so, we were preparing our children for eventual reception into the Church. Since we did not have personal devotion to our Lady, we failed to help our children develop a love and reverence for her.

But when my wife and I were being instructed in the faith, we began to possess the truth about the Blessed Virgin. That is, we began intellectually to accept her role as Mother of the Church, as model Christian, as chief intercessor. We began to learn some of the dozens of titles ascribed to her in Catholic litanies and piety. Once in the Church, following Fenelon's dictum (of which we had no knowledge then), we began to let the truth about our Lady possess us. We began to love her as our mother, mother in a deeper sense than even were our natural mothers.

When as a Catholic I first became aware of the title "co-redemptrix" (not a defined term), I reacted to it negatively. Sensitive to Protestant prejudices regarding Mary, I thought the term is too easily misunderstood, perhaps even by Catholics. I knew that those who use the term pay due attention to Christ's unique mediatorship. I knew also that Pope John Paul II and other members of the hierarchy occasionally used the term as if it were common parlance among Catholics. I knew that use of the title meant that through

10   Quoted by Henri de Lubac, *The Splendour of the Church* (San Francisco: Ignatius Press, 1999), 259, fn. 85.

her identification with her divine Son the Virgin had somehow shared in the redemption He wrought. But that "somehow" still puzzled me. However, in recent years the truth of Mary as co-redemptrix slowly began to possess me. That possession began through long meditation on our Lord's Passion.

Repeatedly I have tried to imagine myself being present at our Lord's scourging, following Him in His excruciating struggle to carry the Cross to Calvary, and standing before Him, my crucified Lord. Because I love Him above all others, I would suffer with Him. But what would be the nature of my suffering? I would be overwhelmed in mental and emotional agony by a deep sense of guilt—a self-centered, horrifying awareness that *my* sin was responsible for His suffering would predominate. And therefore my identification with Jesus' suffering would be weak indeed. I know I could do very little or perhaps even nothing to help Him bear His agony.

In God's providence there was one person present throughout the Passion who was not so handicapped. There was one who could gaze on her divine Son's suffering without the slightest sense of guilt. She who was sinless alone could completely identify with Jesus in His agony. She alone could give Him that immeasurable support of total identification with and in His suffering. And she did. In her devotion to her Son in His Passion, she perfectly fulfilled that duty we can only strive to fulfill: "Bear one another's burdens, and so fulfill the law of Christ" (Gal. 6:2). In her pure love for her divine Son, which He knew so well, our Blessed Mother helped Him bear His burden of the weight of the sins of the world. She surely is Co-Redemptrix.

Submission to Rome is submission to Jesus Christ as He intends us to submit. It is submission to Him personally, to be possessed by all His truth and all His grace. That is what the word *Catholic* means. The common understanding of the word *catholic* is *universal*. That is at best a secondary meaning. The word comes from two Greek words, *kata holou,* that mean "according to the whole." When first used by Ignatius of Antioch at the beginning of the second century, it could not have meant *universal* in a geographic sense. In contrast to sectarian break-offs, the Catholic Church alone has the wholeness of the truth.

After Chesterton's conversion, his friend Hilaire Belloc wrote him, "The Catholic Church is the exponent of *Reality*. It is true. Its doctrines in matters large and small are statements of what is. This it is which the ultimate act of the intelligence accepts. This it is which the will deliberately confirms."[11] This is how a convert takes possession of the truth. And then comes the lifetime of becoming more and more fully possessed by that truth.

---

11   Quoted by Joseph Pearce, *Wisdom and Innocence,* 271.

CHAPTER EIGHTEEN

DOES BEING CATHOLIC
MAKE A DIFFERENCE?

For most converts—and for all who were formerly clergymen—the pilgrimage into the Catholic Church causes pain and suffering. Does becoming Catholic make the disruption of their lives worthwhile? More specifically, does being Catholic make a real difference in a person's life? Does it make an *eternal* difference?

At first glance, perhaps not. Vatican II's *Dogmatic Constitution on the Church* seems to point in that direction. Section 16 names several categories of persons outside the Catholic Church who can be saved. The list includes non-Catholic Christians, Jews, Muslims, those who seek the unknown God, even those who have no explicit knowledge of God. These persons can be saved if they seek to respond to God and to love Him on the basis of the best information available to them.

But note that all the Church teaches about salvation through non-Catholic traditions presupposes that persons in those traditions do not realize the Catholic Church is the one true Church established by Jesus Christ. One who *does* know what the Catholic Church is and still refuses either to remain in her or to enter her "could not be saved."[1]

But there is a profound difference between being Catholic and not. The previous chapter pointed out that only in the Catholic Church can one be assured of responding to Jesus Christ, in faith and obedience, on *His* terms, not ours.

And there is more to consider. Start with our Lord's command about moral and spiritual growth. "You, therefore, must be perfect, as your heavenly

---

1   Vatican II, *Dogmatic Constitution on the Church*, 14.

Father is perfect" (Mt. 5:48). When I was a child, someone gave me a statue of three little monkeys sitting side by side. One covered his mouth, the middle one his eyes, the third one, his ears. This was the proverbial "speak-no-evil, see-no-evil, hear-no-evil" trio. In my early years, I sometimes thought of those monkeys when I read Matthew 5:48. Their message has merit, but is hardly accurate commentary on our Lord's command.

Consider the word we translate "perfect." In Greek, *teleios* does not refer simply to abstract or metaphysical perfection. It is a functional term. To be perfect is for a thing to fully realize the purpose for which it has been produced. *Teleios* comes from the noun *telos*, which means *purpose, end, goal*. "You must be perfect" means that each of us must strive to develop his or her unique potential, under God, to the fullest possible extent. These words are both command and promise. The imperative is laid upon us who follow Christ, but we know that only the grace of God can finally bring about this process of sanctification.

Why this requirement for Christians to seek sanctification in this life? If heaven is our goal, why couldn't our Lord have narrowed the command to "become at least good enough to qualify for heaven"? Why not, unless the degree of fulfillment as a Christian that one achieves in this life has eternal implications?

Protestants have always criticized Catholic teaching on sanctification. On the one hand, Protestants mistakenly assume that striving for sanctification undercuts justification by faith. For most Protestants, in other words, sanctification is a "work," a contribution we make to our salvation. (Traditional Baptists reject the whole concept of sacrament for essentially the same reason.) On the other hand, the Protestant approach to the faith minimizes the *need* for emphasizing growth in sanctity. Once you have accepted Jesus as Savior and Lord, your salvation is assured. At the moment of death, if you are saved, Christ takes you into heaven. And that's it.

But does being Catholic make a difference?

"For we must all appear before the judgment seat of Christ, so that each one may receive good or ill, according to what he has done in the body" (2 Cor. 5:10). ("According to what he has *done in the body*"—not as Luther would have it, justification by faith *alone*.) A proverb has it, "As the tree falls, so it lies." The level of spiritual maturity we have attained at the moment of death is the level at which we shall be perfected through our experience of purgatory. It is the level at which we shall spend eternity.

Our capacity for the beatific vision, therefore, is determined forever at the moment of death. Capacities will vary. Take two containers—one large, one small—and fill each with water. They are equally full, but they hold different amounts of water. So will it be in heaven. There will be varying degrees of blessedness in the lives of the redeemed in heaven. Assuredly there will be no envy there with regard to varying capacities for sharing in the beatific vision. Yet if in one's life on earth one has more and more deeply yearned for union with Christ, in heaven one surely will want the deepest possible union with Him.

The Council of Florence in 1439 taught that those who have incurred no sin after Baptism and those who have been cleansed of all stain of sin will "clearly behold the Triune God as He is, yet one person more perfectly than another according to the difference of their merits." The Greek version of the conciliar teaching ends with the words "according to the worth of their lives."[2]

In the *Letter on Certain Questions Concerning Eschatology* issued by the Congregation for the Doctrine of the Faith in 1979, we are reminded that, with regard to life after death, we "must firmly hold" to the continuity "between our present life in Christ and the future life (charity is the law of the Kingdom of God and our charity on earth will be the measure of our sharing in God's glory in heaven)." The *Dogmatic Constitution on the Church* (49) speaks of the life of the redeemed in heaven: "All in various ways and degrees are in communion in the same charity of God and neighbor and all sing the same hymn." Several "New Testament texts speak of a final destiny of the soul—a destiny which can be different for some and for others" (CCC, 1021).

At this point someone might say, "All I care about is getting into heaven. All I want is to have those pearly gates slam shut *behind* me and not *in front of* me." Sometimes a student will say, "All I want out of this course is a passing grade. I don't care about anything else." If that student does get his passing grade, he will get little else out of the course. As for the man at the pearly gates, with that self-centered attitude he may well see the gates slam shut in front of him.

If spouses truly, deeply love one another, they yearn and work for the closest possible union of life. Pity the poor spouses who say, "We don't really work at our marriage any more. After all, we have enough love going to make sure we won't split up." Not only are they denying themselves the deep joy and fulfillment of marriage, but by their selfish attitudes they have set a collision course with unhappiness and even the breakup of their marriage.

Does being Catholic make a difference?

Consider some of the Church's teaching about herself. Jesus entrusted "all the blessings of the new covenant" to "the apostolic college alone, of which Peter is the head." "For it is through Christ's Catholic Church, which is "the

---

2   Norman Tanner, S.J., ed., *Decrees of the Ecumenical Councils*, vol. 1, *Nicaea I to Lateran V* (Washington, D.C.: Georgetown University Press, 1990), 538.

all-embracing means of salvation,' that they can benefit fully from the means of salvation.[3] The next section of the *Decree* contains these words: "[T]he Catholic Church has been endowed with all divinely revealed truth and with all means of grace." Does it not follow that anyone *not* in the communion of the Catholic Church does *not* have access to all divinely revealed truth? That the non-Catholic does not have access to all the means of grace by which Christ intends to nourish his people?

"Baptism," says the *Decree on Ecumenism*, "establishes a sacramental bond of unity which links all who have been reborn by it" (22). It clarifies this statement by adding that Baptism in itself "is only a beginning, an inauguration." Baptism is "wholly directed toward the acquiring of fullness of life in Christ." That "fullness"—and note the recurring adjective—is "a *complete* profession of faith, a *complete* incorporation into the system of salvation such as Christ willed it to be, and . . . *complete* ingrafting in eucharistic communion."

This can mean only that sincere non-Catholics do not have access to the full truth of the Gospel. Indeed, in their separated state they cannot. If a non-Catholic does believe all that the Church teaches but chooses to remain outside her communion, he is in grave peril of everlasting damnation. The Second Vatican Council teaches that "the Church, now sojourning on earth as an exile, is necessary for salvation: the one Christ is mediator and the way of salvation; he is present to us in his body which is the Church." And then come these words previously quoted: "Whosoever, therefore, knowing that the Catholic Church was made necessary by Christ, would refuse to enter or to remain in it, could not be saved" (*Dogmatic Constitution on the Church,* 14).

The words from the *Decree on Ecumenism* quoted above also can mean only that sincere non-Catholics have not been, and as non-Catholics cannot be, fully incorporated into "the system of salvation such as Christ himself willed it to be." Not having full access to *all* of Christ's gifts to His people prevents a non-Catholic from attaining the greatest possible degree of spiritual maturity, the deepest sanctification, in this life. The fact that an individual non-Catholic's sanctity may—and in many instances probably does—greatly exceed that of many Catholics is beside the point. The point is that non-Catholic will not have developed in this life, by God's grace, the capacity for the beatific vision he could have attained as a Catholic. The mature Christian yearns above all else for, and continually strives for, closest possible union with the Triune God.

Being Catholic makes a difference—an *eternal* difference.

---

3   Vatican II, *Decree on Ecumenism*, 3.

The *Decree on Ecumenism* speaks of the deprivation suffered by non-Catholics. Non-Catholics "are not blessed with that unity which Jesus Christ wished to bestow on all those who through him were born again into one body, and with him quickened to newness of life—that unity which the Holy Scriptures and the ancient Tradition of the Church proclaim" (3). Most serious of all, non-Catholic communities "have not retained the proper reality of the eucharistic mystery in its fullness, especially because of the absence of the sacrament of Orders" (22). And therefore their members are not being fed as Christ intends them to be fed on himself. "[U]nless you eat the flesh of the Son of man and drink his blood, you have no life in you; he who eats my flesh and drinks my blood has eternal life" (Jn. 6:53f). How dare anyone ignore this stark command from the Son of God? Or how dare anyone try to dismiss our Lord's commands by trying to make a metaphor of his words?

All this applies in some measure even to members of the separated Eastern churches. Though they have retained valid sacraments, among themselves and with other traditions they lack the unity that Christ wishes to bestow on all who bear His name. They lack the infallible guidance of the Church's magisterium that would separate truth from error for them in matters of doctrine and morals. One can see the effects of this lack, for example, in their having accepted the dissolubility of marriage and the use of artificial contraception and in their lack of a united stand against abortion.

Being Catholic does make a difference—an eternal difference.

From time to time during my childhood in the depression years, our family would want something, and in many cases need something, for which we simply had no money. My usual childish, impatient response was to ask, "Then what will we *do*?" One of my parents would always answer, "We'll do *without*. *That's* what we'll do." And the subject was closed.

Jesus Christ gives His Church incalculable riches for the benefit of *all* His people. What are non-Catholics to do about much—even most—of this treasure? They simply do without—and through no particular fault of their own. But someone *is* at fault. You and I are at fault for not witnessing more faithfully and zestfully, for making no effort to bring fellow Christians into the fullness of their rightful heritage. The failure (dare I say refusal?) of us Catholics to evangelize calls to mind a pathetic passage in Acts 19:1ff. Paul came to Ephesus and found there some followers of Jesus. He asked if they had received the Holy Spirit when they began believing in Jesus. Their answer was, "No, we have never even heard there *is* a Holy Spirit." They had never heard of the greatest gift God wanted to bestow on them!

For non-Catholic Christians, there are countless gifts waiting for them about which they know nothing. One can imagine their responding to a forthright proclamation of the Catholic faith in a manner somewhat like that of those ancient Ephesians. "We love Jesus, but we have never *heard* we can literally receive Him into our bodies, in His full humanity and divinity." "We know that on Calvary Jesus offered Himself to the Father, but we have never even *heard* that He commands us to join Him in re-presenting Himself to the Father in every Eucharistic celebration." "We know that Jesus has spoken to us through the scriptures, but we have never even *heard* that He speaks to us today directly through the successor of Saint Peter."

Why have they not heard? Why are we not telling them? For many reasons, I suppose. Let me speak of one. For decades, dissenting Catholics and lazy Catholics have used the bugaboo of "triumphalism" to inhibit or at least dilute authentic Catholic excitement about the Church and about the joy of being Catholic. Repeatedly we have been told by these bugaboo-ers that if you say positively the Catholic Church is the one true Church, if you speak enthusiastically of the inestimable benefits and graces of being Catholic, if you seek aggressively to bring others—Christian as well as unbaptized—into the Church, then you're committing the vague "sin" of being "triumphalistic."

The strategy of this bugaboo is to equate articulate, enthusiastic Catholic witness with self-aggrandizing boasting. But we know we can't boast about the Church, because we didn't invent the Catholic faith. All we can do is give thanks for our privilege and witness to non-Catholics.

On this point *The Dogmatic Constitution on the Church* speaks to each of us. "All the Church's children should remember that their exalted status is to be attributed not to their own merits but to the special grace of Christ." (The phrase "exalted status" in context means being inheritors of all the riches of Christ in his Church.) Then in the spirit of Jesus' words "Every one to whom much is given, of him will much be required" (Lk. 12:48), the Council issues a solemn warning. If the children of the Church "fail moreover to respond to that grace in thought, word and deed, not only will they not be saved but they shall be the more severely judged."[4]

Being Catholic makes a difference, an eternal difference—but only if a Catholic is faithful to the Church's teaching.

From time to time most of us receive e-mail warnings about new computer viruses that some psychopaths have unleashed onto the Internet. The effects of these man-made viruses range from mild disruption to widespread loss of information on any computer unwittingly exposed to the virus. To combat these dangers, increasingly sophisticated anti-virus software is continually being produced.

---

4   *Dogmatic Constitution on the Church*, 14.

All Catholics must be on their guard against a far more dangerous virus that can disastrously affect our belief and our faith. Let's call it the "spectrum virus." Like the computer virus, it is also man-made. Infection from this virus is widespread, but the virus itself is not widely recognized. There are countless instances of its ravages in Catholic writing and speaking today. We shall describe the origin of the spectrum virus and point out the chief presence. Then we can examine its deleterious effects in the lives of those who allow it to enter their systems of thought and belief.

In politics and economics, to take the two clearest examples, there is always a range of opinions regarding solutions to the problems a society faces. Each theorist has to make the best case he can for his position. The range of opinions constitutes a wide spectrum, from "conservative" or "reactionary right" to "liberal" or "radical left." In a democracy, everyone has a right to his or her own opinion and to being included in the political or economic spectrum. The spectrum exists necessarily because there are no final answers in these areas.

Enter the spectrum virus. Today many who claim to be Catholic arbitrarily decide which of the Church's teachings they will accept and which they will reject. The common euphemism used for these heretics is *dissenters*. To justify themselves, they try to apply the spectrum model to the Catholic faith. The whole enterprise of dissent is based on this strategy.

Though most dissenters will pay lip-service to the magisterium, they want to keep it in cold storage. They assume—and insist everyone else assume—that, with regard to what authentic Catholicism is, there is and must be a spectrum of opinions. Within that spectrum there will be many disagreements and even contradictions. But, they say, everyone who makes any claim to being "Catholic" has a right to the inclusion of his or her opinions on the spectrum. Catholics simply have to learn to respect one another's opinions.

The spectrum axiom of dissent is false. There can be no spectrum of opinions regarding the authentic Catholic faith, for one good reason. Unlike in politics and economics, in the Catholic Church there *are* final answers to questions about what is the truth revealed in Jesus Christ. And there is a God-given authority to safeguard and interpret those answers.

The chief symptom, indeed the hallmark, of the spectrum virus is the use of labels to describe what those who are infected claim are factions within the Church. For Catholics who are faithful to all the Church's teaching and to the Holy Father, dissenters use such terms as "conservative," "traditionalist," "the right," and so on. In sharp contrast, dissenters are sparing in their use of labels for the pick-and-choosers. Occasionally they may refer to themselves as "liberal" or "progressive," and even on rare occasion as "the left." They scarcely ever call themselves dissenters. As George Weigel has pointed out, the use of labels drawn from the political arena

> has caused endless mischief. Doctrine isn't "liberal" or "conservative." Doctrine is true, or it's heresy. Theology isn't "liberal" or "conservative," either. Theology is thoughtful or dumb, scholarly or shoddy, well-informed or ill-informed. To treat doctrine or theology as essentially political matters distorts the Church's self-understanding [sees the Church primarily as an institution in a secular sense], divides the Church into factions, and promotes the pernicious view that every issue in the Church is, at bottom, a question of power.[5]

Consistent with their theory, those infected by the spectrum virus seldom (if ever) draw a line beyond which one ceases to be Catholic. In their discussion of the most radical departures from Catholic teaching, even in their criticism of them, dissenters never suggest these outlandish opinions are anything but Catholic. One dissenter acknowledges that "on the left" there are "many today who are openly contemptuous of magisterial authority and particularly papal authority." Again, he notes "the Catholic left consists of a broad spectrum [note the key word of dissent] of positions, movements, and theologies." But in his eyes they are all still Catholic and must be listened to.[6]

Furthermore, carriers of the spectrum virus make much of what they call "pluralism" in theology. "The New Testament," says Rausch, "represents not one but many theologies"[7]—meaning the teaching of the New Testament itself is pluralistic. This claim tries to ignore the distinction between two different kinds of pluralism. Dissenters' pluralism involves many contradictory views of doctrine—all, supposedly, legitimately occupying space on the same spectrum. The "pluralism" of the New Testament, and of Catholic theology from the beginning, is like a many-faceted diamond: differing approaches to the same truth—none of them contradictory, all of them complementary.

Even the title of Rausch's book is a symptom of the spectrum virus: *A Divided Church*. The division he describes exists only along the spectrum he imagines. The Church can never be divided; this is her solemn teaching. There is division within the Church, yes, but it is a division between faithful Catholics and unfaithful Catholics.

---

5   George Weigel, "The Mischief of Labeled Catholicism," *The Southern Cross*, June 6, 2002, 31.Weigel gives much of the credit for the use of labels in Catholic doctrinal and moral issues to Father Francis X. Murphy. Father Murphy was a Redemptorist priest who under the pseudonym "Xavier Rynne" published in the *New Yorker* a long series of reports on the Second Vatican Council while it was in session.

6   Thomas P. Rausch, S.J., *Reconciling Faith and Reason: Apologists, Evangelists and Theologians in a Divided Church* (Collegeville, MN: Liturgical Press, 2000), 2.

7   *Ibid.*, 17.

Another jargon term associated with the spectrum theory is *polarization*. Dissenters express great concern about "hardened positions" and claim to seek "middle ground" on which competing viewpoints can agree. A few years ago, a national Catholic magazine carried an advertisement for a forthcoming liturgical conference that claimed this as its object: "Bringing together people from all parts of the theological spectrum [the key word again] to discuss the future of Catholic liturgy and move us closer to the unity all Catholics hope for." For dissenters, the ultimate accolade for a theologian is that he is "mainstream," an adjective that covers a multitude of doctrinal sins. The late Monsignor William Smith of Dunwoodie Seminary once observed, whether being "mainstream" is a good thing depends on what the stream is and where it's going. What if one is "mainstream" in the Niagara River fifty yards above the falls?

Dissenters even have a place for the pope on their spectrum. Often one hears or reads of someone "disagreeing with the pope." This manner of speaking seeks to reduce rejection of defined Church teaching to a matter of personal disagreement and in no sense a disqualification for being Catholic.

One final symptom of spectrum virus infection. Since dissent broke out in force in the late 1960s, its adherents have repeatedly called for "dialogue" on key doctrinal issues. This call seems always to be motivated by their desire to find moral wiggle room. They are asking for acceptance of their divergent opinions regarding the Church's doctrine. Once a matter is settled, what is there to "dialogue" about? Except, maybe, the dissenters' own errors.

Now for the harm the spectrum virus works in those who allow it to enter their thinking.

In May of 1998 Pope John Paul II issued a short apostolic letter, *Ad Tuendam Fidem*. To the codes of canon law of the Roman Catholic Church and of the Eastern Catholic Churches, the letter added clear statements of the obligation to uphold the Church's teaching. Penalties were specified for those who dissent from official teaching. In a commentary on the apostolic letter, speaking for the Congregation for the Doctrine of the Faith and the Holy Father, then-Cardinal Joseph Ratzinger made this point: "Whoever denies these truths [the Church's clear teaching] would be in a position of *rejecting a truth of Catholic doctrine and would therefore no longer be in full communion with the Catholic Church*" (sec. 6; italics in the Saint Paul edition of this commentary).

Why does rejection of one of the Church's official teachings affect so drastically one's communion status in the Catholic Church? Cardinal Ratzinger does not explain his statement, but the reason for it is not hard to see. Try this analogy.

Suppose it were possible to summarize all the Church's official teaching in fifty propositions. Suppose further that a theologian reads down the list and announces that he holds every doctrine except no. 32. (If he's a typical dissenter, no. 32 probably has to do with sexual morality.) Then he concludes by saying that on a grading scale, he has a score of 98. That, he says triumphantly, is an "A" or an "A+" in anybody's class. So basically he's a good Catholic—indeed, a "conservative" Catholic.

But look more closely at what has happened. The dissenter has not only rejected *one* of the Church's teachings, he has made four other fateful decisions. First, in good dissenter fashion, he has applied the false spectrum theory to the whole realm of Catholic teaching. Second, he has rejected another basic Catholic teaching, namely, that the Church speaks with the authority and guidance of Christ in her official teaching. If in one instance she teaches error—and our dissenter has said that no. 32 is in error—she obviously does not, indeed *cannot*, speak authoritatively in Christ's name. Third, he has refused to submit to the Church's authority and has thereby taken up a non-Catholic, essentially Protestant stance toward everything else the Church teaches. Now, he is saying, *he* will decide what authentic Catholicism is. He has made himself the final authority in *all* matters of doctrine and morality. He focuses not on *belief in* the Church's doctrines, but on his own *opinions about* those doctrines. And that's why he is no longer in the full communion of the Catholic Church. He may outwardly conform to Catholicism, but inwardly he is Protestant.

Finally, our hypothetical dissenter has started down a slippery slope of disbelief. Few stop with rejecting only one of the Church's teachings. He will, in the spectrum jargon, become more and more "liberal."

At the heart of all dissent lies the spectrum virus. It works incalculable harm in the lives of countless Catholics. Rausch quotes a dissident archbishop who has written, evidently approvingly, that the majority of Catholics in his archdiocese "seem to ignore much of the Church's teaching on sexuality and make their own decisions on many of these questions [contraception, abortion, homosexual behavior, and so on] using common sense."[8] It is not hard to predict what moral judgments about these issues unfaithful Catholics will make on the basis of their "common sense." Does the judgment pronounced in Matthew 18:6[9] fall on a shepherd who sees his sheep plunging to destruction and seemingly does nothing to stop them?

---

8   *Ibid.*, 71.

9   "If any of you put a stumbling block before one of these little ones who believe in me [or in a position of authority does nothing to remove stumbling blocks one clearly sees], it would be better for you if a great millstone were fastened around your neck and you were drowned in the depth of the sea."

Faithful Catholics can inoculate themselves against the spectrum virus by refusing to use labels. Banish them from your vocabulary. One is either Catholic or one is a dissenter (to use the current euphemism) or heterodox or simply unfaithful. There is no "middle ground" that carriers of the spectrum virus claim they are trying to establish.

We must pray for dissenters. We must ask the Spirit to lead them out of the blind alleys of disbelief into which they have stumbled, infected as they are by the spectrum virus. In rebelling against the vicar of Christ and his teaching, dissenters in fact are rebelling against Jesus Christ Himself. So long as they persist in their error, they can never know the joy of being Catholic.

They can never know the difference—the eternal difference—being Catholic makes.

CHAPTER NINETEEN

NO SALVATION
OUTSIDE THE CHURCH?

The previous chapter recalled the Church's teaching about salvation for non-Catholic Christians and for non-Christians. The Second Vatican Council affirmed that the Holy Spirit can use non-Catholic traditions for the salvation of their members. If in ignorance of the whole truth of the Church these persons serve God as best they can, they can be saved. The Church also teaches that non-Christians can be saved if they strive to serve God with faith on the basis of the best information they have of Him.

And yet, down through the ages, the Church has taught, in the words of Saint Cyprian, *extra ecclesiam nulla salus*: "outside the Church, no salvation."[1] The Second Vatican Council re-affirmed this doctrine: "Basing itself upon Sacred Scripture and Tradition, it [the Council] teaches that the Church, now sojourning on earth as an exile, is necessary for salvation. Christ, present to us in his Body, which is the Church, is the one Mediator and the unique way of salvation."[2]

Several years ago, the Congregation for the Doctrine of the Faith issued a document that states, "With the coming of the Saviour Jesus Christ, God has willed that the Church founded by him be the instrument for the salvation of all humanity."[3] Note that the Church is not saying "*an* instrument"; she is saying "*the* instrument."

---

1   On this subject the Supreme Sacred Congregation of the Holy Office (now known as the Congregation for the Doctrine of the Faith) sent a letter to the Archbishop of Boston in 1949. The letter, entitled *Suprema haec*, spoke of *extra ecclesiam* as "an infallible statement" and as "dogma."

2   *Dogmatic Constitution on the Church*, 14.

3   *Dominus Iesus* (August, 2000), 22.

These two themes seem contradictory at first glance: salvation by Jesus Christ is available to non-Catholic and non-Christians, and yet there is no salvation outside the Catholic Church. Yet proper understanding of *extra ecclesiam* resolves this apparent contradiction. This doctrine says nothing about the *scope* of Christ's salvation. It only designates *how* Jesus Christ makes His salvation available to all human beings.

Start with the fact that Jesus Christ is the redeemer, the *only* redeemer of the world. He revealed Himself in absolute terms: "I am the way, and the truth, and the life; no one comes to the Father, but by me" (Jn. 14:6). Equally categorical is Saint Peter's proclamation of Christ to the Sanhedrin: "[T]here is salvation in no one else, for there is no other name under heaven given among men by which we must be saved" (Acts 4:12). The Congregation for the Doctrine of the Faith speaks of "the one universal gift of salvation offered by the Father through Jesus Christ in the Spirit."[4] God has never left any of His children without some knowledge of Himself (Rom. 1:18ff.).

Wherever you find human beings in any age, you will always find some knowledge of God. God reveals Himself only through His Word. Whatever of God's truth is available to any persons always comes through the revealing activity of the Word. That Word we know in His Incarnation, our Lord Jesus Christ.

Redemption in Jesus Christ has two distinct dimensions. *Objective* redemption of the world was accomplished once for all by Jesus Christ through His life, death, Resurrection, ascension, and gift of the Holy Spirit. Now the benefits of that redemption have to be applied unceasingly to Christ's members throughout their lives. This we may call *subjective* redemption.

In other words, redemption is an ongoing process. "[W]ork out your own salvation in fear and trembling, for God is at work in you" (Phil. 2:12–13). The objective redemption accomplished by Jesus Christ must be worked out continually in the subjective redemption of each person who responds—in whatever way—to the grace of Christ. In the liturgy of the second Sunday in Ordinary Time, the offertory prayer says: "Grant us, O Lord, we pray, that we may participate worthily in these mysteries, for whenever the memorial of this sacrifice is celebrated, the work of our redemption is [being] accomplished."

Non-Catholics generally assume that Jesus Christ's Passion, death, and Resurrection concluded God's redemptive work. The Catholic Church teaches that, in a sense, Jesus Christ's Passion, death, Resurrection, and ascension marked the *beginning* of Christ's redemption. The process of working out His redemption in individual lives will continue until He comes again. The

---

4   *Ibid.,* 13.

question is, *how* does Jesus Christ work out His redemption in individuals? The answer is, through His Mystical Body, the Church.

To fulfill His messianic mission, the second Person of the Blessed Trinity took on human nature from His mother, Mary. He lived a natural life in a human body through which—and only through which—He redeemed the universe. Since His ascension, and until the end of time, Jesus lives a *supernatural* life in another body: the body of His members, the Mystical Body. For Protestants—and I once believed this—the phrase "Body of Christ" is essentially a metaphor. For Catholics, it denotes literal reality.

Here's why. The Catholic Church is not simply Christ's representative on earth, although she is that. The Catholic Church is Christ Himself, living an incarnate life in the bodies of His members who together constitute the Mystical Body of Christ on earth. The Catholic Church is the body in and through which Christ continues to live and love and speak until His Second Coming—indeed, just as truly as when He lived and loved and spoke in the Holy Land two thousand ago.

Our Lord emphasized the supernatural quality of His Church when He said, "I am the vine, you are the branches. He who abides in me, and I in him, he it is that bears much fruit, for apart from me you can do nothing" (Jn. 15:5). The branches express the life of the vine. Branches can do nothing apart from the vine. But the vine can bear fruit only through its branches.

Recall how Jesus identified Himself with His Church when He spoke to Paul on the road to Damascus. Falling to the ground, Paul "heard a voice saying to him, 'Saul, Saul, why do you persecute me?' And he said, 'Who are you, Lord?' And he said, 'I am Jesus, whom you are persecuting'" (Acts 9:4–5). Paul had never laid eyes on Jesus. Yet twice Jesus indicted Paul for persecuting Him. Paul persecuted Jesus when he persecuted the Mystical Body of Christ.

Many years later, writing to Saint Timothy, Paul admits that he had persecuted Jesus by persecuting Jesus' Church. Paul thanks Christ for having appointed him an apostle, "though I formerly blasphemed and persecuted and insulted him, but I received mercy because I had acted ignorantly in unbelief" (1 Tim. 1:12–13). In a joyful outburst, the *Liturgy of the Hours* exults: "When you rose from the dead, Lord Jesus, you formed the Church into your new body and made of it the new Jerusalem, united in your Spirit."[5]

In his encyclical *Mystici Corpus* (1943), Pope Pius XII stressed Jesus' identification with His Church. The Holy Father drew a parallel between the Incarnation and the founding of the Church: "As the Word of God willed to make use of our nature, when . . . he would redeem mankind, so in the same way throughout the centuries he makes use of the Church that the work begun

---

5   Volume 4, p. 1083.

might endure."[6] Redemption, subjectively speaking, is an ongoing process, not a once-for-all event.

Pope Pius emphasized the fact that Christ carries on His redemptive work *through* His Mystical Body. Christ could have imparted all His graces "to mankind directly, but he willed to do so only through a visible Church." And why only through His visible Church? Christ wanted all the members of His Mystical Body to "cooperate with him in dispensing the grace of redemption."[7] *Dispensing*: a continuous process.

The Second Vatican Council underlined Pope Pius XII's parallel between Christ's physical body and His Mystical Body. Just as Jesus used His natural body "as a living organ of salvation," in a similar way "the visible social structure of the Church serve the Spirit of Christ, who vivifies it."[8] Again, Christ constituted a supernatural body out of all His members. And for what purpose? To be the "entity with visible delineation through which he communicated truth and grace to all."[9]

Pope Pius XII rejected the distinction Protestant thought tends to make between the Mystical Body of Christ and any historical institution. The Catholic Church as an historical institution, and the Mystical Body of Christ, are not two separate realities, but one. The fathers of Vatican II made the same point. "[T]he society structure with hierarchical organs and the Mystical Body of Christ . . . form one complex reality which coalesces from a human and a divine element."[10] In the Incarnation, Christ perfectly united His divine nature with a fully human nature. In the Church He established and through which He lives on earth, Christ again unites His divine nature with the human nature of His members. Dare we say that, in a sense, the Catholic Church is a second Incarnation?

Now go back to our Lord's analogy of the vine and the branches. Not only do we know the vine through its branches. It is only through its branches that the vine achieves its purpose, to bear fruit. God has made Christ "head over all things for the church, which is his body, the fullness of him who fills all in all" (Eph. 1:22–23). In other words, Christ *and* His Church constitute the fullness of the Son of God.

Pope Pius XII explained this further. The gifts of Christ unfold in those who are members of His Mystical Body, through which He continues His presence on earth. "Thus the Church . . . becomes as it were, the filling out and

---

6 *Mystici Corpus,* 12.
7 *Ibid.,* 12.
8 *Dogmatic Constitution on the Church,* 8.
9 *Loc. cit.*
10 *Loc. cit.*

the complement of the Redeemer, while Christ in a sense attains through the Church a fullness in all things." Indeed, the Church is "another Christ" which on earth "shows forth his Person." Thus Christ and His Church "constitute one new man, in whom heaven and earth are joined together in perpetuating the saving work of the cross."[11]

Note the word *perpetuating*. The effects of Calvary continuously must be unfolded in human lives. At the same time, Pope Pius XII reminds us that the Church herself contributes nothing to "the immense treasure of the Redemption." Yet in the distribution of those graces, Christ not only shares this work with His Church, He also "wills that in some way it be due to her action."[12] From "earliest times" it has been the tradition of the Fathers that Christ and the Church "form but one mystical person" or, as Saint Augustine put it, "the whole Christ."[13]

Excepting the opening verses of the fourth Gospel, we may say the most exalted passage concerning our Lord comes in the first chapter of Colossians. "He is the image of the invisible God, the first-born of all creation; for in him all things were created, in heaven and on earth, visible and invisible, whether thrones or dominions or principalities or authorities—all things were created through him and for him. He is before all things, and in him all things hold together" (Col. 1:15–17).

Not only is Christ the agent of creation; He is also the goal of creation. He is also the sustainer of the universe. Try to imagine the mysterious order in the universe about which we have some meager knowledge. Then realize that "in him all things hold together"! How is it possible to know this divine Person? The next verse gives us the answer: "He is the head of the body, the church."

Jesus Christ and his Church form one mystical Person. He has entrusted to his Church the treasure of his redemptive love. It is in this context that we can understand the opening words of Vatican II's most important document. The Catholic Church "is in Christ like a sacrament . . . of very closely knit union with God and of the unity of the whole human race."[14] A few sections later, the council teaches that the Catholic Church is Jesus Christ's "instrument for the redemption of all, and is sent forth into the whole world as the light of the world and the salt of the earth."[15] Speaking of the unity of the Church under the Chair of Peter, the Council declared, "[A]ll men

---

11 *Mystici Corpus*, 77.
12 *Ibid.*, 44.
13 *Ibid.*, 67.
14 *Dogmatic Constitution on the Church*, 1.
15 *Ibid.*, 9.

are called to be part of this catholic unity of the people of God which in promoting universal peace presages it. And there belong to or are related to it in various ways, the Catholic faithful, all who believe in Christ, and indeed the whole of mankind, for all men are called by the grace of God to salvation."[16]

In 1992, the Congregation for the Doctrine of the Faith characterized the Church as "the sacrament of salvation." That is, Christ founded her to witness to Him and His truth and "to gather all people and all things into Christ, so as to be for all an 'inseparable sacrament of unity.'"[17] Blessed John Paul II told us that Christ founded His Church to be "his co-worker in the salvation of the world." Again, Christ "carries out his mission through her [the Church]."[18]

We note Blessed John Paul's words that the Church is "the sacrament of salvation for all mankind, and her activity is not limited only to those who accept her message."[19] In the same document, the Holy Father spoke of persons who never have had opportunity to know Christ or to enter His Church. "For such people salvation in Christ is accessible by virtue of a grace which [has] . . . a mysterious relationship to the Church."[20] The Congregation for the Doctrine of the Faith brings to sharpest focus the Church's role in the salvation of humanity. As "the universal sacrament of salvation," the Catholic Church "has, in God's plan, *an indispensable relationship with the salvation of every human being*"[21] (emphasis added).

Early in the first document issued by Vatican II, the Council taught, "[I]t is the liturgy through which the work of our redemption is accomplished, most of all, in the divine sacrifice of the Eucharist.'"[22] In the Church's offering of the Holy Sacrifice, Christ renews—re-presents to the Father—His redemptive sacrifice for the salvation of the human race. We must always remember that the Mass and the Cross are inseparable. The grace of Calvary is poured forth into the world through the offering of the Holy Sacrifice. "Without the cross, the mass would be only an empty ceremony; but without the mass, the cross would be only a sealed fountain."[23]

As successor of the apostles, a bishop is directly responsible for each celebration of the Eucharist in his jurisdiction. At the same time, it is necessary

---

16 *Ibid.*, 13.
17 *Some Aspects of the Church Understood as Communion*, 4.
18 *Mission of the Redeemer*, 9.
19 *Ibid.*, 20.
20 *Ibid.*, 10.
21 *Dominus Iesus*, 20.
22 *Constitution on the Sacred Liturgy*, 2.
23 Roger Hasseveldt, *The Church: A Divine Mystery*, trans. William Storey (Covington, KY: Sisters of Notre Dame, 1962), 260.

that each bishop be in communion with, and responsible to, the successor of Peter. May we not say that each offering of the Holy Sacrifice is ultimately the responsibility of the pope? And we have said that the offering of the Eucharist is central to the salvation of mankind. In the light of these two doctrines, perhaps we can better understand some apparently grandiose words of Pope Boniface VIII. The final sentence of his papal bull *Unam Sanctam* is this: "[W]e declare, we proclaim, we define that it is absolutely necessary for salvation that every human creature be subject to the Roman Pontiff."[24]

"Outside the Church, no salvation." The *Catechism of the Catholic Church* teaches us, "Reformulated positively, it means that all salvation comes from Christ the Head through the Church which is his Body" (846). Wherever the grace of Christ appears—and it appears throughout creation—it always comes, however mysteriously, through His one, holy, catholic, and apostolic Church: His Mystical Body on earth.

---

24 www.fordham.edu/halsall/source/b8-unam.html. 2.

CHAPTER TWENTY

PRIESTLY CELIBACY

The Church's code of cannon law mandates priestly celibacy. "Clerics [all those in Holy Orders] are obliged to observe perfect and perpetual continence for the sake of the kingdom of heaven, and therefore are obliged to observe celibacy. . . ." (Canon 277). As we shall see, this discipline is rooted in the apostolic Church.

In the 1950s Pope Pius XII granted dispensation from this rule to a number of former Lutheran clergy who were married, and allowed them to be ordained to the priesthood. Vatican II extended the scope of this dispensation in authorizing married men to serve as permanent deacons. About thirty years ago the Vatican began allowing former Anglican clergy who were married to be ordained priests with dispensation from celibacy. And now the recent establishment of the Anglican ordinariate will increase further the number of married Catholic priests in this and some other countries. This setting aside one of the Church's laws in a special case has been referred to as an "indult," but the Church has never used the term in allowing dispensation from celibacy.

Yet for thirty years, time after time, in various parts of the country, Catholics have said to me, in words like these, "You're a *married* priest? I didn't know we had any married priests. I think the Church *should* allow her priests to marry." Always I assure such persons that my wife and I strongly believe the Church is carrying on an important and essential apostolic tradition in requiring celibacy. I am deeply grateful for the Church's generosity which allows me to serve in her priesthood. Yet I know that as a married man and father I am not totally free—physically, emotionally, spiritually—to serve the people as is a celibate priest.

The objection usually persists. "But surely a married man is better qualified to teach people about marriage than is a celibate priest." Again, I disagree, politely of course. The purpose of marriage preparation is not to teach couples what the priest has experienced. Catholic couples need and have the right to be instructed in the Church's revealed truth about the meaning of human sexuality and holy matrimony. If both a married and a celibate priest are reasonably mature, and if each teaches in harmony with the Church, the married priest has no essential advantage over the celibate priest in giving marriage instruction.

Then comes the final argument. "Yes, that may be, but if priests could marry, it would solve our priest shortage." My reply is, that assumption has no evidence to support it. If the rule of celibacy is keeping men out of the priesthood, how do you account for the dioceses in this country that have an abundance of priests? As Pope Paul VI said forty years ago, the decline in priestly vocations is due to lack of faith on the part of our people. The dissent that has been rampant in recent decades has created widespread confusion about the Church's teaching, especially with regard to the priesthood.

Unquestionably, sentiment in favor of optional celibacy for priests is fairly widespread, even among faithful Catholics. This sentiment is based on ignorance and/or misunderstanding of the history of priestly celibacy, the Church's commitment to celibacy, and the Church's evaluation of consecrated virginity and celibacy.

An apostolic tradition

People commonly believe that the Church mandated celibacy for priests beginning in the fourth century or the twelfth century or somewhere in between. The fact is, priestly celibacy is an apostolic institution.

The connection of celibacy with priesthood was first revealed in Christ. We see that, in its perfect embodiment, priesthood involves remaining free of all claims of marriage and parenthood. That freedom enabled God's Son to be completely available for the working of the Father's perfect will through Him (cf. Jn. 4:34).

When Christ called His successors, the apostles, "they left everything and followed him" (Lk. 5:11). Later, Peter reminded Jesus, "We have left everything and followed you." Then he asked, with typical candor, "What then will we have?" (Mt. 19:27). Jesus replied, "There is no one who has left house or wife or brothers or parents or children, for the sake of the kingdom of God, who will not receive manifold very much more in this time, and in the age to come eternal life" (Lk. 18:29). Recall also that when Jesus taught the indissolubility of marriage, he also highly commended celibacy (cf. Mt.

19:12). Saint Paul strongly endorsed celibacy for more effectively serving the Lord. Yet there are four passages in the New Testament that seem to support the case for optional celibacy. We will look at these in a moment.

The disciplinary canons of the Council of Elvira (AD 305) are the Church's earliest record regarding priestly celibacy. These canons deal with infractions of the Church's traditional rules. Because the rules themselves were ancient and presumably well known, the council gave no explanation. It simply called for obedience. Canon 33 forbade all married bishops, priests, and deacons to have sexual relations with their wives and beget children. Though the council does not so specify, we learn from somewhat later sources that both the ordinand and his wife would have been required to make a vow of perpetual continence before he could be ordained. The council reminded the married clergy they were bound by this vow. Penalty for breaking that vow was deposition from the ministry. Commenting on this council, Pope Pius XI said these canons, the "first written traces" of the "law of ecclesiastical celibacy," "presuppose a still earlier unwritten practice."[1]

The Council of Arles (314) upheld both the obligation of continence for married clergy and the penalty for non-conforming, as stated by the Council of Elvira. The Council of Nicaea (325) took for granted priestly celibacy for unmarried and married clergy. Canon 3 stated, "This great synod absolutely forbids a bishop, presbyter, deacon, or any of the clergy to keep a woman who has been brought in to live with him, with the exception of course of his mother or sister or aunt, or of any person who is above suspicion."[2] On the basis of fourth- and fifth-century evidence, Father Christian Cochini, S.J., holds that the phrase "any person who is above suspicion" includes wives of clergy who with their spouses had taken vows of continence before their husbands were ordained.[3]

Near the end of the fourth century, a Spanish bishop wrote to the pope, asking for help in dealing with married clergy who were having children with their wives. In his response in 385, Pope Siricius reminded all married clergy (in Spain and presumably everywhere) that their vows of perpetual continence are "indissoluble."[4] In 386, the Pope issued a decretal repeating his ruling of

---

1   *Ad catholici sacerdotii*, 43 (1935). A Russian Orthodox archbishop, Peter l'Huillier, claims that Canon 33, along with other canons, was not promulgated by the Council of Elvira, but was added later. He gives no support for this statement, nor does he say when he thinks the canons were added. See *The Church of the Ancient Councils* (Crestwood, NY: Saint Vladimir's Seminary Press, 1996), 36. Yet in footnote 123, p. 89, he admits "it is unquestionable that the canon [33] wants to express a prohibition of marital relations ... for bishops, priests and deacons." But see below: the canon must have been added before 314, when the Council of Arles practically quoted it.

2   Norman P. Tanner, S.J., ed., *Decrees of the Ecumenical Councils*, vol.1 (Washington, D.C.: Georgetown University Press, 1990), 7.

3   Christian Cochini; S.J., *Apostolic Origins of Priestly Celibacy* (San Francisco: Ignatius Press, 1990), 185-195.

4   *Ibid.*, 9.

the previous year regarding clerical celibacy. He insisted he was not giving new rulings but was rather re-calling the clergy to rules long established in the Church.

Some of the married clergy tried to defend their continuing conjugal life. There was no tradition of optional celibacy to which they could appeal. To justify their conjugal union with their wives, they appealed rather to 1 Timothy 3:2, Titus 1:6 and 1 Timothy 3:12. These verses specify that a bishop, priest, or deacon must have been "married only once" (must be *unius uxoris vir*, "husband of one wife"). In response, Pope Siricius declared that "married only once" does *not* mean that after their ordination married clergy could continue conjugal relations with their wives. The true meaning, he said, is this. A man faithful to one wife reasonably could be expected to be mature enough to live the perpetual continence required of him and his wife after his ordination.

This is the original magisterial exegesis of these passages. Pope Siricius's teaching finds clear echoes in the writings of the Fathers of this era: Ambrose, Epiphanius of Salamis, Ambrosiaster.[5]

Another passage that has been used to buttress the case for optional celibacy is 1 Corinthians 9:5. Referring to his prerogatives as an apostle, Saint Paul asks (seemingly rhetorically), "Do we not have the right to be accompanied by a believing wife, as do the other apostles and the brothers of the Lord and Cephas?" (NRSV). The Greek words behind "believing wife" in this translation do not mean wife in the ordinary sense. The phrase means a *sister wife*, or a *sister as wife*. In the early centuries, the term *sister* (as in 1 Cor. 9:5) was used to designate a wife of a clergyman who with him had vowed perpetual continence before his ordination. Their relation was that of brother and sister.

Departing from our chronology momentarily, we should glance briefly at the *Directory on the Ministry and Life of Priests*, issued in 1994 by the Congregation for the Clergy. Section 59 affirms Pope Siricius's exegesis of the passages in Timothy and Titus. It also cites several early councils that required continence for married as well as for unmarried clergy. Then come these words: "[T]he Church, from apostolic times, has wished to conserve the gift of perpetual continence of the clergy and choose the candidates for Holy Orders from among the celibate faithful." "The celibate faithful" clearly would include married men who with their wives had vowed to observe perpetual continence after the men were ordained.

---

5   *Ibid.*, footnote 18, p. 12.

Back to the fourth century. The Council of Carthage (390), involving the whole African hierarchy, restated the rule of perpetual continence for all married clergy. It declared it was simply restating the Church's unbroken tradition. In explaining its decree, the presiding bishop (Genethlius) urged that "what the apostles taught and what antiquity itself observed, let us also endeavor to keep."[6]

A decretal, *Dominus Inter*, was issued in the early fifth century by a synod led probably by Pope Innocent I. Responding to questions raised by bishops from Gaul, canon 16 repeats the Church's rule of perpetual continence for married clergy.[7] We find the same teaching by pontiffs who succeeded Innocent I, such as Leo the Great. Jerome, Augustine, and Ambrose all stressed this same teaching. So did the councils of Tours (461), Gerona (517), and Auvergne (535). So did Pope Gregory the Great (c. 540–604). The requirement of perpetual continence for married clergy appears in the penitential books of the Celtic churches as well.

In the eleventh and twelfth centuries, the Gregorian reform dealt with violations of the norm of clerical celibacy. The Second Lateran Council (1139) was part of this movement. From this fact, some Catholics (and non-Catholics) have wrongly concluded that this council *originated* clerical celibacy. Like all its predecessors that dealt with the issue, the Lateran Council sought to enforce the apostolic ban on conjugal life for the clergy.

Apologists for the separated Eastern Churches' practice of mixed celibacy (married priests and deacons, celibate bishops) ignore these councils' declarations that they were upholding an apostolic tradition. Instead, those apologists continue to hold that these councils *originated* priestly celibacy.

But if these councils did originate the rule of priestly celibacy, why did they lie by insisting they were only upholding ancient tradition? Even more to the point is this. If celibacy was optional prior to the early fourth century, why would the council fathers and those of later councils impose on themselves and on the other married clergy such a discipline? Why did *no one* object that the conciliar rulings were unprecedented?

Or put the issue on a more personal level. Assume for the moment that these councils *did* impose a new rule of perpetual continence for married clergy. Imagine a married bishop going home from Elvira or from Arles or from Carthage. He goes through the front door and says, "Honey, I'm home!" After his wife greets him, she asks, "So what did you guys do in the council?" The bishop says, "Sit down. I've got some news." Then he tells her they decreed perpetual continence for all married clergy. The wife bursts out, "You decided *what*?"

6   *Ibid.,* 5.
7   *Ibid.,* 15.

At this point perhaps we should stop eavesdropping. However, we can be certain that scenes like this would have taken place in many clerical homes after the councils—*if,* that is, the separated Eastern apologists are right in rejecting what the councils themselves said in reminding married clergy of their obligation of perpetual continence.

In more recent times, the predecessor of the Sacred Congregation for the Doctrine of the Faith issued an instruction in 1858 that said this about celibacy: "Whoever ponders diligently the true tradition of celibacy and clerical continence will indeed find that, from the first centuries of the Catholic Church, if not by a general and explicit law, at least by behaviour and custom, it was firmly established that not only bishops and priests, but [all] clergy in Holy Orders were to preserve inviolate virginity or perpetual continence."[8] That priestly celibacy is an apostolic tradition "is shown clearly and convincingly" by the work of Stickler, Cochini, Heid, and others. This is the verdict of then-Cardinal Joseph Ratzinger.[9]

What, then, of optional celibacy in the separated Eastern Churches and the Eastern Catholic Churches?

The Eastern discipline of optional celibacy for priests and deacons (it is required for bishops) was formulated in the seventh century. Prior to that time, all the Eastern Churches followed the apostolic tradition of mandatory continence for both married and unmarried clergy. The Council of Trullo in 692 radically changed the discipline of celibacy. One of its canons did retain the prohibition of bishops, priests and deacons marrying after ordination. It also partly preserved the apostolic tradition in requiring perpetual continence of married men who were installed in the episcopate. But it decreed that married men ordained to the diaconate and priesthood could continue their conjugal life *after* ordination. In doing so, the council explicitly and polemically rejected the clerical discipline of Rome.

To justify this departure from the apostolic tradition, Trullo quoted the canons of the Council of Carthage (397). That council, as we have seen, had restated the rule of perpetual continence for all married clergy by appealing to what it called the apostolic tradition. Its records were widely available. Trullo changed the wording of the Carthaginian canons so that they mandated only *temporary* continence for married clergy *only* on days when they served at the altar. (This is the Old Testament law for levitical priests who served in the Temple.) Despite this radical alteration of the Carthage council's ruling,

---

8   Quoted by Roman Cholij, "Celibacy, Married Clergy, and the Oriental Code," *Eastern Churches Journal,* vol. 3, no. 3 (Autumn, 1996), 112.

9   Cardinal Joseph Ratzinger, "The Theological Locus of Ecclesial Movements," *Communio* (Fall, 1998), footnote 2, p. 483.

the Council of Trullo assured all who would listen that by its decrees it was only "preserving the ancient rule and apostolic perfection and order."[10] The Catholic Church, of course, has never recognized the Council of Trullo.

For an outsider, the Trullan rulings raise questions. If a married man can be ordained and live in conjugal union, why can't a celibate clergyman marry? If a married man can be ordained a deacon and priest and continue in his marital union, why can't a bishop be married and live with his wife? These apparent inconsistencies are due to the separated Eastern Churches' and the Eastern Catholic Churches' having retained only portions of the ancient tradition. Today some Eastern Orthodox theologians and even an occasional bishop are urging further changes in clerical celibacy. They contend that single priests and deacons should be allowed to marry after ordination. They contend further that bishops should be allowed to marry. If adopted, these measures would sever all Eastern Orthodox ties with the apostolic tradition of priestly celibacy.

In her magisterial statements regarding the Eastern practice of celibacy, the Catholic Church uses guarded language. She does not want to widen the breach between the separated churches and the Catholic Church. But she has never even hinted that the Eastern practice stands on a par with her own discipline regarding celibacy. Typical of her attitude is the language of Pope Pius XII in his 1935 encyclical on the Catholic priesthood that was quoted earlier. After extolling the glories of priestly celibacy, he said he was not criticizing the Oriental discipline. "What we have said has been meant solely to exalt in the Lord something we consider one of the purest glories of the Catholic priesthood; something which seems to us to correspond better to the desires of the Sacred Heart of Jesus and his purposes in regard to priestly souls" (sec. 47).

Another example of the magisterial attitude is section 16 of Vatican II's *Decree on the Ministry and Life of Priests*. While it "commends ecclesiastical celibacy," the council fathers denied any intention of changing the rule of the Eastern Catholic Churches or of denigrating the rule of the separated Eastern Churches. Indeed, they said the council "permanently exhorts all those who have received the priesthood and marriage to persevere in their holy vocation so that they may fully and generously continue to expend themselves for the sake of the flock commended to them."

But note the next sentence. It begins a new paragraph with these words: "Indeed, celibacy has a many-faceted suitability for the priesthood." Then follows a list of at least ten reasons for a celibate priesthood. Almost all of them are expressed in comparative terms (that is, in contrast with married

---

10 Quoted by Roman Cholij, *Clerical Celibacy in East and West* (Herefordshire, UK: Fowler Wright Books, 1988), 115.

priesthood). For example, celibate priests "are consecrated to Christ by a new and exceptional reason. They adhere to him more easily with undivided heart, and they dedicate themselves more freely" to Christ and his people. They "more expeditiously minister to his kingdom." They "apt to accept, in a broad sense, paternity in Christ." They give witness to and "commit themselves faithfully to one man." They recall the "mysterious marriage" between Christ and his Church. They are "a living sign of the world to come, . . . in which the children of the resurrection neither marry nor take wives."

Roman Cholij, himself an Eastern Catholic, characterizes the Catholic Church's attitude toward the Eastern discipline of celibacy in these words: "[I]t is clear that the Oriental discipline of married clergy was always regarded as an exception to general law, toward which Rome showed its indulgence. If this discipline was merely tolerated—and there are good reasons for believing this to have been the case—then the discipline was but a cusâtom of fact, devoid of any legal force."[11] Cholij suggests the Church's acceptance of the differing Eastern discipline of celibacy is in the nature of an indult. But, he reminds us, "There is no question of abrogation of the law of which the indult is an exception."[12]

A different kind of discipline

It is misleading to characterize the rule of celibacy as only a discipline. True, in the sense that the requirement of priestly celibacy is not clearly part of the deposit of faith, it is part of the Church's discipline. But it is quite unlike all her other disciplines. Take the Church's rules about fasting before receiving the Eucharist, or about allowing meat on Friday if one otherwise fulfills the obligation of penance, or about being allowed to register in a parish when one lives outside the parish bounds. Changes to these disciplines in recent decades have no real theological rationale or consequences.

But the "discipline" of theology is quite different. Theoretically, if he chose, overnight the pope could set aside the rule of priestly celibacy. If he did, however, it would have a profound negative effect on the Church's understanding of herself and of the priesthood.

The Church is both human and divine, a duality of structure (organization) and the presence and power of the Holy Spirit. Or we may speak of institution and charism. That which gives the Church her permanency of structure is itself a sacrament, the Sacrament of Orders. This means that the Church's structure is continuously created by God's unfailing action through the Sacrament. The Church as an institution cannot herself choose those who will serve in the hierarchy. The call to holy orders comes from God, and the

11 *Ibid.*, 187.
12 *Ibid.*, 187.

Church can only recognize that call. Thus our Lord commanded us, "pray therefore the Lord of the harvest to send laborers into his harvest" (Mt. 9:37).

So the priestly ministry has a "strictly charismatic character," in the words of Pope Benedict XVI. The Church emphasizes that fact by "linking . . . priesthood with virginity, which clearly can be understood only as a personal charism, never simply as an official qualification." Any attempt to separate priesthood from celibacy ("the demand for their uncoupling") would in effect deny the charismatic nature of priesthood. It would reduce it to an office completely under the control of the institution. Thus the Church in effect would be regarded as a purely human institution.[13]

In his 1967 encyclical *Sacerdotalis Caelibatus* ("The Celibacy of the Priest"), Pope Paul VI quoted these words of Pope John XXIII from an address to a Roman synod in 1960: "It deeply hurts us that . . . anyone could dream that the Church will deliberately or even suitably renounce what from time immemorial has been, and still remains, one of the purest and noblest glories of her priesthood" (sec.37). Pope Paul himself spoke of the law of priestly celibacy as "ancient, sacred, and providential" (sec.17). He invited all to study the Church's teaching about priesthood and celibacy so that, in his words, "the bond between the priesthood and celibacy" will be seen ever more clearly. (sec.25).

Again, "[W]e consider that the present law of celibacy should today continue to be linked to the ecclesiastical ministry" (sec. 14). Vatican II had made it possible to ordain mature married men to the diaconate. This provision, Pope Paul declared, "does not signify a relaxation of the existing law, and must not be interpreted as a prelude to its abolition" (sec. 43).

Pope John Paul II, in his 1992 encyclical on the priesthood (*I Will Give You Shepherds*), repeatedly speaks of clerical celibacy as a gift: "a priceless gift," "a precious gift," "a gift of God for the Church"—a gift, in other words, to be cherished, not to be ignored or given away. He sees a necessary connection between priesthood and celibacy. The law of priestly celibacy expresses the will of the Church. "But the will of the Church finds its ultimate motivation in the link between celibacy and sacred ordination, which configures the priest to Jesus Christ the head and spouse of the Church." (Does not this mean that the law of celibacy is something more than a merely disciplinary issue?) In strong words the Holy Father adds, "The Church, as the spouse of Jesus Christ, wishes to be loved by the priest *in the total and exclusive manner* in which Jesus Christ her head and spouse loved her" (sec. 29; emphasis added).

Previous reference has been made to the Congregation for the Clergy's *Directory on the Ministry and Life of Priests*. It echoes Pope John Paul II's

---

13 Ratzinger, *op. cit.*, 483.

teaching that celibacy is a gift from God. "Celibacy, in fact, is a gift which the Church has received and desires to retain, convinced that it is a good for the Church itself and for the world" (sec. 57). Earlier we noted a passage from the *Directory* that declares, "the Church, from apostolic times, has wished to conserve the gift of perpetual continence of the clergy" (sec. 59).

The Synod of Bishops in 1990 issued what is perhaps the ultimate statement in modern times on the Church's commitment to priestly celibacy. "The synod would like to see celibacy presented and explained in the fullness of its biblical, theological, and spiritual richness, as a precious gift given by God to his Church and as a sign of the kingdom which is not of this world—a sign of God's love for this world and of the undivided love of the priest for God and for God's people, with the result that celibacy is seen as a positive enrichment of the priesthood." Said the synod, the Church is totally committed to maintaining priestly celibacy. "The synod does not wish to leave any doubts in the mind of anyone regarding the Church's firm will to maintain the law that demands perpetual and freely chosen celibacy for present and future candidates for priestly ordination in the Latin rite"[14] (proposition 11).

Celibacy and consecrated virginity

In its canons on the Sacrament of Marriage, the Council of Trent decreed: "If anyone says the married state is to be preferred to that of virginity or celibacy, and that it is no better or more blessed to persevere in virginity and celibacy than to be joined in marriage, let him be anathema"[15] (session 24). Pope Pius XII, in his 1954 encyclical, *Sacred Virginity*, taught:

> This doctrine of the excellence of virginity and of celibacy and of their superiority over the married state . . . was revealed by our Divine Redeemer and by the Apostle of the Gentiles [referring to 1 Corinthians 7]; so too, it was *solemnly defined as a dogma of divine faith* by the holy council of Trent, and explained in the same way by all the holy Fathers and doctors of the Church. Finally, We and Our Predecessors have often expounded it and earnestly advocated it whenever occasion offered (sec. 32, emphasis added).

Several documents of Vatican II stress the superiority of the charism of virginity and celibacy over that of marriage. The *Dogmatic Constitution on the Church*, speaking of the counsels Jesus enjoined on his disciples, says, "An eminent position among these [counsels] is held by virginity or the celibate

14 Quoted by John Paul II, *I Will Give You Shepherds*, 29.
15 Tanner, *op. cit.*, vol. 2, 755.

state. This is a precious gift of divine grace given by the Father to certain souls, whereby they may devote themselves to God alone more easily, due to an undivided heart in virginity or celibacy" (sec. 42). The *Decree on the Training of Priests* requires that seminarians be trained in the duties and dignity of Christian marriage. At the same time, "Let them recognize, however, the surpassing excellence of virginity consecrated to Christ, so that with a maturely deliberate and generous choice they may consecrate themselves to the Lord by a complete gift of body and soul" (sec. 10). The *Decree on the Ministry and Life of Priests* contains half a dozen or more similar statements of the superiority of the virginal or celibate state over that of marriage.

The 1967 Synod of Bishops' statement on *The Ministerial Priesthood* contains these words: "While the value of the sign and holiness of Christian marriage is fully recognized, celibacy for the sake of the Kingdom nevertheless more clearly displays that spiritual fruitfulness or generative power of the New Law by which the apostle knows that in Christ he is the father and mother of his communities" (4b). Moreover, said the bishops, "Through celibacy, priests are more easily able to serve God with undivided heart and spend themselves for their sheep, and as a result they are able more fully to be promoters of evangelization and of the Church's unity."[16]

Pope Paul VI, in his previously mentioned 1967 encyclical, acknowledged that the married state is a way of sanctity for couples called to matrimony. "But Christ has also opened a new way [celibacy], in which the human creature adheres wholly and directly to the Lord, and is concerned only with Him and His affairs. . . ; thus he manifests in a clearer and more complete way the profoundly transforming reality of the New Testament" (sec. 20).

Pope John Paul II reiterated the Church's teaching quite simply in 1981 in *The Role of the Christian Family in the Modern World*: "[T]he Church, throughout her history, has always defended the superiority of this charism [virginity or celibacy] to that of marriage, by reason of the wholly singular link which it has with the Kingdom of God" (sec. 16).

Finally, the 1983 *Code of Canon Law* twice asserts the superiority of the charism of virginity or celibacy. Canon 277(1) describes celibacy as "a special gift of God by which sacred ministers can adhere more easily to Christ with an undivided heart and are able to dedicate themselves more freely to the service of God and humanity." Canon 599 speaks in similar terms.

The regard consistently shown to priestly celibacy by the magisterium reveals it is not merely one of the Church's disciplines. Given the fact that priestly celibacy is an apostolic tradition; given the Church's commitment

---

16 Austin Flannery, O.P., ed., *Vatican Council II: More Post-Conciliar Documents* (Northport, NY: Costello Publishing Co, 1982).

to celibacy; given the Church's appreciation of virginity and celibacy as the highest of all human callings; given all this, it seems certain that the Church will always cherish and preserve this precious gift that God has given her.

Optional celibacy?

Forget it.

EPILOGUE

Like millions of other parents, we read to our children C.S. Lewis' seven volumes of fairytales known as the Chronicles of Narnia. All the children worked through the books again on their own. One of the most charming characters is Reepicheep, a valiant, two-foot-tall talking mouse. (Lewis admitted that, apart from the main character, Aslan—a huge talking lion who is a figure of Christ—Reepicheep was his favorite.)

Early in *The Voyage of the Dawn Treader*, Reepicheep recalls that when he was in his cradle at Dryad, a wood woman spoke these lines over him:

> Where sky and water meet,
> Where the waves grow sweet,
> Doubt not, Reepicheep,
> To find all you seek,
> There in the utter East.

In the unfolding of the story, Reepicheep learns that though Aslan appears in Narnia to those who know him, his home is in the "utter East." The company of the Dawn Treader discovers that to break an enchantment binding three lords of Narnia, it will be necessary to sail to the world's end and leave one of the company behind. Reepicheep eagerly volunteers.

"That is my heart's desire," he said, to go to Aslan's country. So eager was he that he never thought the ship sailed fast enough. He spent his days sitting on the prow, gazing toward the east, sometimes softly singing the song the Dryad had given him. We read that when Reepicheep parted from the company to go alone to Aslan's country, "he was quivering with happiness."

Though not as impatient with the passage of time as Reepicheep, I, too, am sailing toward Aslan's country. At this writing I am very near that country.

I share Reepicheep's excitement at the prospect of being forever with Aslan—with Jesus Christ—in His country.

Come, Lord Jesus.

Biography

Oklahoma native Father Ray Ryland, Ph.D., J.D., was an Episcopal clergyman from 1950–1963. In 1963 he was received with his wife, Ruth, and their five children into the Catholic Church. Twenty years later, he was ordained to the priesthood of the Catholic Church, with a dispensation from the rule of celibacy under the Pastoral Provision.

Fr. Ryland served as a naval officer in WWII, as professor of theology at the University of San Diego from 1969–1991, and as adjunct professor of theology at Franciscan University of Steubenville from 1991–1994 and 1998–2000. He has been chaplain and board member of Catholics United for the Faith and the Coming Home Network International for over a decade.

Fr. Ryland earned his bachelor's degree from Phillips University in 1942. He studied at Harvard Divinity School and Union Theological Seminary in New York, where he received his master's of divinity degree. He also studied at Columbia University, Virginia Theological Seminary, University of the South, and the University of San Francisco. In 1969 he received his doctorate in religious studies at Marquette University. In 1975 he received his law degree from the law school at the University of San Diego and was admitted to California Bar Association.

Fr. Ryland lives with his wife in Steubenville, Ohio. They have twenty-two grandchildren and three great-grandchildren.